Not in Oz Anymore

Jeffery P. Dennis

Not in Oz Anymore ii

Preface

Residents call it Oz, Xanadu, Heaven, or just Here: a collection of urban neighborhoods, college towns, and resort areas where most gay people live, or have lived in the past, or plan to live someday.

It is surrounded on all sides by "Kansas," not the U.S. state but a vast expanse of cities, towns, farms, and forests, where straight people live and speak and are visible. Some gay people live there, too, but they are generally silent and invisible.

After 17 years in Oz, Joe returned to Kansas for a job. It was a like exploring a new, alien planet, where the basic rules and conventions of the life he knew are turned upside down.

The most pervasive rule was erasure. Friends, co-workers, his doctor, his auto mechanic, movies, tv programs, magazines, novels, college classes, all of them proclaimed, over and over, day after day, with giddy certainty, that gay people did not exist.

As the weeks and months passed, Joe conducted a systematic study of erasure, and found erasure in every area of human endeavour, from the most trivial to the most profound, in the past and in the future, in the human realm and the spiritual realm. Even gay people seemed eager to contribute to the notion that they did not exist.

Joe is a composite of many people with many stories. All names, dates, and locations have been modified.

Table of Contents

Chapter One
His Wife?

This story begins with a casual question from a man Joe had never seen before and would never see again.

Joe grew up in a small town in the Midwest and graduated from a small Midwestern college, barely aware that gay people existed, certainly not aware that they had their own magazines, newspapers, churches, and community centers, that there were places where rainbow flags waved from porches and gay couples strolled hand in hand. There were urban neighborhoods, college towns, and resort areas scattered across the United States, Canada, Europe, and Latin America. Residents called it Oz, Xanadu, Heaven, or simply "Here."

The moment Joe found out, Joe piled suitcases and books into his car and drove 1800 miles cross-country to Oz. He timed his arrival for Gay Pride Day, June 29th.

For the next thirteen years, he lived in the heart of Oz, near the corner of Larrabee and Santa Monica Boulevard in West Hollywood. He marched in every Gay Pride Parade. He read *Frontiers* instead of *The Los Angeles Times*. On vacation, he visited other parts of Oz: Castro Street in San Francisco, the West Village in New York, le Marais in Paris.

All of his friends were gay; so were all of his neighbors; as far as he knew, so was the guy on the next treadmill at the Hollywood Spa, the woman pricing t-shirts at Don't

Panic, and the couple sorting coupons in the check out line at the Safeway. Straights were the enemy, screaming "God hates you!" from behind security fences at Gay Pride, or asking simpering, insulting questions like "What do they think causes that?"

He ventured among them when absolutely necessary, for a job downtown or a class at USC, but afterwards it was always a relief to come home again.

Joe stopped by the Different Light Bookstore on Santa Monica Boulevard almost every day, and bought almost every new book about gay history and culture. During the 1980s, only a few appeared every year – *Byron and Greek Love*, *Ganymede in the Renaissance*, *Homosexuality in Shakespearean England* -- but each was an event, being read in booths at the Café Etoille, displayed prominently on coffee tables, discussed at parties, pressed into the hands of friends, hailed as a victory.

Then, suddenly, in the 1990s, dozens of new books began to appear, then hundreds, more than anyone could ever read or read about, on every conceivable topic, from music to biology, from business to religion. A whole world, previously hidden from view, was becoming visible, and he wanted to be one of the explorers. That meant going back to graduate school and getting a Ph.D.

Joe had already abandoned one graduate program, in English, when coming out made "Ode on a Grecian Urn" seem trivial and irrelevant, and he was forced out of another, in History, for "making an issue of it," that is, refusing to lie back and take homophobic jibes. But this time he would not have to choose between being gay and being a scholar; being gay would *be* his scholarship.

He didn't want to spend hours cramming for the GRE exams in English or History again, so he chose Sociology. He applied to ten schools, all in or near Oz, and finally he ended up at the State University of New York at Stony Brook, a hotbed of radical thought where two important scholars in the field of Gay Studies were teaching.

For the next four years, Joe continued to live in the heart of Oz, the West Village in Manhattan, a few blocks from the Stonewall Inn, where Gay Liberation began. Again, he marched in every Gay Pride Parade. He read *The Edge* instead of *The New Yorker*. On vacation, he visited other parts of Oz, South Bay in Miami, Dupont Circle in Washington DC, the Rue ste. Catherine in Montreal. All of his friends were gay; so were all of his neighbors; as far as he knew, so was the guy on the next treadmill at the New York Sports Club, the woman pricing scented candles at Blue Nile, and the couple buying vitamin supplements at the CVS Pharmacy.

Straights were still the enemy, still screaming "fag" from speeding cars in the dead of night, or intoning that "I don't have a problem with it," as if they had achieved something remarkable. He ventured among them when absolutely necessary, for his classes at Stony Brook or a job in Hempstead, but afterwards it was always a relief to come home to the West Village again.

At the start of the new millennium, Joe received his Ph.D. in sociology with a concentration in Gay Studies and a minor in Criminology, "just in case," and set out to find a teaching job at a college. Only two Gay Studies jobs were advertised that recruitment season, and one was at Yale, far out of his league. He was offered the other: a temporary "visiting" position at New England College in central Maine, three hours and three states away from the nearest part of Oz, in Boston. Too far to come home to every night.

If Joe accepted the position, then for the first time in seventeen years, the first time in his adult life, he would be living and working, buying groceries and going to the gym, finding friends and lovers, falling asleep every night and waking up every morning in Kansas.

"Kansas" wasn't the U.S. state, the flat, black-and-white place where Dorothy lived a dull, drab life before she escaped to Oz, the small towns and suburbs and endless cornfields where everyone in Oz came from – or escaped from.

Joe's friends advised him to stay in the West Village, find a part-time teaching job somewhere, and try again next year. He had forgotten what Kansas was like, they said. In or near Oz, most straights were polite bigots, asking "Which of you is the boy and which is the girl?" or at their worst refusing to photocopy your gay organization's brochure at Kinko's. But in Kansas, they were all screamers, like the ones at Gay Pride Parades, but with no barricades to restrain them. They all dreamed of shipping us all off to concentration camps. They spoke wistfully of how fun it would be to kill us.

If Joe dared to live among them, he would be spat on, called names, harassed by the police, refused medical care, kicked out of his apartment, fired from his job. His car's tires would be slashed. Rocks would be hurled through his kitchen window. One day he would be murdered, no doubt about it, and his assassin would get the lightest possible sentence, as the judge said, "It's a pity that ridding the world of an abomination must be punished at all."

Why did we all flee from our birth towns in Kansas, five, ten, or twenty years ago? they asked. To stay alive.

Joe thought his friends were exaggerating. Surely, so many years after Stonewall, genocidal ranting was rare, even in Kansas. Surely most straights were polite bigots, even in Kansas, their façade of "I don't have a problem with it" fading into hatred only when they were especially tired or depressed. Even then, they would surely be able to restrain themselves from killing him, unless a preacher incited their bloodlust with a cry of "God wills it!"

Besides, Kansas could not possibly be empty of gay people. Not everyone moves to Oz the moment he or she hears that it exists. 10% of the U.S. population would never fit. Not even 5%. For every gay person who grew up in central Maine and then fled to Oz, there must be a dozen who stayed home, and now fly rainbow flags from their porches, stroll down the street hand-in-hand with their partners, create glimmers of freedom in the darkness.

Did Your Wife Come With You?

Three hours before dawn on a dull grey morning in mid-August, Joe loaded a rental car with suitcases and books and drove north out of the West Village, past outposts of Oz glittering in the darkness, New Haven and Hartford and Boston, and then through the northwoods of Maine to Derry, population 21,000. After checking into the Travelers Inn, he made his way to the ancient, red-bricked Massachusetts Hall on the New England College campus. He was anxious to meet actual residents of Kansas, people who managed to live and breathe and find friends and lovers nowhere near Oz.

He didn't have to wait long: a retiring professor, a fat, sweating demographer named Dr. Dean,[1] was busily clearing out his office so Joe could move in. They chatted while he was kneeling on the floor, taping up the last of his boxes and fielding telephone calls from someone he called "Honey." He asked how Joe liked Maine.

"I like it fine so far," he said.

Then, preoccupied with masking tape, not looking up, Dr. Dean asked: "Did your wife come with you?"

My wife? Gay men had *partners, spouses, lovers,* but never *wives.* But why would Dr. Dean think that he was straight? He hadn't mentioned a wife, or any woman. He hadn't kissed or hugged a woman in his presence. He was not wearing a wedding ring.

But Dr. Dean showed no sign of looking for evidence. He showed no sign of making any decisions about Joe's sexual orientation at all. He asked purely by rote, with utter nonchalance, as if "Did your wife come with you?" was mere small talk, the precise equivalent of "How do you like Maine?"

Joe had quick, witty, withering responses prepared for the polite bigot's questions about "which of you is the boy?" and for the homophobe's rant of "God hates you!", but he had no response for someone who was completely unaware that he existed. Not once, since he first set foot in Oz, had anyone asked about his "girlfriend" or his "wife." No one, as far as he knew, had ever assumed that he was straight, not in West Hollywood, not in the West Village, not downtown Los Angeles, not in Stony Brook. Their statements and questions applied to everyone: "You and a guest are invited to his party"; "Do you have a boyfriend or a girlfriend?"; "Is there anyone at home we should call?"

Poet and scholar Adrienne Rich decried "the total neglect of lesbian existence in a wide range of writings, including feminist scholarship," and gave us the term "compulsory heterosexuality" for the tendency to devalue or ignore gay people.

Judy Grahn spoke of "the compulsory illusion of heterosexuality."

Monique Wittig wrote that the straight is not even capable of linguistically understanding the term "man" apart from "desiring women," and "woman" apart from "desiring men."[2]

Joe had read all of the scholarship, he knew all the concepts. But no scholar had mentioned this nonchalance, this blithe confidence that every man has a wife, and every woman a husband, that no one who is gay exists.

"Uh. . .I'm not. . .I don't. . . ." he stammered.

Dr. Dean looked up, frowning, surprised at his hesitation. "Or haven't you met the right woman yet?" he offered in a kindly tone.

Finally collecting his wits, Joe responded, "There *is* no right woman. I last dated a girl when I was sixteen years old. I am not interested in women."

Dr. Dean stared, mouth gaping, utterly taken aback. He would have been less surprised to see a leprechaun strolling the corridors of Massachusetts Hall than to discover that the new visiting professor of Gay Studies was gay!

"Don't give up," he said softly, returning to the box that he was taping up. "Everyone has a soul mate somewhere."

Now it was Joe's turn to stare. Dr. Dean was not shocked about meeting a gay person at all – he still thought he was straight! The fact that he last dated a girl when he was sixteen years old did not tell him that he dated boys, but that he never dated at all. The fact that he was not interested in women did not tell him that he was interested in men, but that he was a heterosexual who had given up on finding "the one."

Later Joe sat in his new office – it was a nice one, with a bank of three open windows that looked out over the green campus with buildings like ornate Gothic mansions.

There was a broad walnut desk, a real, solid bookcase instead of those pitiable hanging shelves, and two chairs embossed with the New England College logo. Soon the bookcase would be crowded with his books on gay history and culture, and the chairs would be occupied by students asking questions about their assignments in Gay Studies. Would they, too, be asking or thinking, "Did your wife come with you?"

Maybe Dr. Dean based his question on statistical probability. Only 10% of the population is gay, and most of them abandoned Kansas the moment they heard that Oz existed, so perhaps only 5% of the men one encounters in central Maine don't have wives or girlfriends, or want them. But then why would Dr. Dean refuse to believe that Joe belonged to that 5% after his "There is no right woman speech"? Surely there are many more gay men in the world than straight men who last dated women at age sixteen.

If you wish a new acquaintance "Merry Christmas" based on the statistical probability that 90% of the American population is Christian, the statement "I don't celebrate Christmas" would certainly make you think that your acquaintance is Jewish, Muslim, Buddhist, or Hindu, not a Christian discouraged by the commercialism of the holiday. No, Dr. Dean must not be aware that gay people exist at all!

But wait – in the 1950s, it may have been possible to live an entire lifetime without ever learning that gay people exist, but not today. They appeared in movies and on television, albeit as bizarre stereotypes. They were raged against in Congress. Pride Parades got first-page newspaper coverage. Of course Dr. Dean *knew*. Why wasn't the information retrieved to explain a man who was not interested in women?

Perhaps the knowledge that gay people exist was linked only to a very specific memory, such as frilly queens gossiping in the lobby of the Winter Garden Theatre after a performance of *Mame* that he saw thirty years ago, but not to anything in his everyday life, not to anyone he might encounter on his own campus. Or perhaps he didn't *want* to know, so he would repress the knowledge whenever possible, literally forgetting that gay people exist if there was any other possible explanation, even the most bizarre.

Are You a Convicted Felon?

Dr. Dean was not unique. During his first few weeks in Kansas, Joe heard about "his wife" often.

The assistant manager who signed him up for a membership at the World Gym told him that his wife could work out with him for free.

The pastor at St. Paul's Episcopal Church mentioned the clubs she might be interested in.

The clerk who signed him up for a Super Value Discount Card at Hannaford's Supermarket offered him a second card to take home for her.

The DMV employee who issued his new driver's license asked if she liked cold winters.

Colleagues, student assistants, new neighbors, church parishioners, and random people at the gym or the bank asked "Are you married?" or "Do you have a wife?" within a sentence or two of "Hello."

It was simply how one made conversation in Kansas, foolproof because it could never result in an awkward silence. If a man had a wife, he could launch into detailed descriptions of her tastes and interests that would suggest more conversational cues ("So she is collects Byzantine ceramics? Well, his wife. . . ."). If he had no wife, he could describe his girlfriend, or the kind of woman he was looking for. Only if he was aching from a bitter divorce or despondent over his failure to meet a woman would he find the question disconcerting, but then he could be reassured, like Dr. Dean reassured him: "The right woman is out there. You just have to keep looking."

No one in Kansas ever asked "Do you have a boyfriend or girlfriend?" No assistant manager who signed him up for a gym membership told him that "your partner" could work out for free, no pastor mentioned the clubs "your wife or significant other" might be interested in, and no grocery store clerk gave him a second Super Value Discount Cart for "your domestic partner." Regardless of whether they were young or old, uneducated or educated, screamers or polite bigots or gay-friendly, they "knew" that the person standing in front of them right now was straight. One professor who asked "Do you have a wife?" ironically had a "GLBT Safe Space" sticker affixed to her office door.

Joe usually refused to respond, "I do not have a wife, I am gay," since that would imply that he had been "passing," pretending to be straight.

In Oz, they despised gay people who passed, who refused to hold their date's hands at the movies until the lights dimmed, who kept no photos of their partner on their desk at work, who walked down the street with their copy of *The Advocate* facing inward, lest someone see the words "gay and lesbian" on the cover. They were worse than homophobes. Passing was a betrayal of their heritage, a slap in the face of all "real" gay people, an assertion that being gay was shameful. To be accused of passing was unthinkable.

Instead, he rolled his eyes – here we go again! – and responded as if the questioner weren't assigning him an unwelcome alien identity. To any question with the word "wife" in it ("Did your wife come with you?"; "How does your wife like it here?"; "Do you have a wife?"), he answered, "We actually call them partners. 'Wife' only refers to women."

No one got it. They always said something like, "Ok, Mr. Politically Correct, *partner*. How does she like it here?"

To "Are you married?", he answered, "No, I'm not allowed to get married in this state. It's illegal."

That response caused a flurry of speculation, as the questioner tried to tease out the "mystery" with increasingly unlikely guesses: "You can't get married because you're already married?" "Because you're not a citizen?" "Because you're a convicted felon?" "Because you owe money to the IRS?" "Because you have a venereal disease?" The most bizarre guess came from a retired professor at a faculty party: "Because you are under age?"

Even when they had to mull it over, they were so accustomed to believing that everyone on Earth is straight that they simply could not think of: "You are gay." Or they refused to think of it, struggling for any other possible explanation. He was an illegal alien, or a convicted felon, or a fifteen year old with a Ph.D., anything but gay.

Occasionally Joe found their refusal to know so annoying that he relented and said, "No, I can't get married in this state because I'm gay." Then some of the questioners recoiled in homophobic panic, and others became angry – "Oh, that! Why did you just say so, instead of making him go through this rigmarole?" But most laughed. "Of course! How stupid of him! How could he have missed that?"

This book is about how they could have missed it.

---

[1] To preserve their privacy, most names of people, organizations, colleges, and cities are pseudonyms. Some incidents have been modified for narrative purposes.

[2] Rich, Adrienne. "Compulsory Heterosexuality and Lesbian Existence." *Bread, Blood, and Poetry: Selected Prose 1978-1985.* New York: Norton, 1991; Grahn, Judy. *Another Mother Tongue..* Boston: Beacon Press, 1984. Warner, Michael. "Fear of a Queer Planet." *Social Text* 9.4 (1991): 3-17; Norton, 1994; Wittig, Monique. *The Straight Mind.* Boston: Beacon Press, 1992.

Chapter Two
A Bar Called Somewhere

Derry was an iconic New England town, cluttered with arching Colonial houses where one would almost expect to find men in tricorner hats discussing *The Federalist Papers* over their pints of ale. There was a green square, the Mall, where they held a weekly farmer's market, and a massive Parish Church where string quartets held concerts. Mariner Street reminded Joe of Bleeker Street in the West Village, lined with antique shops, art galleries, and tiny cafés with outdoor seating in the summer. All that was missing were the gay people.

No rainbow flags flew from any of the arching Colonials on Main Street. Joe walked the Mall amid droves of men and women holding hands, clutching each other's shoulders, reigning in their kids and dogs; no one else walked the Mall alone. The outdoor cafés on Elm Street were crowded with elderly men and women drinking coffee with milk and discussing their grandkids, their 401Ks, and the other effluvia of long heterosexual lives. No car parked at the Parish Church had a lambda bumper sticker.

Inside, he struck up a conversation with a lean, bearded young man who seemed to be alone, but a moment later a girl arrived and kissed him on the cheek and grinned at him. *Not gay,* he thought.

Statistically, 2,100 of the 21,000 residents of Derry should be gay. Even if a third of them, 700, were still children, being raised as if they were straight by oblivious parents, and another 1,000 had long since packed their things and moved to Oz, that still left 500.

There should be at least four men in pink-triangle t-shirts wandering amid the hundred on the Mall, at least one lesbian couple among the fifty sitting at outdoor cafés on Mariner Street, twelve gay people in the audience at the Parish Church. But Joe saw none at all. Where were they?

Maybe they were passing. Even though pretending to be straight was a grievous sin in Oz, it might be a necessary evil in harsh straight world, where holding hands at an outdoor café would cause the manager to telephone the police, where a rainbow flag flying from a porch would invite firebombs, where straights who overheard the word "gay" on the Mall would start screaming death threats.

But Joe didn't even see pairs of men or women skittishly avoiding each others' bodies and dropping the word "gay" from their conversations. He saw no pairs of men or women at all, nor, for that matter, any men and women who were alone or tagalong "gay friends' to a straight couple. In restaurants, movies, concerts, all of the places where one might go with a partner, *everyone,* without exception, was accompanied by someone of the other sex. No wonder they asked so often about his wife; in all of their lives they had never met any man who was not accompanied by a woman, any woman who was not accompanied by a man.

Maybe the 500 gay adults who remained in Derry were not merely passing, they were completely submerged beneath a straight façade. Some might not even realize that they were gay.

Once in West Hollywood, a spry white-haired Methodist minister and his wife appeared at the All Saints MCC, having driving 100 miles from Palmdale. He explained that he had just realized that he was gay, at the age of 62. He had been attracted to men all his life and had never once been attracted to a woman, but he believed that everyone on Earth felt the same way, so he followed the crowd and married his best friend. They continued like that for 38 years, hearing occasionally about gay people but never making the connection, until one day she returned from a trip to the Palmdale Public Library with a very old book, *Familiar Faces, Hidden Lives: Gay Men in America Today*. "I figured out your problem," she announced. "You're gay."

Maybe the 500 gay residents of Derry were likewise spending their lives ignoring their same-sex loves or dismissing them as mere friendships, convinced that there was no one else on Earth who failed to swoon over the other sex, believing that they were in fact straight. Maybe they were sitting at this moment with their husbands or wives at the cafés on Market Street, kissing the cheeks of boyfriends or girlfriends at a concert in the Parish Church, reigning in children and dogs on the Mall, wondering why they were so lonely and sad.

How does one go about finding the gay residents of Kansas, when almost all of them are passing, and most are so entirely submerged beneath a straight façade that they don't even know that they are gay?

Citizens for Equal Protection

The best place, Joe figured, was through gay community organizations. Surely one has to be aware of one's identity to join the Gay Pride Committee, or even a social group like a Gay Bowling League.

But in Kansas, gay organizations are very few, and most try to pass with nondescript names:

Alliance for Full Acceptance
Citizens for Equal Protection
Quad Citians Affirming Diversity
Your Family, Friends, and Neighbors

Maybe they had no choice; maybe the word "gay" in their name would cause death threats and firebombs; but still, after seventeen years in Oz, Joe found it hard not to look at them with disdain, as "traitors."

Other than the Rainbow Coalition, for college students, the only gay organization in Derry was a local chapter of PFLAG (Parents, Families, and Friends of Lesbians and Gays), the organization founded in 1973 by Jeanne Manford for straight parents trying to understand and support their gay children. Later the focus expanded to include straight friends, and finally the straight children of gay parents. It was the largest gay advocacy organizations in the world, with 200,000 members in 500 local chapters, working on dozens of different issues, from homophobia in high schools to discrimination in the workplace.[1] Gay people were not turned away at the door – no one asked if you are parent, child, or friend – but still, it was for pro-gay straights, not for gay people themselves.

Somewhere

In the absence of organizations, the second-best place to find gay people was at a gay-specific bar or nightclub. Every city in Kansas had several, and most small towns had at least one. Since gay children growing up learn nothing about gay culture except, perhaps, for the existence of bars, they were traditionally the first stop on the road into community; many "coming out" stories began with circling the local gay bar a dozen times, afraid to go in.

Even in Oz, bars were reliable, comfortable places for just being around your own people. At clubs and organizations, you have to listen to speeches or discuss issues, but at the bars you don't have to do anything at all.

But successful bars in Oz must always be fully open to the view of curious passersby, lest anyone accuse the patrons of trying to pass.

In West Hollywood, Joe lived around the corner from the Rage, with its name sprawling in a splash of rainbow letters and louvered French doors that opened to the street, so you could sit at one of the little tables and be seen, your gayness visible to the world.

In the West Village, he lived a few blocks from the Eagle, a leather bar with its name emblazoned on the likeness of a giant eagle outside, and a patio open in the summer, where you could stand in both literal sunlight and in the figurative brightness of gay pride.

But in Derry the nearest gay bar, thirty miles south in Portland, emphasized its passing with the cleverly closeted name "Somewhere" ("Where were you last night?" "Somewhere"). The front door was not locked, but he never saw anyone use it; they always went around to the back-alley entrance, lest passersby see them going in and recognize them as gay.

There were no windows facing the street, lest passersby peer through and identify a coworker or neighbor within.

But no doubt most of the straights in town had no clue that the nondescript façade crammed between an insurance agency and a doddering stationery store was a gay bar, or a bar of any sort, or a gay venue of any sort.

Was Kansas trapped in a pre-Stonewall time warp? Did gay people still live under the threat of being fired from their jobs, kicked out of their apartments, rejected by family and friends, arrested, remanded to mental hospitals? Was passing still necessary for survival?

Joe soon discovered that the patrons of Somewhere never thought about whether passing was necessary or not. It was simply a fact of life. Being gay was by definition a secret. Surely, they asked, people who live in Oz weren't foolish enough to tell just anyone? You might "come out" to a very close friend, perhaps to your sister, but never to your parents, certainly not to your neighbors or coworkers – and being visibly gay to strangers on the street – are you insane?

But passing wasn't an unfortunate necessity, the lesser of two evils. It was a fun game! The patrons of Somewhere spent many happy hours telling him their tips on how to be "gay in plain sight," keep the straights guessing or oblivious.

One night Frank, a 32-year old salesman from Portland, said that when his boyfriend called him at work for some reason, he told the receptionist that the mysterious caller was his brother-in-law, his sister's husband, helping plan her surprise birthday party! He chuckled at the complexity of his fabrication. "I just might bring him to the office Christmas party, say that his sister is out of town and he's lonely. Maybe we'll even flirt with some of the women, really play it up for them!"

When Joe told Frank that in Oz they never passed, or if we did, they were criticized as traitors, he was incredulous. "You'd actually introduce your boyfriend around the office as your boyfriend?"

"I have, many times. Danced with him at office parties. As a matter of fact, he used to kiss him goodbye at the airport."

Frank laughed. "Now, you know you're making that up! Where would this airport be, in Never-Never Land?"

On another night at Somewhere, Joe sidled up to a blue-collar type looking lost and lonely on the wrong side of the bar. They started talking about passing, and Joe told the story, by now part of his regular repertoire, about kissing his boyfriend goodbye at the airport. But instead of expressing the usual incredulity, he became angry: "Why do you have to flaunt your sexuality like that and make everyone uncomfortable? Straight people don't do that!"

Joe was flabbergasted. True, patrons of Somewhere never really believed his stories of gay people dancing, holding hands, or kissing in plain sight of straights, unless they had visited Oz themselves, but usually the idea made them pensive and sad, thinking, "I know you're just making it up, but if only such a place existed!" To be criticized for *not* hiding was bizarre.

Once a patron of Somewhere even criticized Gay Pride. "If there weren't so many of those damned parades," he said, "The straights would accept us more. Standing on a float, wiggling your behind and telling everyone that you like to suck cock! How ridiculous!"

Since Joe had helped plan eight Gay Pride Festivals and marched in well over a dozen Parades, he bristled. Pride has nothing to do with one's sexual activities, he yelled. It is about celebrating our fight against oppression, our common history, our common destiny. But he had already moved on to talk to someone who would understand the virtue of allowing straights to believe that they were alone in the world.

In a year of assiduous searching, Joe managed to find only five gay people at Somewhere, and perhaps all of central Maine, who didn't spend their lives pretending that they were straight.

Warren, a short, very portly nurse, and his partner, a tall, very skinny art history major at the University of Maine, invited him to their apartment on the south side of Derry. They watched *I, Claudius* on dvd and ate Thai food, and Warren told him, "Maine isn't New York. People just aren't political up here, gay or straight. They just don't make an issue of it."

Jesse, slim, bearded, and extremely fey, ran an antique shop on Main Street in Derry. He had lived in the same house his entire life, a large Victorian now cut up into studio apartments. He had Joe over for dinner amid 40-odd years of paraphernalia, magazines piled to the ceiling, an old cast-iron stove, shelvesful of ceramic frogs. They listened to whiney torch songs. When he asked for something a little more upbeat, he browsed through an extensive collection and found a single upbeat track on a single cd. As he got increasingly depressed, Jesse talked about how he was just looking "a man to take care of him and keep him warm."

Randy, a carpenter and upholsterer, grew up in Portland and moved to Boston the moment he turned eighteen, but came home two years ago, with his partner Juan in tow. They claimed to belong to a "small gay church," but when Joe attended, he found wall-to-wall straight couples.

When he asked about that inconsistency, Randy said he meant "pro-gay," and Juan added, "What do you care? Do you go to church to worship the Lord or to get laid?" The only conceivable reason to be around other gay people, they believed, was to get laid. Since they already had each other, they were perfectly happy living among straights, in a straight-only world.

In *Uncle Tom's Cabin* (1852), the pre-Civil War bestseller, elderly slave Uncle Tom approves of his slavery and does everything he can to help maintain the Peculiar Institution. Civil Rights activists later adopted the name for African-Americans who work to maintain the policies that keep them oppressed. Somewhere had its own brand of Uncle Toms, men who kept no photos of their partners in their wallets or on their desk at work, went alone to their office parties, introduced same-sex dates as "friends," invented straight romances. They even, in a weird 1984 doublespeak, tried to make passing seem like a positive way to achieve liberation. Randy told Joe: "As long as we make being gay this big, important thing, the straights are going to dislike us. But it's really just a tiny detail. Why cares who I sleep with? I'm so much more than that."

Something So Very Personal

Since many gay people in central Maine believed that their gayness was a terrible secret, they were horrified by the idea that someone might inform straights, either by accident or by devilish design.

When two members of the Rainbow Coalition at New England College visited Joe's class, they offered this bit of staggeringly bad advice: "When you are in public, do not say hello to the people you have met at Rainbow Coalition. Pretend that you don't know them. They might not be out yet, and their straight friends will wonder why they know someone gay."

"Number One," Joe complained, "Why would you hang out with straights who are so homophobic that they get upset over a fellow straight knowing someone gay? Number

Two, why would you snub a gay friend just to avoid upsetting such horrible bigots? Number Three, if you're lying to your friends about being gay, you must not think much of them."

They stared at him. "But most members of the Rainbow Coalition are still in the closet," one suggested.

"Closets are for terrible secrets."

Joe checked Miss Manners, the etiquette doyenne, and discovered that she was not homophobic. She suggested that at dinner parties one avoid boy-girl seating arrangements, to accommodate guests who may be partnered with persons of the same sex. However, she also advised never informing anyone of a friend's gayness. If one was asked directly, one should state, in an indignant tone, "Why, I have no idea! I would never dream of asking something so very personal!"[2]

That is how Joe would respond if he were asked about another's bedroom practices. But being gay was not about a bedroom. Straight desire was very public; straight loves received announcements in newspapers; husbands and wives, boyfriends and girlfriends introduced each other openly and eagerly; in the absence of an introduction, rings on fingers told us instantly that a person is straight.

It was the presumption that being gay is uniquely "personal," too intimate to inform others about, that allowed straights to forget that gay people exist at all, and allowed gay people to be complicit in their own oppression.

Does He Know Dorothy?

In the years before Stonewall, all sorts of code words were available to refer to gay men without acknowledging their existence: *sensitive, artistic, musical, that way,* even *you know,* accompanied by a hand flutter. Gay people themselves had a repertoire of code words and phrases to use to avoid tipping off eavesdroppers and being remanded to jail or the mental hospital. Even the word *gay* was code. In 1954, the straight who heard "I was at a gay party last night" from the next table at a café would conclude only "festive."[3]

Joe thought that speaking in code was a relic of past oppression, like contractual marriages and green carnations, until he met a gay man named Jerome at Somewhere. Jerome was middle aged, graying, but no older than fifty. He must have been a child at Stonewall. He must have spent his adolescence in the first flurry of gay liberation, his young adulthood in the halcyon days of *Making Love* and *The Front Runner*. He had never had to pass in order to survive. Yet he did pass, even among other gay people. He had somehow acquired a vocabulary full of codes and circumlocutions. When Joe mentioned a friend back in the West Village, Jerome asked:

"Does he belong to the fraternity?"

He was mystified. "What fraternity? I never belonged to a fraternity in college."

"No, no," Jerome said, marveling at his denseness. "I mean, does he know Dorothy?"

Joe knew about Dorothy Gale, of course, the protagonist of Frank L. Baum's classic *Wizard of Oz* novel. The 1939 movie adaptation, with its campy catchphrase "I don't think we're in Kansas anymore," was the probable origin of the terms "Oz" for the gay world and "Kansas" for the straight world.

And he knew that Judy Garland, who played Dorothy and then became a performer with a repertoire of throaty, depressing torch songs. She was a favorite of the tortured, depressed gays of the 1950's closet. Some speculated that grief over her death in 1969 sparked the resistance to police harassment that led to the Stonewall Riots.

Her name still popped up from time to time in homo-phobic stereotypes.

A polite bigot once asked Joe, "Why do gay men like Judy Garland?"

In the movie *Cruel Intentions,* a gay high school student tries to "go straight" by discarding his collection of Judy Garland cds.

On the tv series *Will and Grace,* Grace's elderly mother asks if "[gay men] still make out to Judy?"

But what bizarre circumlocution led from Judy Garland's antediluvian fanbase to Dorothy Gale, and thence to "knowing Dorothy" as a euphemism for gay? Joe had never heard it before, and with no other *Wizard of Oz* reference, he was stumped.

"Dorothy who?" he asked.

Now Jerome was getting visibly frustrated, as he tried to think of even more obscure code phases. "I mean, does he go to our church?"

In the days when gay people could never, ever set foot in a church, lest they be torn to shreds by the blathering homophobes therein, this phrase may have been useful, but surely it is meaningless when thousands of local congregations and a dozen denominations have gone on record as "welcoming" or "affirming" gay people. Joe had never heard it before.

"What church?" he responded. "I used to go to the MCC, but here in Maine I'm stuck with Unitarian."

"Not *church,* church!" Jerome exclaimed. "Is he. . .you know. . .one of us?"

Finally he caught on. "You mean, is he *gay*?" He spoke very loudly, bellowing the word "gay." Jerome had evidently never heard it spoken aloud before, not even in a gay bar. His jaw dropped, his eyes bulged, and he nearly knocked over the bar stool in his haste to reach the exit.

By saying the word aloud, by breaking the silence, he was acknowledging that gay people exist, and that was a major taboo. They must all pretend that there is no one gay, not here, not now, not even at Somewhere.

Must Be Discrete

The third best place to find gay people, or at least gay men, was in an internet chatroom. Gay chat websites offer at least one room, usually several, for every big city, but small towns are all lumped together into "Upstate New York" or "All of Colorado Except Denver." Chatting with people from everywhere in Maine, from Portland, thirty miles south, to Aroostook County, three hundred miles north, hardly fosters local friendship. Nevertheless, Joe forged ahead, logging on almost every night, ignoring the hustlers ("Model available"), con artists, and barely-literate homophobes who would burst into the room, type "Your all faggs??? That's nasty!!!!!" and rush out again. And he answered the question of the 500 missing gay people, at least the 250 men.

There were 238 profiles from men living in or near Derry, almost precisely the number he anticipated. They were obviously aware that they were gay, but still, most had wives or girlfriends, or planned to get them for the sake of passing.

Jean, age 45, a teacher (he wouldn't say where, or what subject), identified himself as a MWM, a Married White Man. No one "knew," not his wife, not his kids, not his parents or friends, and he had no intention of telling anyone - if he came out, he told him, he would lose his wife, his kids, his house, his job -- "it would be the end of me!" Yet he was unable to completely ignore his need for same-sex intimacy. He was not looking for friends or romance; he wanted sex, with "no strings," no names, no evidence that he was gay, not even the faintest light in the darkness.

Robbie, age 22, a New England College student majoring in biology and planning to go to medical school, identified himself as "bi-curious." Perhaps he was genuinely attracted to both men and women, perhaps not, but he led an indefatigably straight public life: dining and dancing with girls, a string of steady girlfriends. His parents, friends, and classmates had no idea about his "secret." He fully intended to marry a woman someday; no doubt she, too, would have no idea. He wanted to meet a man for sex, preferably a regular encounter, but again there must be no strings, no names, no evidence. Everyone must pretend that no gay people exist.

TJ, age 32, worked at an insurance agency and was thinking of going back to school for an MBA. He was gay, but "not out to anyone," not even his parents: "My mother would have a heart attack and drop dead, seriously!" He was dating a woman from the office, what they used to call a "beard," except that she didn't realize that she was being used to maintain a straight facade. "She thinks it's serious, but I know it won't go anywhere."

He wouldn't meet at one of the cafés on Mariner Street (his agency was only a few blocks away!), or on the Mall (his brother lived nearby!), or at his apartment (what if a neighbor saw his car parked outside?), or at his apartment (his roommate was at work, but what if he came home early?). There must be no evidence, however tenuous, that might "implicate" him as possibly gay.

The missing gay men in Derry were missing because they were horrified by the idea that someone might "find out." They were skulking in a 1950s closet, believing, irrationally, that discovery would be mean losing their jobs, losing their friends, maybe even jail time. Thus, they were married, or they intended to marry, or at least spend their lives being seen on the arm of a woman, and no one, parent, child, wife, neighbor, social scientist conducting a survey, or passerby on Market Street, must ever suspect.

Straight Friends

Some of the patrons at Somewhere were astonished that Joe was expending so much time and energy looking for gay people, when he could find straights so much more easily. "How can you limit yourself to one tiny segment of society?" they would ask. "How can you cut yourself off from so much human experience?"

He countered that Oz contained more than enough human experience for a dozen lifetimes.

In West Hollywood, he knew a professional model from Norway with a degree in art history, a busboy from Guatemala who spoke little English, the star of a popular tv sitcom, and the lieutenant governor of the state of California.

In the West Village, he knew the minister of a spiritualist church, a psychiatrist who owned a million-dollar apartment, a seventeen-year comic book collector who had been with his partner for three years, and an Anglican priest.

Would his life really become so much richer if he added some men who have sex with women or some women who have sex with men to his social calendar?

But maybe, in Kansas, they were right. The gay people in Derry, at least the ones Joe managed to find, were all of a type, quiet, conservative, traditional, cowering. If he wanted pro-gay friends, maybe he could find them among straights.

Straight women were out. In spite of the mythology about "fag hags," straight women who seek out close friendships with gay men, in all his years in Oz, Joe encountered only two such couples:

A middle aged lawyer who invariably dined with an older woman in grotesquely heavy makeup.

A young middle school teacher who came to a party with his "best gal," a portly fellow teacher who referred to gay people as "homos" (she was not invited back).

They believed that gay men with straight female best friends had, at best, been brainwashed by a homophobic culture into believing that a man is incomplete without a woman at his side. They might even be trying to pass! Joe couldn't abide the idea of being accused of passing, so he sought out no straight women. That left men.

Straight men were easy to find and easy to talk to. They were eager to extend a sweaty hand from the next treadmill at the gym, or to help him complain about the long line at the bank, or to strike up a conversation from the next table in the faculty dining room. But moving from casual conversations to invitations to "do something" proved daunting. Their nights and weekends were thoroughly occupied by wives and children, or, if they were unmarried, by their obsessive quest after "the one."

What they called "friends" were really acquaintances, same-sex neighbors and coworkers, sources of friendly conversations over the hedge or cubicle wall, but not much else. At most they occasionally invited a group of "buds" to the house to watch "the game." One-on-one friendships, pairs of friends going out to dinner or to a movie or to the clubs, were completely unknown.

Some straight men did recall sweetly passionate "best friends" from childhood. The bond may have lasted through adolescence, in a cool, cordial form, but eventually it faded away to yearbook memories. Now they recalled those boyhood friendships with a bemused incomprehension: could they ever have been so ignorant of what really matters in life?[4]

Oddfellows

Giving up on finding straight men on the street who were willing or able to take the leap from "game bud" to "friend," Joe decided to join some local community organizations. As you drive into any small town, you'll see a welcome sign emblazoned with the symbols of a dozen fraternal brotherhoods like Moose, Elks, Oddfellows, and Masons; service organizations like Toastmasters and the Junior Chamber of Commerce; and hobbyist clubs, like bowlers and bird watchers.

A hundred years ago, these groups were the mainstay of American social life, places of social networking, homosocial bonding, and arcane rituals.[5] Joe's great-grandfather was an 11th level Oddfellow in the Lagrange, Indiana Lodge, and his wife belonged to the ladies' auxiliary, the Rebekahs.

Since World War II, membership in fraternal and service groups has been steadily shrinking, along with the decline in participation evident everywhere in America, as more and more people assume that friendships are irrelevant, that a husband or wife and kids is all anyone should ever want or need.[6] In big cities, the vast Masonic Temples and B.P.O.E. Halls have been transformed into restaurants, theaters, apartment complexes, or sites of gun shows; or they stand empty, mysterious, probably haunted, eliciting curious glances from passersby. But in small towns, they are likely to be bright and noisy with activity; about a quarter of small-town men still belong, more if they're middle aged or elderly. And it's easy to find straight men in them, since they do not believe that gay men exist.

The March meeting of the Derry Rotary Club involved discussions of wellness, empowering youth, and providing financial security "for your family," followed by a patriotic song, "She's a Grand Old Flag," and then coffee, cookies, and endless "small talk" queries of "Are you married?"

Habitat for Humanity, which builds homes for the homeless, sounded more expansive, in theory: it does not discriminate against gay people in employment decisions, and the Arcus Foundation awarded the Kalamazoo Valley chapter $40,000 for its work with the GLBT community.[7] But in Derry, Maine, the meeting involved needy families, all apparently straight, and afterwards coffee, cookies, and a repeat of the "Are you married?" litany.

Joe was afraid to walk into a meeting of a fraternal organization without an invitation, but a search on the websites of the Benevolent and Protective Order of Elks, Moose International, and the Toastmasters revealed that many activities and announcements presumed universal straightness; indeed, they seemed obsessed with wives and kids.

A keyword search for *gay* revealed only halls festooned in "gay colors" for Christmas, as if no other meaning for the term had ever existed. A search for *lesbian* and *homosexual* was fruitless. Non-discrimination clauses mentioned only "color, creed, or nationality," omitting "sexual orientation." The erasure did not necessarily imply that individual members or groups were homophobic; he found no rules condemning "homosexuality," no news stories of gay people refused membership. In January 2006, Moose Lodge 318, in Huntington, Long Island, even allowed Bravo's *Queer Eye for the Straight Guy* to give them makeovers and photograph them for a fundraising calendar.[8] Nevertheless, in the everyday life of the lodge, they behaved as if gay people did not exist.[9]

Big Brothers

Organizations for adults who wanted to nurture and mentor youth sounded promising. Derry had Big Brothers/Big Sisters, Junior Achievement, and the YMCA, and in Portland, thirty miles south, there were Boys and Girls Clubs, Campfire Boys and Girls, Youthbuild, and Young Life. But the refusal to believe that gay people exist was, if anything, more prevalent in organizations for youth. The counselor at Big Brothers advised him that he should make sure "his wife" was ok with the time commitment, and, more disturbingly, assumed that not one of the needy children or adolescents in the program could possibly be gay: "He's thirteen, so he hasn't discovered girls yet"; "He's fifteen, so you'll have to handle boy-girl issues."

Junior Achievement, a group for high school entrepreneurs and their adult mentors, notes on its website that it is open to all, without regard to race, color, creed, or "any protected characteristic as required by law," but that coy way of not having to mention sexual orientation may backfire, since discrimination against gay people was legal in most cases. The counselor at the Junior Achievement office did not ask about "his wife," and suggested that he teach sexual orientation-neutral career planning. But in the sample session he attended, the conversations, jokes, and asides between mentor and student were all about boys liking girls.

Other youth-oriented organizations were as certain as the Rotary Club that gay people, youth or adult, do not exist. Even though the YMCA has been using the double-entendre-laden Village People number "Y.M.C.A." in its television commercials, its website consists entirely of smiling nuclear families, with gay people not mentioned at all, except in the human resources department. There may be no discrimination on the basis of sexual orientation in hiring decisions, but on the gym floor, everyone was assumed straight.[10]

The farm-friendly Four H Program admitted gay youth and volunteers, but you would never know from their official website. The Girl Scouts had a "don't ask, don't tell" policy: "We do not permit the advocacy or promotion of a personal lifestyle or sexual orientation" (that is, other than straight).

Only Campfire U.S.A. stated that everyone was welcome, "regardless of race, gender, socioeconomic status, disability, sexual orientation, or other aspect of diversity." Not coincidentally, its official website showed two grinning boys rather than a nuclear family, along with a slogan asserting that it builds "integrity, responsibility, [and] tolerance."[11]

Even the overtly homophobic Boy Scouts of America managed to assume that gay people do not exist. The controversial ban of gay scouts and adult volunteers was not justified anywhere on the official website – indeed, it was not mentioned at all. There was a mission statement about BSA's "Support of Diversity" that proclaimed scouting's "value. . .to all people, regardless of background" without ever clarifying that some backgrounds are unwelcome.[12] An anti-Semitic organization surely couldn't manage to avoid mentioning its dislike of Jews, nor a racist organization the race that it finds distasteful. How was it possible for Boy Scouts to avoid mentioning the very group they oppose? Because they did not have a specific homophobic intent. When called on it, most of the 4.7 million boy scouts and their 1.7

million adult leaders would no doubt admit to a dislike of gay people, but they were never called on it, never think about it at all. They spent their lives believing that every scout, every leader, every human being is straight.

Guys are Guys

When he did manage to make social contacts in central Maine, Joe assumed that it would not be necessary to state "I am gay" immediately after "Hello." Surely Dr. Dean was a fluke, elderly, isolated, and preoccupied the day they spoke. Surely most younger men, not taken by surprise, would wait to assign him a sexual orientation until they heard him talk of a boyfriend or girlfriend or saw him gaze with appreciation at a passing man or woman. Surely, in the absence of evidence, they would leave the question moot, or simply ask. But in fact, they behaved precisely like Dr. Dean. They never weighed the evidence, they never left the question moot, and they never asked. They assumed he was straight from the moment we met, and nothing short of a jarring "I am gay!" could make them "remember" that gay people exist.

Joe first saw Benny, an English instructor working on his doctoral dissertation on the Beat Generation, in the locker room of the campus gym, stripping out of a plaid shirt, suspenders, and a ridiculous red bowtie. Joe concluded that he was straight almost immediately, through the gleaming, new-looking ring on his finger and his casual references to his wife. Surely Benny concluded that he was gay almost immediately, from his answer to the questions "What's your field?" (Gay Studies) and " What are you working on now?" ("religion and gay people"), or from the shelves of gay books, rainbow flag mouse pad, and gay pride poster in his office.

But no, when an attractive girl passed, Bennie nudged him so he could look. Joe said "I only look at guys."

That wasn't enough.

Benny commented on one of his wife's eccentricities with "Wait until you're married!" Joe said "I can't get married in this state, it's illegal."

That wasn't enough.

Finally Joe invited him over for pizza and trotted out every clue he could think of.

He invited him to select a movie to watch from his collection of 200-odd DVDS. Other than a few classics, they all had gay characters, gay subtexts, or covers displaying muscular guys with their shirts off. Without a word or even an odd look, he selected Alfred Hitchcock's *North by Northwest,* which has none.

Benny sat on his couch, directly behind a coffee table containing a pile of gay magazines. On top was an issue of *The Advocate,* selected deliberately because the word "Gay" was written on the cover several times in big, bold letters. Surely it was unmistakable.

It wasn't enough.

After the movie, they were channel surfing, when an attractive man appeared on the screen. "Wait – go back," Joe exclaimed. "That guy was totally hot!"Benny said "Don't be funny."

So Joe said, in a loud, clear voice, "I am gay."

Benny replied, "Really? I had no idea! You hide it so well."

Hide it?

Is She Hot?

After they "found out," Joe straight friends continued to behave as if he were straight.[13] They expected him to nod knowingly when he referred to the details of his life with a woman, the tampons, the panty-hose, the lipstick. They expected him to help him rate potential partners or evaluate his latest triumph; but he became "uncomfortable" when he asked his assistance in rating his potential partners or evaluating his triumphs.

Did they want him to continue to pass, even after he was "out"? Had they simply forgotten to make the mental adjustment – "guys are guys, and guys like girls, with the single exception of the guy right here in front of me." Or did they think that straight desire and practice was a constant: "guys are guys, and guys like girls, even gay guys."

Two incidents support the "guys like girls, even gay guys" theory. When Benny asked about his "first time," he evoked a college boyfriend.

He quickly said, "No, no, he meant first time with a woman."

"I've never had sex with a woman. Gay, remember?"

"How do you know you don't like it if you've never tried it?" he said, like a mother trying to convince her child to try some noisome vegetable.

"How do you know you don't like men, if you've never been with one?"

He ignored the parallelism and persisted: "You should try it at least one before making your decision."

One night another straight friend, Richard, asked if Joe would kick a certain female celebrity out of bed.

Joe explained that he would kick every female celebrity on the planet out of bed, that his bed was reserved for the exclusive use of men. If she really needed a place to sleep, he might offer her his couch.

Richard grinned, nodded, feeling special – chosen to be privy to his "secret," learning about Oz that none of his straight friends knew existed. But a moment later, another female celebrity appeared on tv, and he asked again if he would kick her out of bed.

Joe was included, invited along, confided in, with no homophobic discomfort. Richard was a bit skittish about sitting too close to him on the couch, apprehensive of a lustful lunge, but Benny would strip down next to him at the gym without even bothering to shield his penis from his admiring gaze. Once he noticed Joe's attempt to sneak a peek, graciously displayed himself, and said "So, what do you think? Could I get a boyfriend?"

But when it came to the particulars of the male straight experience, rating girls in bikinis or nodding knowingly about pantyhose draped on shower curtains, then Joe suddenly became straight. They were so accustomed to universalizing straight experience that they could not conceive of anyone who did not share it. Being gay did not mean liking men *instead of* women, it meant liking men *in addition* to women. Everyone, everywhere is straight, but this person right here in front of me is *also* gay.

One Date is Enough

Gay children grow up being told over and over, a hundred times a day, that they are straight, "like everyone else on Earth." It often takes years of struggle and self-examination for them to realize that they have been lied to, and more years to get around to telling family, friends, and the people who keep calling them for dates. If the struggle lasts into adolescence, they will probably go out on a few boy-girl dates, because they haven't figured it out yet or because they want to fit in with their straight peers.

But in central Maine Joe quickly learned to never admit to the slightest straight practice, no matter how trivial, like a single evening spent sitting next to a girl at a high school basketball game twenty years ago. People would cling desperately to the incident as proof that he was not gay at all; he was confused or discouraged, but straight.

When the date to a basketball game twenty years ago came up, Benny sighed with palpable relief. "So you do date girls!" he exclaimed. "You do date girls! How can you be gay?"

Startled, Joe thought for a moment about how best to respond. "I had five dates with girls in high school, when he wasn't out yet, and there was tremendous pressure to date, everyone always asking 'What girl do you like?' and 'What girl are you taking to the dance?' I started dating guys in college, and since then, I've gone on about one date per week, or two or three when I'm in a relationship."

Joe went to his computer and calculated. "Let's see. . . that's 2,232 dates. Five with girls -- that's 0.22%. And not one since I was sixteen!"

Benny was not dissuaded by his statistics. "But if you thought a girl was cute enough to ask out, you must be able to notice. How can you just give up on being. . .on women, without even trying?" He stopped himself from saying "normal."

Joe kept calculating. "I had sex for the first time a few weeks after my twenty-first birthday. Since then, most dates have ended with sex, and of course when I'm in a relationship we have sex almost every day, so let's say. . .4,634 sexual experiences, every single one of them with a man. I did kiss two girls, in high school."

"So you've kissed girls!" Benny exclaimed in triumph. "You're not immune!"

"But I wasn't out yet. I had no idea that there was such a thing as being gay."

Todd shook his head, as if to say "irrelevant." He was so desperate to believe that gay people do not exist that he was willing to judge kissing two girls at the age of seventeen a more reliable measure of his sexual orientation than a lifetime of 4,634 sexual experiences with men. Sighing, Joe gave up.

---

[1] PFLAG Official Website, http://www.pflag.org/

[2] Martin, Judith. *Miss Manners' Guide to Excruciatingly Correct Behavior*. New York: Norton, 1985. Her latest edition omits the offending statement, but still suggests that one assume heterosexuality under all circumstances, until one has been specifically informed to the contrary.

[3] Reuter, Donald F. *Gay-2-Zee: A Dictionary of Sex, Subtext, and the Sublime*. New York: St. Martin's Press, 2006.

[4] Walker, Karen. "Men, women, and Friendship: What They Say, What They Do" *Gender and Society* 8.2 (1994): 246-265

[5] Adams, James E. *Dandies and Desert Saints: Styles of Victorian Masculinity*. Ithaca, NY: Cornell University Press, 1995.

[6] Putnam, Robert. *Bowling Alone: The Collapse and Revival of American Community*. New York: Simon & Schuster, 2001.

[7] Habitat for Humanity International Recruitment, http://www.habitat.org/hr/; Arcus Foundation, http://www.arcus foundation.org

[8] "Queer Eye for the Moose Guys," *Moose Magazine Online,* February 2006, http://www.mooseintl.org. Of course, allowing gay men to give you grooming tips is quite different from embracing them as lodge brothers.

[9] BPO Elks USA, http://www.elks.org/; Loyal Order of Moose, http://www.mooseintl.org; Toastmasters International, http://www.toastmasters.org/

[10] Junior Achievement, Inc, http://www.ja.org; YMCA, http://www.ymca.net/

[11] Girl Scouts USA, http://www.girlscouts.org/; "Girl Scouts and Discrimination," http://www.bsa-discrimination.org/html/gsusa.html; Big Brothers-Big Sisters of America, http://www.bbbs.org; National 4-H Council, http://www.fourhcouncil.edu/; "All About Us," Campfire USA, http://www.campfire.org.

[12] Boy Scouts of America National Council, www.scouting.org

[13] See Price, Jammie. *Navigating Differences: Friendships Between Gay and Straight Men.* Binghamton, NY: Harrington Park Press, 1999.

Chapter Three
The Best Books Ever Written

The insistence that gay people do not exist, or if they do, they "notice" the other sex as much as straights, couldn't be based merely on the absence of rainbow flags flying from porches or the lack of men or women holding hands at band concerts. Only 1.4% of the population of Derry was African-American, yet there can be little doubt that the white people in town knew that African-Americans exist. If they rarely saw racial minorities on the street, then they at least heard about them in school, or saw them on television, or read about them in books.

Joe sat in his office in Massachusetts Hall on a cool November afternoon, and watched the grey-streaked clouds outside, and the small, ice-tinged flakes falling onto the bare quad. He could see dozens of students below, meandering west toward the Student Union with its gigantic statue of a polar bear, or north toward the red brick library, or south toward the dorms. All of them, without exception, were carrying armloads or backpack-loads of books.

Did none of those books mention that gay people exist? At some point every college student will certainly read about Jews, at least for an assignment about the Holocaust, and about African-Americans, at least for an assignment about slavery. But would they ever read about gay people? And afterwards, during a lifetime of Book Clubs and jaunts to the public library and clicking on the Recommended Titles at Amazon.com, would gay people ever appear?

Before his year in Derry ended, he would find out.

Money and Marriage

Joe had always had a fondness for the *classic novel*, the "serious" sort of book-length fiction that appears on the syllabi of English classes, on lists of "The Best Books Ever Written," and eventually on the "To Do Before he Die" lists that we compile during our midlife crises:

1. See Paris
2. Read *The Grapes of Wrath.*

Though it is the goal of vast numbers of wannabes who register for creative writing classes, the classic novel is extremely limited in theme and structure. It must be naturalistic (no elves, fairies, or time machines) and character-driven (not a lot of action), and the plot, as Terry Eagleton points out, must be about "money and marriage, social mobility and the nuclear family,"[1] that is, topics of pressing interest to elite, upwardly-mobile straights. Not coincidentally, this is the group most likely to become teachers and college professors and write the lists of "The Best Books Ever Written." Topics of interest to gay people, same-sex romance, commitments, even friendships, are almost entirely absent.

Fortunately, Joe, like almost every gay person, learned at an early age to "queer" fictional texts, to look in the margins, to listen to the unspoken, to find undercurrents of same-sex desire where literary critics, English teachers, and the authors themselves cry "Nothing like that is intended!"[2] Gay people may find meaning in same-sex friendships of particular intensity and permanence, or same-sex friendships of any sort, men storming into dungeons to rescue men, or women rescuing women. Gay men also seek out the rare description of male beauty amid the endless evocations of women's breasts. Some of the classic novels that Joe read in high school or college became lifelong companions, packed in boxes whenever he moved, reread every few years, precisely because they offered something more than the deadening litany of marriage and inheritance:

In Jane Austen's *Pride and Prejudice*, Mr. Darcy decides to court Elizabeth Bennett because his "friend" Mr. Bingley is courting her sister, a classic triangulation which allows same-sex partners to stay together forever while meeting the social requirement of straight marriage. All of Jane Austen's novels seem to include at least one young man with a passionate devotion to a male friend and no interest in women, though he may marry for the sake of the inheritance: Robert Ferrars in *Sense and Sensibility*, Tom Bertram in *Mansfield Park*, Frank Churchill in *Emma*. No wonder, as a Jane Austen blog points out, most of her male fans are gay.[3]

When Charles Dickens wrote about straight relationships, he often stumbled into bathos, but his evocations of same-sex friendships are intimate and touching. Early in *Great Expectations*, Pip becomes interested in Estella, but he is much more emotionally invested in Herbert Pocket, and at the end of the novel he has become an "old bachelor," eschewing the company of ladies altogether. James R. Kincaid agrees that the novel is "about men. . .there are powerful moments of homoerotic bonding."[4] The same could be said for *Oliver Twist*, *Nicholas Nickleby*, and *David Copperfield*.

Kidnapped, by Robert Louis Stevenson, is usually relegated to junior high English classes. Perhaps it is considered inappropriate for adults because there is no straight courtship or marriage. Instead, it offers David Balfour and Alan Breck learning to care for each other while adventuring in the wild Scottish highlands.[5]

The Great Gatsby, F. Scott Fitzgerald's tale of the jazz age, is "about" Jay Gatsby's obsession with Daisy Buchanan, who is married to someone else. However, narrator Nick Carraway, who exhibits not a whit of straight interest, seems rather taken by Gatsby himself. When he famously evokes the "orgiastic green light," is he really thinking of Gatsby and Daisy, or of an unrequited love of his own?[6]

But Joe soon discovered that most classic novels are not so easily queered.

What is *Madame Bovary* but the chronicle of Charles and Emma Bovary's marriage woes?

Crime and Punishment features not a moment of same-sex tenderness, nor even a positive same-sex friendship; instead, Raskolnikov's salvation comes through the love of the prostitute Sonya.

In *The Sun Also Rises*, the subtle homoeroticism of Bill Gorton's attraction to Jake Barnes is overwhelmed by endless descriptions of what girls look like.

The editors of The Modern Library apparently selected the list of the Top 100 Novels of the Twentieth Century[7] because of their ability to forestall queering, so assiduously did these tomes omit not only gay people but same-sex friendships, in order to obsess over the minutiae of straight relationships.

In Aldous Huxley's *Brave New World*, sex is the chief recreation of the oppressed proletariat of a near-future dystopia, yet no one considers anything but straight sex.

In John O'Hara's *Appointment in Samarra*, a small-town salesman ignores his wife, tries to pick up women, describes ladies' breasts in great detail, and never has a tender thought about a man.

Portnoy's Complaint, by Philip Roth, is about a middle-aged man whose neurosis leads to "extreme sexual longings, often of a perverse nature," but always straight; same-sex desire does not appear in the novel except for a few "fairy" and "fag" slurs.

Only a few of the novels on the list could be effectively queered, and real, actual, overt gay characters did not appear in any of them. Three novels did evoke same-sex practice, as a symbol of debauchery and moral decay, but so subtly that most readers would never notice.

In *I, Claudius*, Robert Graves assigns the decadent, insane Emperor Caligula a laundry-list of sexual practices, including bestiality and incest, but only hints at his interest in men, as if it is by far the most disgusting of the lot.

The Heart is a Lonely Hunter, by Carson McCullers, tells of the mute John Singer, who loses his partner – *possibly* his lover -- to insanity and subsequently takes up with a number of small-town outcasts, some of whom may *possibly* become his sexual partners.

Vladimir Nabokov's experimental novel *Pale Fire* consists of an epic poem plus commentary, supposedly edited by college professor Charles Kinbote, who is insane: he suffers from a "homosexuality" so gingerly described that no one will notice who is not looking for it.

A fourth, *Brideshead Revisited*, by Evelyn Waugh, is a little more open about the sexual "debauchery" of teddy bear-toting wastrel Sebastian Flyte. However, it remains a story of a straight relationship. Protagonist Charles Ryder, a naïve Oxford undergraduate, does experience something of a crush on Sebastian, and *may possibly* have sex with him, but it is mere British schoolboy homoeroticism, fleeting, age-specific, a presage to the true, real, permanent loves of men and women. In the end Sebastian is merely a plot device to get Charles invited to Brideshead, so he can meet the "girl of his dreams."

The massive classic novels praised as encapsulating "all of human experience," such as *The Decameron, Gargantua et Pantagruel, Der Zauberberge,* and *The Ship of Fools,* were most problematic. Joe found that "all of human experience" meant "straight experience only."

One of his undergraduate professors proclaimed once that if Western civilization were ever destroyed, we could rebuild it simply by reading James Joyce's *Ulysses.* Within its pages are every philosopher, every poetic genre, every bit of European history, all the best that had ever been written or thought. However, a civilization recreated from *Ulysses* would be entirely gay-free.

The day in the lives of Stephen Dedalus in 1904 Dublin contains endless scenes of men gazing at ladies and discussing ladies, a visit to a brothel, and a nine-page long stream-of-consciousness sentence that depicts Molly Bloom's thoughts during an act of heterosexual intercourse. But there is only one tangential reference to same-sex practice: Buck Mulligan is asked his opinion of "the charge of pederasty" sometimes brought against William Shakespeare. He thinks it's ridiculous.[8]

Bestsellers

Academic books usually sell less than 2,000 copies to their audience of college professors and graduate students. Trade books, hidden away in bookstores for browsers to stumble upon by accident, may sell 5,000. But novels that a publishing company deems worthy of the big guns, reviews, book signings, lecture tours, and display-racks in chain stores, may become bestsellers, with a million or more copies filtering off the shelves onto coffee tables, then to nightstands, and finally to the remainder bins at Half Price Books.

Bestsellers usually aspire to become classic novels, though not one in a hundred makes it. (*The Great Gatsby* didn't make it; readers in 1925 were too busy grabbing up copies of *The Constant Nymph, The Keeper of the Bees,* and *The Glorious Apollo.*) Therefore they mimic the conventions of the classic novel: they are naturalistic and character-driven, with plots involving straight courtship, marriage, and relationships.

During February of his year in Maine, Joe read the top ten novels on the *New York Times* fiction bestseller list. They all featured one or more men and women undergoing a courtship or marriage, usually while proclaiming that all people everywhere are straight, or as John Grisham tells us in *A Painted House,* "It's only natural for boys to look at girls."

None of the novels included any significant same-sex friendships; indeed, most of the authors took great pains to scrape every last hint of same-sex potential from their dismal, lonely worlds.

Lone Eagle, by Daniele Steele, traces the on-off romance of two straights from the days of Pearl Harbor through the 1950s and the turmoil of the 1960s, but excludes Gore Vidal, Tennessee Williams, the Beat Generation, or the emergence of Gay Liberation.

Fall on Your Knees, by Ann-Marie MacDonald, is about four sisters involved in lifetimes of straight relationships in Cape Breton, Nova Scotia; one of them spends time in New York City in the gay-friendly 1920s, but fails to visit a rent party in Harlem or to meet any of the gay actors on Broadway.

In *A Walk to Remember,* by Nicholas Sparks, the protagonist reminisces about high school in 1958, where he fancied himself a rebel without a cause like James Dean. "All of the boys" in his high school were wild about girls, and none had the slightest interest in boys except as antagonists and competitors. No gay people exist, in the 1950s or in 2002. Not even Sal Mineo. Not even James Dean.

Amy Tan's *The Bonesetter's Daughter* is set in San Francisco, an iconic gay city, and the protagonist, hard-as-nails career woman Ruth, knows that gay people exist. In fat, she "suspects" her partner in yoga class because he has a beard, his nails are clean, and he wears a wedding ring on the "wrong" hand. But a few pages later, he turns out to be straight. The clues merely provide a brief conflict, as Ruth finds herself attracted to a man she believes to be "off limits." But then she learns the truth and happily falls in love with him, and the reader happily continues, assured that there are no actual gay people in San Francisco.

Choosing settings where gay people should logically appear, and then omitting them, sounded to Joe like a deliberate decision by the authors: "See, no gay people exist, not even here!" But, he conceded, it was also possible that Anne-Marie MacDonald had no idea that 1920s New York was a gay mecca, Nicholas Sparks had no idea that James Dean was bisexual, and Amy Tan did not realize that San Francisco has a large gay population.

Or perhaps they never even thought of including gay people in their novels because there were none in their everyday lives. No matter how much background research they do, authors base characters, themes, settings, and situations to a great extent on their own experiences. If during the last week or the last month every friend they have lunched with, every couple they have seen strolling through the park, every expert they have consulted for a background detail has been straight or passing, if gay people have appeared only in an occasional news item or a catty stereotype in a movie, or nowhere at all, then when they sit down in the study of their rambling New England farmhouse, switch on their computer, and begin to write Chapter Six, the world of their imagination will be irredeemable straight.

The Cat Who Was Straight

If upwardly-mobile straights are drawn toward the classic novel and the best seller, what about downwardly-mobile and socially-stalled straights? Joe's uncle liked horror novel, his mother mysteries, and his sister Harlequin Romances. These were all "genre fiction," so-called because they follow carefully delineated conventions – horror must involve a supernatural threat, mysteries an unsolved murder, and so on – though good writers often challenge or transcend the conventions.

Genre fiction is deemed "mindless" by English professors and snubbed by Top 100 Novel lists because it breaks the cardinal rules of the classic novel: it is fantastic rather than naturalistic, with spaceships, demonic dogs, and murder victims in rooms locked from the inside; and it is plot-driven rather than character-driven; we read to find out what will happen next, not what the protagonist is feeling inside. Did it break the third rule, too, Joe wondered, or was it as obsessed as the classic novel and the bestseller with straight courtship and marriage?

He started with his mother's favorite genre, the murder mystery. At the Barnes and Noble in Augusta, Maine, he bought ten of Lilian Jackson Braun's *Cat Who...* series, about cats who "solve" the murder: they knock over a vase containing a secret message, curl up on a book with the killer's identity hidden in the title, yowl to draw attention to a vital clue, and so on. He chose them because they were extremely popular, each installment selling millions of copies, and because the setting of Moose County, "four hundred miles north of everywhere," reminded him of Cicely, Alaska of the television show *Northern Exposure*, which numbered gay people among its "eccentric" residents.

The *Cat Who...* novels were pleasantly written, as charming and cozy as an English high tea, with nothing harsh or troubling, not even the murders (the victim was always an outsider, no one you cared about, and the culprit was always thoroughly reprehensible, about to foreclose on an orphanage or open a fast-food franchise in town). Braun described Moose County with precision, consistency, and wit. However, she introduced every character with the match-making fervor of an elderly yenta, as someone's straight husband or wife, girlfriend or boyfriend, as married, engaged, divorced, widowed, or "single and available." Those who were single invariably embarked on a straight romance before the cats yowled at the third clue. Not only were there no gay people, there were no significant same-sex friendships at all; all human association in Moose County, from the most casual to the most intimate, occurred exclusively between men and women.

The only potential queering came from protagonist Jim Qwilleran, formerly a crime reporter in the Big City, who inherited a billion-dollar fortune and moved north to bankroll civic improvement projects and solve murders. A "confirmed bachelor," he dates but never tries to kiss his "lady friend," librarian Polly Duncan. He is a devotee of the theater and the arts. He named his Siamese cats Koko and Yum-Yum, after characters from Gilbert and Sullivan's *Mikado*. He sounded to Joe like a 1950s gay stereotype – you couldn't even say his name without lisping. But no fan apparently ever considered the possibility that Qwilleran could be gay. He was a "nice boy," a gentleman, a cat lover, there-fore obviously straight, just like Liberace.[9]

A parody, *The Cat Who Killed Lilian Jackson Braun,* had the murder take place in a gay bar. Fans were livid with rage that something so sordid as "homosexuality" would be al-lowed to intrude upon their picture-perfect, i.e., straight, world. A Lilian Jackson Braun online encyclopedia called it "mental garbage," and summarized the plot with a single sentence: "you don't want to know." [10]

Straight mystery fans certainly knew that gay people exist. But they didn't *want* to know. They read murder mys-teries in the first place in order to forget.

Forbidden Passion

Joe's next stop at the Barnes and Noble in Augusta was the romance aisle. It was a paradise of beefcake, cover after cover of muscular torsos bursting out of lumberjack shirts or British redcoat uniforms, bulging biceps, six-pack abs, rugged jaws, piercing eyes. But every man was depicted with a swooning woman in his arms. Of course classic no-vels and bestsellers always evoke heterosexual passion, but in the genre of the romance, which accounts for a fifth of all books sold in the United States every year, heterosexual pas-sion drives the plot. The protagonist, always female, spends hundreds of pages falling for, kissing, thinking about, break-ing up with, and reconciling with a man who has the sculpted physique of a Greek god but has a dark secret or is afraid to love. The fun for readers is in seeing the same basic situation played out in new, unusual settings, such as in a small-town travel agency or in the world of competitive dog shows.

Joe read two novels by Linda Howard, a well-recognized master of modern romance.

Dream Man, which tied for first place on the Romance Reader website's list of Top 100 Novels, stars Marlie Keen, a sweet-natured clairvoyant who longs to lose her gift and embark upon a "normal" life, that is, find a man. When she starts seeing through the eyes of a serial killer, she must team up with a macho detective named Dane Hollister.

Though setting is present-day Orlando, Florida, there are no gay characters, and gay people are mentioned only two times. Dane denigrates a house for being painted in "ice cream colors, which only women and gays knew the names of"; and the killer explains that he prefers female victims because he isn't "queer."

Open Season stars Daisy Minor, a prim librarian who reaches her 34th birthday and realizes that she still isn't married, so she tries to attract a man by hanging out in seedy bars on the wrong side of town. She sees too much, and must team up with a macho police chief named Dane. . .um, Jack Russo. He grudgingly falls in with her.

Daisy has a male best friend, antiques dealer Todd Lawrence, whom she seeks out for hair and makeup tips. She suspects that he is gay, but he turns out to be straight. Macho cop or fey antique dealer, conventional or rebellious, guys are guys, all waiting, without exception, to be redeemed through the love of a woman.[11]

Not a Child Molester

Joe knew that gay men are not entirely absent from the genre of horror fiction. They are the villains, the leering transvestites, the killer clowns, the bug-eyed child molesters, the effeminate antique dealers who may or may not be vampires.[12] They storm out of the shadows into "our" real, normal, straight world, threatening to kill, eat, pervert, or otherwise destroy innocents. The protagonists, stalwart straight men or women, must then rise up, battle the effeminacy, banish the gayness, and restore straight normalcy to the world.

In the movie *Silence of the Lambs,* after FBI agent Clarice Starling triumphs over the creepily effete cannibal Hannibal Lecter and the woman-killing transvestite Buffalo Bill, a straight colleague with the grandiosely symbolic name Noble Pilcher offers her a retreat at his sister's house. There she recovers amid the wholesomeness of siblings and pets and heterosexual intercourse: "On the bed are many large quilts, and on the quilts and under them are several large dogs. . .additional mounds beneath the covers may or may not be Noble Pilcher. . .but the face on the pillow, rosy in the firelight, is certainly that of Clarice Starling."

In the 1970s, Stephen King almost single-handedly revitalized the moribund genre of horror fiction by using contemporary settings, small-town high schools and supermarkets instead of castles in Transylvania, throwing in vast numbers of pop culture references, and making his protagonists "total guys" who listen to rock music, watch the Boston Celtics, and drink Budweiser, not mild-mannered scholars translating eldrich lore from the Assyrian. But he failed to modernize the homophobia: the Bad Thing that come in from outside is always transvestite, effeminate, pedophile, or an amorphous, leering nightmare of gayness.

In *The Shining,* the Overlook Hotel in Colorado is haunted chiefly because it was the site of unimaginable depravity during the Jazz Age. There was even sex *between men!*

In *It,* the monster takes on the most terrifying form imaginable, a leering, effeminate, pedophile Clown.

In *The Tommyknockers,* a mincing, lisping gay stereotype who also happens to be a necrophiliac and probably a pedophile receives a gory, well-deserved punishment.

In *Everything's Eventual*, a man who stakes out a highway rest stop in the hope of engaging in depraved, disgusting acts *with other men!* receives a gory, well-deserved punishment.[13]

Cell has no gay monster. Tom, one of the three survivors who band together when everyone with a cell phone turns into a murderous zombie, is certainly a stereotype, a throwback to the "confirmed bachelors" of 1960s comedy: mild-mannered, soft-spoken, with long, nimble fingers and King's usual "something of a lisp" (one wonders where King got the idea that all gay men lisp. Did his research consist of watching the old Jack Benny program?)

Yet Tom displays hidden reserves of courage, he becomes an invaluable member of the group, and straight protagonist Clay likes him – the highest praise a gay man can hope for! King even addresses the pedophilia libel by giving Tom a paternal bond with twelve-year computer geek Jordan (see, gay men aren't all pedophiles after all).

But Tom is identified as "gay" only twice, both times during the denouement (by that time, King no doubt reasoned, his homophobic readers would be too engrossed in the story to toss the book aside in disgust). Otherwise you have to parse out Tom's gayness through the stereotypes, or through subtle hints. When they take refuge at Tom's house, Clay notes the fastidious neatness and muses that it is characteristic of men whose lives "don't necessarily include women." When Tom plans to spend the night with a hysterical teenage girl, to comfort her, he says, "You know I'm safe with her, right?" Clay nods; he understands that Tom actually means "I won't try anything sexual because I'm gay."

Those readers who do figure it out will find a gay man who is a welcome change from King's earlier villains, but still an effeminate stereotype, and still utterly alone in the world – no lover, no friends, just a pet cat. When Clay suggests a dangerous, zombie-ridden trek from Boston to Maine to search for his estranged wife and son, Tom eagerly agrees to come along. Why does he never suggest seeking out his local friends, or at least checking to see if they survived? Perhaps he has none, or perhaps Clay's quest is infinitely more important.   Home, hearth, and happiness, the world we are striving to rebuild, is still exclusively straight.[14]

Always Male and Female

Science fiction plots are driven by technological marvels or intriguing far-future societies, not by marriages and inheritances. Fantasy plots are driven by magical marvels or intriguing Elfland societies, not by the battle of good versus gayness. But straight romance is still in the air. Joe checked a half century of science fiction novels, and found that they nearly always end with a man and a woman falling into each other's arms.

A. E. Van Vogt, *Two Hundred Million A.D.* (1943): "L'onee was waiting. Together they closed and sealed the door. Together, they went up out of the darkness into the light."

Raymond Jones, *Man of Two Worlds* (1951): " 'I want to marry you] more than anything else in the world," Elta said. She drew close and laid her head against his shoulder. 'More than anything else.'"

Michael Moorcock, *The Wrecks of Time* (1966): "She winked at him. He grinned and winked back. They walked into the house."

John Brunner, *Interstellar Empire* (1976): "She came down the steps to Ordovic, and put her arm around his waist, smiling."

R. M. Meluch, *Wind Dancers* (1981): " 'Shall we go to bed together, get drunk, gamble away what money we still have, or start a fight in a bar?' Roxanne hooked his arms. 'One of those.'"

Ben Bova, *Mars* (1992): "His gaze ended with Joanna, standing slightly aside from all the others, strong and proud. Her eyes gleamed back at him."

Timothy Zahn, *Night Train to Rigel* (2006): "'Would you. . .I mean. . .' 'Like a little companionship?' I finished for her. 'I thought you'd never ask!'

On and on, interchangeably, as if every story is really the same story, as if the spaceships or magic swords are just colorful background details, like travel agencies and dog shows in romance, as if the real goal of science fiction and fantasy is to display straight romance.

Women in science fiction and fantasy occasionally form strong, passionate bonds with each other, but not one novel in a hundred features a friendship between men. When two men approach each other as anything but sneering competitors in the quest after glory or women, Joe was amazed, and scurried to find everything else the author had written. When two men actually decided to stay together at the end of their journey, he felt jubilant, yet nervous, as if someone might steal the scene away, or it would turn out to be a dream.

Alan E. Nourse, *Raiders from the Rings* (1962): "'I hope you realize what you're buying into,' Ben warned. Tom grinned at his spacer friend. Side by side they crossed the glittering concourse and started down the ramp toward the spaceport."

Christopher Stasheff, *A Wizard in Bedlam* (1979): "[Gar asked:] 'Can you stand a hitchhiker?' Dirk found himself grinning. 'I thought we were supposed to be rivals.' Gar shook his head. 'Friends, right from the start.'"

Diana Wynne Jones, *Deep Secret* (1997): "Rob is someone I can talk to. There aren't many other people that I can tell real stuff to, but Rob's always going to be one. I've been over to see him quite a lot since all this happened, and we've talked of *everything*."

Often it did turn out to be a dream. In later installments of Christopher Stasheff's *Wizard* series, Gar abandons Dirk to marry a woman and "settle down" on an amenable planet. In spite of his assurance that Rob is always going to be in his life, Nick does not mention him at all in the sequel to *Deep Secret*, nor does he form any new homoromantic relationships. Instead, he meets a girl.

If only one science fiction novel in a hundred contained even the inchoate gayness of a pair of buddies, and even that bond is likely to vanish in the sequels, how many novels contained real, self-affirming gay characters? Joe found a few bisexuals, a few lesbians, but virtually no gay men at all.

Since the "new wave" of sociological speculation in the 1970s, many science fiction stories have depicted some form of "alternative sexuality." There are species with three or more sexes or none at all, species whose sex organs change every season or at random, societies where technology makes changing one's sex as easy as changing one's shoes. Nevertheless, every sexual encounter, every romance involves a being who is male (right now) and one who is female (right now). The message is clear: one can be attracted only to beings with complementary sex organs; same-sex desire does not exist.

Some stories were set in future or magical societies in which bisexuality is "accepted," but not people drawn exclusively to the same sex, not gay people, especially not gay men, and any characters who happen to mention in passing that they are bisexual experienced only straight passion during the course of this particular story.

The vast majority of science fiction and fantasy stories that Joe read did not bother with "alternative" sexualities at all, or even with offhand references to bisexuality being "accepted": there were straight men and women, period.

In the thirty-plus volumes of Piers Anthony's *Xanth* series, whimsical adventures set in a pun-ridden fantasy land, there was not even one same-sex romance, not even when one of the partners could change gender at will, nor even a single reference to same-sex desire or practice.

Stork Naked (2006) proposes that in Xanth, the old tale of babies coming from storks is true; prospective parents simply send the proper forms to the stork headquarters, and wait nine months for delivery. Since no straight intercourse is required, one would expect same-sex partners to apply for babies quite often; but only male-female couples are mentioned. Every reference to desire, love, or romantic relationships in the book, and in all Xanth books, carefully specifies that it is straight. When a fairy tells the adventurers about a strange lake filled with "love water," they ask: "Standard love elixir? Male loves nearest female, and vice versa?"

Lest readers still not catch on that same-sex practices are utterly absent from Xanth, the fairy answers: "Yes. I have seen creatures there. I couldn't make out exactly what they were doing, but always male and female."[15]

Piers Anthony could easily let his "standard love elixirs" target the nearest *person,* and have the fairy say "they were *usually* male and female." But he was doggedly determined to keep Xanth gay-free. In his newsletter, he offered three responses to a fan's criticism of the ongoing erasure.

First, as someone who is "110% straight," whatever that means, he could never create believable gay characters (yet he was easily able to create ogres, demons, centaurs, mermaids, and talking storks).

Second, he was afraid that his publisher would not permit such a "controversial" move (but Avon Books had no such homophobic policy, and published many novels with gay characters, including the works of important gay authors Paul Monette and Gordon Merrick).

Third, he was afraid that including a gay character would ruin sales.

Straight science fiction fans did seem to be more homophobic than usual. On an online forum, a fan who asked why so many gay men like science fiction was told that it gives them hope: "since sf has new inventions and discoveries, there would be a great possibility for a cure for it."

A guide to Science Fiction Conventions advised straights who are subject to a same-sex advance to "refuse politely and clearly" instead of physically attacking their "assailant."[16]

Once Piers Anthony wrote in his newsletter that fellow science fiction writer Stephen R. Donaldson was gay (he was mistaken, having looked up the wrong Stephen Donaldson online).[17] Fans were livid: how dare he print "malicious slander" that "labeled a bestselling author as a homosexual!" A slightly less rabid homophobe worried that the "slander" would cause Donaldson to lose readers: "I have nothing against homosexuality myself," he wrote, "But. . .the general public is, in the vast majority, against it."[18]

Perhaps this was the reason for the absence of gay characters in genre fiction, Joe concluded: authors are concerned about sales more than any other love, and they are not willing to risk having even a single fan with "nothing against homosexuality" toss their book aside with a groan of disgust and walk out of the Barnes and Noble in Augusta, Maine empty-handed. But wouldn't a book with positive gay characters draw a dozen gay readers, or a hundred, for every homophobe who rejects it? The authors do not consider this possibility for an instant – they believe implicitly that their audience is 110% straight and 110% homophobic.

No Gay Muggles

Since childhood Joe had been collecting boys' books – not the picture-books for toddlers, but fast-paced adventure novels for middle schoolers, with titles suggesting stalwart heroes, exotic dangers, and cliff-hanging escapes: *Cannibal Adventure, Secret of Skull Island, Tom Stetson and the Giant Jungle Ants, Trapped in Death Cave.* After thirty years, even with frequent moves, gleaning, and discarding, he owned nearly 500. He preferred them to genre fiction for adults, since they omit the descriptions of women lounging about in bikinis, there is no climactic rescue of a woman from the villain's clutches, and there is no fade-out promise of straight marriage. Indeed, women are usually absent altogether, and the boy-meets-boy plotlines can be easily read as romance.

For instance, in *The Secret of Skeleton Island* (1949), the teenage Ken Holt, son of a famous journalist, escapes from kidnappers and stumbles into the office of a small-town newspaper, where he meets the editor's son, the massively muscular Sandy. The next day, they are both re-captured by the kidnappers. Although he became involved in the adventure only by accident, Sandy does not scram the moment he gets his hands untied; he sticks by Ken through many close-calls and run-ins with the bad guys, rescuing him and being rescued by him, right through the final cliffhanger. In the last chapter, Ken's father arrives to explain the mystery and write it up for his newspaper. Then, instead of saying good-bye with a mere promise to visit sometime, Sandy asks that Ken stay with him, come live with him forever. Ken is so overcome with emotion that he can barely assent. Most novels end with the promise of a permanent relationship, but here it is two boys, not a boy and a girl, who will live happily ever after.

However, the recent children's books that Joe read did not offer the safe harbor of same-sex romance: the children within were as straightly active as their elders, as prone to straight crushes and dates, and though sex scenes were omitted, they were quite likely to kiss.

In the thirteen volumes of the popular *Series of Unfortunate Events*, Lemony Snicket envisions a world of complete gender equality: there are offhand comments about burglars or surgeons being "she" that disrupt sexist assumptions that these jobs are always occupied by men; fourteen-year old Violet, the oldest of the unfortunate orphans, is somewhat "masculine," forceful, aggressive, a whiz at mechanics, while her brother, twelve-year old Klaus, is soft, passive, somewhat "feminine." Yet gender equality does not translate into gay equality: everyone in this world is straight. As the series progresses, Violet gets a boyfriend, and Klaus a girlfriend; the effeminate villain, Count Orlof, gets a girlfriend; and the narrator moans endlessly over his lost love Beatrice.

In *The Sea of Trolls*, by Nancy Farmer, a boy named Jack, living in Saxony in 753 AD, is kidnapped by Vikings and transported to their homeland as a slave. When he meets a Viking boy named Thorgill, one thinks, "Finally, a same-sex friendship!" But Thorgill is quickly revealed to be a girl, and Jack, of course, falls in love with her: "She looked truly beautiful in the firelight. Her eyes shone, and her hair. . .framed her face like a dandelion puff. . .Jack felt an ache in his heart." His world has no room for same-sex love or even same-sex friendship.[19]

During the first few installments of J. M. Rowling's *Harry Potter* series, the teenage wizard-in-training has a remarkably loving friendship with his Hogwarts Academy classmate, Ron Weasley. When a wizarding contest asks Harry to rescue the "person he loves the most" from an underwater abduction, that person turns out to be Ron. Surely a romance is not beyond all imagining. Perhaps in an attempt to squelch the homoromantic potential, later in the series Rowling makes both Harry and Ron obsess over girls. As if that wasn't enough, Harry learns that there will be a Wizard's Ball at Hogwarts, and he – like every student -- must bring a date "of the opposite sex."

The rule would not even exist unless the question of same-sex dating had come up before, and it had been banned by a homophobic administration. Rowling does not believe that everyone on Earth is straight, necessarily, but if you are gay, you must pass, bring an opposite-sex date to the Wizard's Ball, enter into a marriage of convenience, never for an instant let the world know. Harry may have escaped from his closet, but every gay wizard, every gay muggle is doomed to stay there forever.

The last scene in the last book of the series depicts all the major characters as adults. Harry has married Ron's sister Ginny, so they are now brothers-in-law. Isn't that what they really wanted all along? Meanwhile, Ron has married their other friend Hermione, and the effeminate antagonist Draco has married an unspecified woman. All loose ends are tied, all connections are made, everyone is straight or passing. Rowling concludes: "All was well."

After all of the books in the series were published, Rowling informed the world that Dumbledore, headmaster of Hogwarts, is – was – gay. No such revelation appears in any of the books, though one could "queer" the text, particularly in the last installment. But Joe found himself admiring the carefully placed layers of invisibility.

Dumbledore is an adult, not one of the children; children are always straight.

His gayness is revealed after he is dead, so there is no problem of having to deal with a living gay man.

None of the other characters were apparently aware that he was gay.

He lived his very long life constantly passing, lying to chums about the girls he liked, bringing opposite-sex dates to every Wizard's Ball, letting the gay students at Hogwarts believe that they were utterly alone in the world.

A few realistic children's books, dedicated to exploring all of the "problems" of contemporary youth culture, such as drug addiction, date rape, and gang violence, did think of the "problem" of gay people, but they face howls of outrage from straights. According to the American Library Association, children's books with gay characters were challenged, censored, or banned in the United States 6,000 times between 1990 and 2000.

Some 6,000 parents or teachers believed that letting children become aware of the existence of gay people would destroy them (most likely "turn" the straight ones gay). Others believed that books with gay characters were "unsuitable to the age group," or "sexually explicit," since straights may fall in love, marry, and kiss with a G-rating, but the word "gay" always evokes a bedroom.

The gay characters in these novels were almost always adults.

In *Tiger Flowers* (1994), by Patricia Quinlan, a boy's uncle and his partner both have AIDS.

In *Ironman* (1995), by Chris Crutcher, a high school athlete discovers that his coach is gay.

In *The Skull of Truth* (1997), by Bruce Coville, a boy finds a skull that forces people to tell the truth, and thereby learns his uncle's "secret."

Again and again, a straight kid faced the "problem" of accepting a gay father, uncle, teacher, coach, or older brother, an adult intruding upon the universal straightness of childhood. When Joe found a children's book in which an underaged character was gay, the cover carefully stated that "this is not a gay story, it's a human story. . .it's about friendship, love, being human."

What novel about straights was ever praised with: "This is not a straight story, it's a human story!" Straights were by default human, their loves the loves of all humanity.

To My Wife, My Lover, My Reason for Living

One could spend a lifetime avidly reading classic novels, bestsellers, genre fiction, and children's fiction, and never encounter a gay character, or any indication that gay people exist. But it was not merely an absence, not merely an oversight; authors went to considerable trouble to exclude gay people, and proclaim, loudly, jubilantly, aggressively, that everyone on earth is straight.

Even the packaging of a book proclaimed universal heterosexuality.

On a bright, cool day in January, Joe was reviewing the books for his classes, when he noticed that *Criminology, 7th edition* contained a preface announcing that author John E. Conklin was straight. He stated that he was married to Sarah Belcher Conklin, and he had four children. Thus, unless the children are adopted, he was informing readers that he had engaged in heterosexual intercourse at least four times.

Why, Joe wondered, did Conklin think readers would want to know about his sexual activities? If Joe ever began a lecture with a summary of whom he had slept with the previous evening, he would be sitting in the Dean's office before the day was out. Yet thousands of students in hundreds of colleges walk into Criminology class fully apprised of where Professor Conklin's penis has been.

Had he found yet another place for straights to assert their domination? Intrigued, he checked some of the other textbooks on his office bookshelf. Sure enough, in the preface to *The Basics of Social Research*, Earle Babbie reminisced about how, early in his career, he married Sheila and "created Aaron," a gratuitous evocation of the renowned scholar's orgasm. However, we heard nothing of the orgasms of either Roger N. Lancaster or Micaela di Leonardo, editors of *The Gender/Sexuality Reader*, perhaps because it was intended for Gay Studies courses, and the authors were either gay themselves or unwilling to brag about their heterosexuality to such an audience.

Next Joe checked the most recent 100 or so books in his home library, excluding those on gay topics.

Steve Otfinoski, author of *The Golden Age of Novelty Songs*, lives "in Connecticut with his wife, Beverly, and their two children, Daniel and Martha."

Orville Schell, author of *Virtual Tibet: Searching for Shangri-La from the Himalayas to Hollywood*, lives "with his wife and children in the San Francisco Bay Area" (at least he spared us the precise number of his orgasms).

Karl Beckson dedicates *Aesthetes and Decadents of the 1890's* to "his wife, Estelle, and his sons, Mace and Eric," and then helpfully informs us that "they are neither aesthetes nor decadents" (that is, not gay).

Harry Harrison, author of *Return to Eden*, "lives with his wife in County Wicklow, Ireland, where he is at work on his next novel."

About 50% of the authors of books in Joe's home library bragged about engaging in heterosexual intercourse. Men were more likely to brag than women, new authors more than established authors, and Americans more than Europeans. Not surprisingly, these were the same groups most likely to believe that no gay people exist. When they invited readers to judge them on the basis of their straight practice rather than the quality of their book, they did not intend to snub gay people, but to sway straights. But why would straights be impressed by a boast of straight orgasms? Surely they had engaged in heterosexual intercourse as well.

When a publishing company accepts a book, it asks the author to write a brief biography, to be used as the preface or as a back cover blurb. Authors are free to include any information that they believe readers would find interesting or useful. Thus, journalists mention their awards, fiction writers their cats (necessary to stir the creative juices), and an authority on pirates his home "by the sea." Perhaps the enumeration of straight practices derives from the Family Man Syndrome, the belief that straight men who have married and reproduced are infinitely more competent than those who have not.

If he is not an established author with awards or previous bestsellers, the male author will simply point out that he has married and reproduced, that he is a Family Man, therefore competent enough to sway the undecided at the Barnes and Noble.

Inside the book or outside, in the story or the cover blurb, Joe found a wasteland of straight desire, world after world where every man longs for women, every woman longs for men. There may be dragons, unicorns, interstellar empires, underground cabals, murders solved by prim English ladies, a thousand impossible things before breakfast, but gay people are beyond the possible, beyond the boundaries of what can be imagined.

---

[1] Eagleton, Terry. *The English Novel: An Introduction.* Oxford: Blackwell, 2004: 2.

[2] See, for instance, Sedgwick, Eve Kosofsky, ed., *Novel Gazing: Queer Readings in Fiction.* Durham, NC: Duke University Press, 1997, and his own *Queering Teen Culture: All-American Boys and Same-Sex Desire in Film and Television.* Binghamton, NY: Haworth, 2006.

[3] Duncan, Rebecca Stephens. "Sense and Sensibility: A Convergence of Readers/ Viewers/ Browsers." Pp. 1-17 in Laura Cooner Lambden & Robert Thomas Lambden, eds. *A Companion to Jane Austen Studies.* Boulder, CO: Greenwood Press, 2000: 14. Jane Austen Blog, http://www.austenblog.com/2008/06/23/weekend-bookblogging-jane-austen-lives-edition/

[4] Interviewed in Epstein, Norrie. *The Friendly Dickens.* New York: Penguin, 2001: 146.

[5] Buckton, Oliver S. "Reanimating Stevenson's Corpus." *Nineteenth Century Literature* 55.1 (2000): 22-58.

[6] For the homoerotics of *Gatsby*, see Kerr, Frances. "Feeling 'Half Feminine': Modernism and the Politics of Emotion in *The Great Gatsby.*" *American Literature* 68.2 (1996): 405-431.

[7] 100 Best Novels, http://www.randomhouse.com /modernlibrary/100bestnovels.html.

[8] James Joyce, *Ulysses*. New York: Vintage, 1990: 201.

[9] Unofficial Lilian Jackson Braun Fan Club, http://www.geocities.com/heartland/estates/6371/lillian.htm

[10] Lilian Jackson Braun Encyclopedia, http://home.att.net/~RACapowski/catFAQ.htm#ending

[11] Linda Howard Interview, http://www.likesbooks.com/lindahoward.html

[12] Benshoff, Harry. *Monsters in the Closet: Homosexuality and the Horror Film*. St.Martin's Press, 1997.

[13] Keesey, Doug. " 'The Face of Mr. Flip': Homophobia in the Horror of Stephen King." In T. Magistrali, Ed., *The Dark Descent: Essays Defining Stephen King's Horrorscape*. Greenwood Press, 1992.

[14] Tronolone, Thomas. "Stephen King Calls. Should Gay Men Answer?" After Elton, February 9, 2006. http://www.afterelton.com/print/2006/2/stephenking.html

[15] Anthony, Piers. *Stork Naked*. New York: Tor Books, 2006: 48.

[16] Science Fiction Convention Survival Guide for Newbies, http://www.locksley.com/neofans/mainpage.htm?

[17] "Ogre's Den," http://www.hipiers.com/newsletter.html ; "Piers Anthony Unbound," Slashdot.com, July 14th, 2002, http://interviews.slashdot.org.

[18] Piers Anthony Forum, http://www.voy.com/2066/40.html

[19] Farmer, Nancy. *The Sea of Trolls*. New York: Simon & Schuster, 2004: 433.

Chapter Four
Are You Ever Mistaken for Gay?

Joe's job at New England College would last for only a year, so during the spring semester it was time to start looking again. He scoured the joblists in the *Chronicle of Higher Education* and *The American Sociological Association*, and applied for everything, both visiting and tenure-track, not only in Gay Studies (there were only three, all recruitment season), but in gender, deviance, criminology, media studies, social theory, whatever he thought he might be able to doubletalk into "his main research interest."

He omitted the most prestigious universities (out of his league), and religious colleges (where the recruitment committee would probably try to exorcise the demons out of his application). Otherwise his only rule was that the college had to be within an hour's drive of Oz. If something appeared within commuting distance, even better... But he was not prepared to give up the lifeline of weekly visits and strike out into the wilderness, hundreds of miles from normalcy, from sanity, from home.

Academic jobhunting was a time consuming process. He needed:

- A letter explaining in detail how this job was the fulfillment of his destiny
- Three or four reference letters from colleagues proclaiming that he walked on water.

- Copies of his publications.
- An essay describing his teaching interests and research plans for the next five years.
- Course syllabi.
- An essay about his teaching philosophy, whatever that meant.
- Student evaluations and syllabi of the courses he had taught.

Thus, a complete application packet could easily run to hundreds of pages. Still, even the most soul-destroying, suicide-inducing one-years at Redneck State Technological College and Football Stadium received at least a hundred applications, and since Oz was an A-list destination for both gays and straights, a tenure-track there would receive over four hundred.

The twenty applicants who made it through the initial screening were called for telephone interviews, with questions ranging from the vague ("What are you working on now?") to the nitpicking ("How do you handle students who complain about their grades?")

The three or four who were able to correctly guess the answers that the search committee wanted were invited to the campus for a two-day visit. There they gave a lecture about their research, taught a sample class, or both. They were taken out to two breakfasts, one lunch, and two dinners, tour the campus and the community, introduced around at informal receptions, and interviewed by about a dozen people: the search committee, other faculty members, graduate students, the Dean, the Provost, and sometimes the President.

Between January and June of his year in Maine, Joe sent out 87 application packets. He had fifteen telephone interviews and thirteen offers of campus visits. He actually visited ten colleges, so during the round of dinners, receptions, tours, and formal interviews, he talked to nearly 200 people. Every one of them sat in on his lecture on gay youth or heard him talk about his research on gay youth, or saw his application packet, with two books and thirteen articles in Gay Studies. Yet still nearly twenty of them, nearly 10%, thought that he was straight.

Human relations law prohibits asking directly about an applicant's marital status or children, to protect straight applicants from the Family Man Syndrome, the belief that men who have married and reproduced are infinitely more competent than those who are not (they're "settled down" and stable), while women are infinitely less competent (they will no doubt be worrying about their children's sore throats or school marks rather than attending to their sales presentations). Still, Joe was asked "Are you married?" three times and "Do you have a girlfriend?" twice. He was asked "Do you have kids?", "How old are your kids?", and "How do your kids adjust to you moving around so much?" (Many gay men do have children, either adopted or the product of straight liaisons before they came out, but it is unlikely the questioners knew this; certainly it comes as an utter shock to his students.)

Three times he was told, "This is a great town for raising a family!", and half a dozen times he was bragged to about the quality of the local school system. He was shown a local Presbyterian church with an active singles' group. At dinner, he was nudged and told, "That waitress liked you!" On visit after visit, from the moment he was picked up at the airport to the moment he was dropped off again, an occasional question, comment, or aside betrayed an assurance that he must be a single straight or a married straight, that no other possibilities existed.

At a research university near Cleveland, a hefty bear of a graduate student listened intently to Joe's lecture on gay teenagers. He nodded, grinned, asked questions, as if a whole new world was opening up for him, and he sensed a budding Gay Studies scholar. But at the reception afterwards, he waylaid him, a plateful of mini-sandwiches in one hand and a plastic cup of slimy-looking punch in the other, and asked, "Do you have any teenagers of your own?"

Giving him the benefit of the doubt, Joe said that when he was in his twenties, gay men were almost never permitted to adopt. He never even thought about it. Oblivious, the grad student continued: "Lots of older people adopt nowadays. How old is your wife?"

At the same research university, an energetic, almost hyperactive professor of Women's Studies took Joe on a tour of the vast campus on a very cold day. She had not attended his lecture yesterday, so as they walked through the inside of every building to avoid freezing to death, he rattled on about gay teenagers. Oblivious, she asked, "Will your family be moving with you?"

Joe pretended to assume that she meant his family of origin: "No, my parents are very happy where they are."

"Will your wife be moving with you?"

"No, my *boyfriend* will probably stay in Maine."

This time she got it. With a knowing grin, as if she had just deciphered the phrase "friend of Dorothy," she told him that her husband's cousin was gay.

In a distant suburb of Philadelphia, actually closer to Newark, Delaware, an elderly golf-fanatic professor took Joe to lunch at a pub called Rock Solid, which was occupied entirely by tables full of boisterous fratboys from his liberal arts college.

Joe was pleasantly surprised: surely his host chose this place in order to gawk at the beefcake. But then he asked, "Don't you worry that, spending so much time around homosexuals will. . .you know, convince you to try it?"

Joe took a large bite of his hamburger to give him enough time to mull over an appropriately acidic response. Finally he said, "Not at all. I'm around straight people all the time, and I've never had any interest in trying *that*."

He blinked, stared for a moment, and started talking about his wife and kids.

At the second-best Mexican restaurant in a town near San Antonio, a very young professor, in his first year at the state university, insisted that Joe try a chimichanga the size of the Yucatan Peninsula, deep-fried and slathered with cheese. While trying to cram it down, Joe talked about his research. Suddenly the very young professor asked, "Given your research interests, does anyone ever mistake you for gay?"

Laughing, Joe answered quite truthfully, "No, no one ever mistakes me for gay."

At a liberal arts college near St. Louis, he chatted with the department secretary while waiting for a criminology professor to finish teaching his class so they could go to dinner. He finally arrived, led Joe into the hallway, then leaned close and said in a low voice, "She's single. Another perk, if you come here, right?" It took him a moment to realize that he was talking about the secretary!

Later, over burgers and pale ale at a microbrewery, he asked, "Are the girls in Maine hot?"

"I don't know, I'm not interested in girls."

Not comprehending, he promised that, if Joe took the job, they could go to a nightclub in St. Louis where the hottest girls in town hung out.

Joe's publications in Gay Studies made the erasure particularly puzzling: weren't they proof that he was gay? In the 1960s, when anyone revealed as gay would be fired instantly, the few scholars working on "homosexuality" always maintained an elaborate pretense of straightness, beginning their books or articles with gushing dedications to someone of the other sex -- "to his love, his life, his soulmate, the person whose glance still make him tremble" (when the political climate became less oppressive, they usually confessed that they had been bisexual or gay all along).

But now the opposite was true: campus politics, the desire to "present the right image," effectively limited scholars to studying groups that they belong to. Men who hoped to specialize in Women's Studies, or Caucasians in African-American Studies, or Roman Catholics in Jewish Studies, must reconcile themselves to being forever unemployable. Joe had never met a scholar in Gay Studies who was not personally gay or lesbian, except for Eve Sedgwick, the doyenne of queer theory – but she was tenured many years ago, and besides, she goes through great theoretical lengths to explain that she should be taken as "queer" in spite of accidentally liking men.[1]

Some of the questioners were probably unaware of his teaching and research interests – the details of the application packets must blur together after awhile. Some were probably testing him, to see if he would "make an issue of it" and assert himself rather than meekly pretending not to exist. But most probably thought of gay people as a distant, exotic group, like the Sami, formerly called Lapps, who herd their reindeer on the northern edges of Scandinavia: they certainly exist, and if we travel far enough, we might encounter them, but they are alien to everyday experience. The job of the scholar is to venture to the northern edges of Scandinavia, conduct some interviews, and return to campus with a neat, well-organized powerpoint presentation about Sami lives. It would be absurd to think that the scholar, or anyone else who roams college campuses in our world, might be Sami. He might research gay people, but it would be absurd to think that he might personally be gay.

Do You Believe in God at All?

Every campus visit required an airport shuttle to and from the Portland airport, and if no one at the college had volunteered to pick him up, another shuttle from the destination airport to his hotel and back; in all, between January and June, he rode in thirty-two shuttles, limousines, and taxi cabs. The drivers were always male, and either very young, just out of high school, or elderly, feeling useful during their retirement years.

The moment Joe strapped on his seatbelt, they would ask one of two questions: if they were on our way to the airport, "Where are you headed? Then, whatever town or state he named, about half would immediately chirp, "There sure are some hot girls there!" If they were on our way to the hotel, they would ask, "Where are you coming from?" Then, whatever town or state he named, about half would chirp, "Are the girls there hot?"

No one ever stopped to determine if he was straight before beginning the litany, though once another passenger asked the driver, "Do you like girls?", before beginning his hour of graphic tales about the accommodating young ladies of Saipan Island.

In Detroit, Joe answered, "I'm not interested in girls, I only like boys."

The driver looked so stunned that he thought he had misinterpreted the term *boys,* so he quickly clarified: "Not little boys, of course, adults, I only like adult men."

But the driver wasn't thinking of pedophilia at all; he was stunned by the realization that a gay person had emerged from the realm of movie stereotypes and homo- phobic jokes to take a place in his shuttle, complete with suitcase and carry-on bag. The subsequent forty minutes consisted of grim, grueling silence, broken only by "Do you believe in God at all?" and "I've seen God heal a lot of afflic- tions. Why don't you just ask Him to. . . ." he pretended to be engrossed in his book.

In Philadelphia, Joe answered, "I'm not interested in girls," leaving out the boys.

But then the driver seemed to conclude that "not in- terested" meant "pretending to be not interested out of mis- guided loyalty to his girlfriend back home." He said, "Come on, you can't tell him that you never look at a girl! What about at the beach? Some hot girl in a bikini passes right by your blanket, and you're not gonna sneak a peek?"

When Joe ignored the question altogether, the young- er drivers continued with nonstop avowals of their own he- terosexual mania. One driver ended every avowal with a re- quest for his approval:

"Man, she is fine, am I right?"

"I really like blondes, but he wouldn't kick Angelina Jolie out of bed, am I right?"

"If you don't think she's hot, you'd better check your pulse, am I right?"

The retired drivers usually switched to a discussion of their wives and kids and grandkids, but one told him," This job is great! Who wouldn't want a job where you get to look at pretty girls all day?"

When there were female passengers, the drivers never asked about girls, but once a carload of men in business suits turned into an endless explication of feminine hotness: "Is she hot?" "Sure, she's hot, but what about her friend?" "Are you kidding? She's not nearly as hot!"

Eventually all Joe heard was a continuous murmur of "hot. . .hot. . .hot. . .hot."

What was the function of this litany? Probably the driver wanted to make the trip pleasant, for himself and for the passenger, by chatting about a common interest, and since he was unaware that gay people exist, there was only one interest that he could be absolutely certain he shared with every male passenger: girls.

Of course, thousands of gay men used airport shuttles, limousine services, and taxi cabs. Surely every driver had had at least one gay male customer, been told "I'm not interested in girls" at the start of the litany at least one. Yet he always ignored them or misunderstood, so certain was he that guys are guys, and all guys like girls, am he right?

Aren't You Happy You're Flying Today?

By the time Joe reached the airport, the litany had gone on so long that he was desperate to buy a copy of *The Advocate, Out, Genre,* or *XY* to restore his sanity. But though straight men could buy *Maxim, Esquire,* and even *Playboy* and *Penthouse* at the newsstands nestled between gates, he was unable to find any gay magazine anywhere, except once, a pile of *Advocates* on sale in a concourse at the Philadelphia Airport.

Newsstand managers can order magazines separately, but usually they hire to distribution services, and neither of the two major airport distributors includes gay magazines on its list. They may believe that there is no market – no one will read them aboard an airplane, for fear of a violent re-prisal from the homophobe in the next seat – or else that they are inappropriate, not "family-friendly" like *Playboy* and *Penthouse*.

Joe's twenty-seven airplane flights during recruitment season were mostly free from erasure, if he ignored the men and women who felt free to hold hands, cuddle, and kiss, while two men traveling together were constrained to "touch not, taste not, handle not." No seatmate ever asked "Are you married?," though one said, as they were landing after a bumpy flight, "Won't you be glad to be home with your wife and kids?"

Oddly, it was the male flight attendants who most of-ten expressed their certainty that Joe was straight – perhaps they were gay themselves, and overcompensating in their attempt to "pass."

On a flight from Detroit to San Antonio, Joe began a cordial conversation with the supermodel who had plopped down next to him in the first-class section (most colleges ex-pect candidates to fly coach, but a few spring for first class). Meanwhile, a flight attendant named Alex, a flamboyantly feminine blond with a diamond earring in one ear, could hardly contain his enthusiasm over the prospect of orches-trating a hetero-romance at 30,000 feet. He sidled up with unsolicited refills of their sodas, then put a hand on Joe's shoulder and whispered, "Aren't you happy you're flying today?"

Later, when the supermodel was in the bathroom, Alex sidled up again and said "Things are going well, I see."

On the way back to Detroit, Joe was seated next to an extremely attractive man, and they had a far more stumbling, embarrassed sort of conversation, the sort you have when you are overwhelmed by physical attraction. A different flight attendant said not a word except "What would you like to drink?"

Mancations

Since his interview in Texas came just before spring break, Joe thought about flying on to Mexico or the Caribbean for a few days. The trip never happened, mostly because he was too tired from dozens of other flights, and because his credit cards were getting over-extended (applicants usually pay for their own expenses and get reimbursed later – weeks or months later). But planning it gave him the opportunity to explore erasure in the travel industry.

Tours, cruises, and independent jaunts to anywhere outside of Europe were advertised through a limited repertoire of just four images, corresponding to the intended audience. Often all four appeared in the same brochure, poster, or tv commercial:

A middle-aged straight couple on a "second honeymoon" laughs, dances, and clicks wine glasses, to draw middle-aged straight couples; presumably they would book a Caribbean cruise or a hotel in Acapulco in order to "fall in love all over again."

A young woman in a bikini lounges on a beach, sometimes with a man by her side, often not, to draw young straight men; presumably they could be seduced into traveling to Barbados or the Philippines only if they were promised ample views of young women in bikinis.

A young woman with an exotic "native" appearance, long black hair and large eyes, gazes seductively at the camera, to draw straight men of all ages to Fiji or Costa Rica, where presumably they could meet and have sex with local women.

The young woman's little brother, or at least a little boy with the same exotic "native" appearance, short black hair and large eyes, grins at the camera. He is not intended to draw pedophiles, but to assuage potential visitors' fears about civil unrest in Sri Lanka, terrorism in Indonesia, or crime in Brazil, proclaiming that the "natives" are all like children, cute, friendly, and harmless.

No brochure, poster, or tv commercial ever portrayed a muscular man in a swimsuit, or a young man with an exotic "native" appearance gazing seductively at the camera.

Advertising agencies believed that straight men have all the money and make all of the travel plans, with minimal input from their girlfriends and wives, so they portray what all men on Earth want to see: seductive women. Gay men were summarily excluded from the gaze.

Gay men and lesbians were perfectly welcome to book a cruise on the Royal Caribbean to the Mexican Riviera, Celebrity to Bermuda, or Costa to the Greek Isles, as long as it was not for "couples only" (that is, straight couples only). Customers reported a minimum of homophobic incidents, and those few were rude rather than dangerous, surly staff members and staring passengers rather than hate crimes.[2]

But the advertising brochures, posters, and tv commercials Joe saw contained no same-sex couples, or for that matter men of any sort who were not paired with women. They displayed either a pair of delighted straights clicking wine glasses at each other or a bikini-clad lady lounging languorously on the beach, the first two of the repertoire of images, and nothing else.

Some resorts offered "mancations," vacation trips for men who want to engage in "masculine activities such as sports, camping, gambling, chasing women and drinking, without the presence of wives, mistresses or girlfriends."[3] They assumed that all men everywhere have wives, mistresses, or girlfriends, and that no men anywhere have boyfriends.

Guide books were slightly more inclusive. The stodgy *Frommer's* completely erased gay people from their guide books, as did Rick Steves, perhaps because he was overcompensating: his soft-spoken, flamboyantly feminine presence on his PBS travel series, not to mention the numerous hunky young men who guide him around the cities, has many tongues speculating about his sexual orientation. *Let's Go, The Rough Guide,* and *Fodor's* all contained a few tips for gay travelers, usually next to the tips for blind and wheelchair-bound travelers in the chapter on "special needs." However, most forgot later on in the book, and presumed that all travelers – and all locals – were straight.

Bring a Lady Friend

In April of Joe's year in Maine, shortly after he returned from St. Louis, the department secretary, a tall, overly made up woman named Margaret, who kept a dozen photos of children and grandchildren in her office and droned on about her daughter's upcoming wedding to anyone who failed to walk past quickly enough, came around with a clipboard to see if he would be attending the annual faculty banquet.

"Probably," he said, "But I have to check my schedule of campus interviews first. They're coming like once a week now."

"Well, this will be next month, when recruitment season is over," she chirped. "You have two tickets reserved, so you can bring a lady friend."

Lady friend?

Margaret had met his date at a faculty party just two weeks before; granted, he introduced him only as Ted, without specifying a relationship, but he put his arm around him frequently during the afternoon, and besides, she was standing right next to her husband, a grinning, gray-haired man who worked behind the meat counter at Piggly Wiggly, when he asked "How long have you boys known each other?", surely acknowledging that they were a gay couple (complete with "boys" to imply that gay men never really grow up).

Even if she hadn't noticed Ted or talked to her husband about them, Margaret handled all of the departmental mail, so she had certainly seen the prepublication announcement for his book. She had approved postage on three application packets to Gay Studies programs. Surely after all that she still didn't think he was straight?

Absolutely. Either she hadn't been paying attention, or else she simply concluded that he was a straight guy who researched gay communities, like most of the faculty at the colleges where he interviewed.

As "lady friend" hung in the air like an obscenity, Joe considered his options. Saying "Ok, thanks" was out of the question: it would leave Margaret with the misimpression that he was straight.

Nor was he going to say, "I'm gay"; if he could deduce her heterosexuality from the 10,300 photographs of her children and grandchildren attached to every square inch of her office wall, why couldn't she deduce his gayness, or at least leave the question open?

So he said: "I don't have a lady friend."

Matchmaking fervor lit in Margaret's eyes. She glanced around his office, at his shelves of gay-themed books, rainbow flag mouse pad, and gay pride poster from France, noticing only the absence of photos of his wife and children, and chirped, "Well, we're just going to have to take care of that. I know lots of single women who are about your age. . . ."

"I don't date women," he interrupted.

She frowned. "Never?"

"Well, I had five dates with girls in high school, but they don't really count. I called two of them hoping that they would say 'no' and I would get to borrow my parents' car for the evening anyway, but they said 'yes.' And three of them I dated on only because a cute boy asked him to double. He was on the football team."

Surely anyone would get it after such a speech, Joe thought.

Not Margaret. He doubted that she was even listening; her brow furrowed, she imagined a lifetime of tv dinners in empty apartments, telephones that never ring, a man anguished by loneliness and yet unwilling to "take a chance on love," and finally the worst fear in the straight handbook, "dying alone" (he never understood that one. Doesn't everyone die alone?)

Slowly, sadly, Margaret returned to her clipboard. "You'll only be needing one ticket, then. . . ."

"No, I'll bring a date."

Now Margaret was completely mystified. "But you said. . . ."

"I'll bring a date, just not a woman."

The wheels churned as she tried to figure out what he meant. What other kind of being could a man go out on a date with? A teddy bear? A cocker spaniel? But, amazingly, she never reached the conclusion: "A man." Same-sex dating was beyond the realm of what can be conceived, what can be known. She wrote "Two tickets," and vanished, still pondering the conundrum of a man who never dates women, yet has a date for the banquet.

Within a few days, the mystified looks gave way to knowing smiles, as if we were co-conspirators, privy to secret knowledge. Evidently Margaret had asked around, and someone had had revealed "his secret." For some residents of Kansas, there is no other way to know.

In June Joe finally received an offer of a tenure-track assistant professor position (leading to tenure and permanence, a goal heavily desired but usually unattainable to today's gypsy academics). It was not Gay Studies but in the Sociology of Culture, at Florida University in Boca del Gato, a flat town of pink stucco houses and vast highways north of Fort Lauderdale. He would still have to live and work in Kansas, but Oz, Wilton Manors in Fort Lauderdale, was only fifty miles south, easily accessible for evening and weekend visits. He would at least be close to home.

---

[1] Kerr, Mark, & Kristin O'Rourke. "Sedgwick Sense and Sensibility." *Threshholds: Viewing Culture* 9 (1995).

[2] "Gay on a Straight Cruise," Cruisemates, http://www.cruisemates.com/forum, August 15, 2006.

[3] "Guys on Vacation Equal Mancations", Matt Sedensky, Associated Press, September 16, 2006.

Chapter Five
The Sunrise Cinemas

One evening shortly after he arrived in Boca del Gato, Joe and a friend decided to rent the horror movie *28 Days Later,* because it was rumored to feature frontal nudity. And sure enough, in the first scene, an attractive young man named Jim lies naked in a hospital bed. He awakens from a month-long coma to discover that while he was sleeping, the world ended. Most people have been transformed into bloodthirsty zombies, who roam the streets, attacking anyone "normal." Soon Jim teams up with two other survivors, Mark and Selena.

Suddenly Joe said, "I know how the movie will end. Jim and Selena are hooking up. Mark is doomed."

"Oh, how do you know?" his friend asked. "Are you an expert on zombie movies?"

Joe was not an expert on zombie movies; he disliked horror movies in general, and especially post-apocalyptic nightmares. He had never heard of the writer, the director, or any of the stars. Only about five minutes of screen time had passed. Yet still he knew, without any doubt, that the movie would end with Mark nowhere in sight, and Jim and Selena in each other's arms.

A moment later, Mark was killed, just as he predicted. Selena immediately told Jim, "Just because we're the only two people left on Earth doesn't mean I'm going to fuck you."

It did, too.

By the end of the movie they were in love, living together on an abandoned farm. They even had a "daughter," an orphaned girl whom they picked up along the way.

Joe knew what would happen because it happened in every movie in Kansas. Whether it was serious or frivolous, artistic or hack, good or bad, comedy, tragedy, or drama, it always faded out to a man and a woman living happily ever after. Even if the "real" plot was about something else, like saving the world from zombies, there would be a straight embrace.

Later they tried to watch *Love, Actually*, but ended up fast-forwarding to the end, in which *sixteen* men and women "find love," fading out to hundreds of pixel-sized shots of straight extras kissing, hugging, and celebrating the absence of gay people from the universe, until the pixels combine to depict a gigantic heart.

If classic novels and bestsellers in Kansas were about a man and a woman in the midst of a romance, married or long-term lovers, then film in Kansas was about the beginning of that romance, about a boy meeting a girl.

The difference was no doubt due to the intended audience. Classic novels and bestsellers were aimed at straight adults, presumably married with children, already negotiating their straight romances. But movies were aimed chiefly at straight teenagers and young adults, presumably unmarried, and in danger of deciding that they prefer to remain single; they might even recognize that they are not straight at all. Thus, they must be told, over and over, that their lives now are merely a prelude, that their real lives will begin with a fade-out heterosexual embrace; that their story, like every story, is about a boy meeting a girl.

But there was another difference, Joe reasoned. Straight novelists tend to do their writing in the small towns and rural hideaways of Kansas, like Stephen King's Bangor, Maine or Piers Anthony's farm in the north Florida boondocks, where everyone is straight or passing. They can easily believe that every man has, or wants, a wife, that every woman has, or wants, a husband. But movies are scripted, cast, shot, edited, and marketed in L.A. Straight actors party at the Viper Room on Sunset Boulevard, less than four blocks north of Oz. Straight directors power-lunch on *costata di manzo* and *tagliatelle al Carciofi* at Ago's Ristorante on Melrose Boulevard, less than eight blocks south. They can see gay people at the other tables, on the street, at parties, on the set. Some of their fellow actors and directors themselves are gay. Why would they be so certain that everyone's story is about a boy and a girl?

He had already investigated the world of fiction. Now it was time to look at movies.

The Greatest American Movies

Joe's first stop was the 100 Greatest American Movies of All Time, as compiled by the American Film Institute.

Over half literally end with a fade-out kiss or embrace, and 89 of the 100 feature men and women meeting and falling in love, recognizing that a "platonic" friendship is really a romance, realizing how much they care about each other, or reconciling after a breakup, even when the something far more interesting is happening in the background.[1]

Gone with the Wind makes the Civil War play second fiddle to Clark Gable wooing, winning, and leaving Vivien Leigh.

Casablanca uses the underground resistance of World War II as mere local color, to add zest to the tale of Humphrey Bogart and Ingrid Bergman ruminating endlessly over their lost love.

No one remembers that *Singin' in the Rain* is about the difficult transition from silent movies to talkies, so overwhelming is the bicker-romance between Gene Kelly and Debbie Reynolds.

No one remembers that *The Graduate* is about the angst of 1960s youth, so overwhelming is collegiate Dustin Hoffman's affair with middle-aged Anne Bancroft and subsequent discovery of "true love" with Katharine Ross.

Eleven of the 100 minimize hetero-romance, but only one omits it altogether: *The Wizard of Oz.*

Many starry-eyed men and women serenade each other in L. Frank Baum's original novels and in their various stage adaptations, but the film contains only one extremely muted straight relationship; Dorothy's Aunt Em and Uncle Henry. There are no other straight marriages, romances, or flirtations. No male-female couples can be seen among the Munchkins, or on the streets of the Emerald City. Indeed, no one in Oz appears to have the slightest idea that heterosexual desire exists at all. No wonder it is a gay favorite.

None of the Top 100 contain any major gay characters, although a few of the comedies allude to a vague, generally humorous dysfunction that makes men giddy, girlish, and unwilling or unable to engage in straight practice.

Bringing Up Baby has Cary Grant in a woman's frilly nightgown exclaiming "I've just gone gay all of a sudden!"

In *Some Like It Hot*, Tony Curtis pretends to be. . .you know. . .so Marilyn Monroe will be motivated to "cure" him.

In *M*A*S*H*, a soldier who suffered from "stage fright" during a night of straight sex concludes that he must have "homosexual tendencies," and therefore decides to commit suicide.

Time magazine's list of the 100 Greatest Movies of All Time was not limited to Hollywood, but the global industry was apparently no more inclusive. 85 of the 100 featured men and women falling in love. Again, no major characters were gay, but a few minor characters displayed a disturbing or humorous gender transgression: fops in *The Discreet Charm of the Bourgeois* and "fags" in *Goodfellas,* a murderous transvestite in *Psycho* and a murdered "homosexual" in *Berlin Alexanderplatz.*

Premiere magazine's list of the 100 Greatest Movie Characters of All Time drew from every time period and genre, mixing Michael Corleone and Margo Channing, Raymond Babbit and Dr. Evil, Norman Bates and Ace Ventura. None of them were actually gay, but several expressed that same vaguely-defined disruption of gender polarities. The most blatant was Dil in *The Crying Game,* living as a woman, but somehow also a man.[2]

One of the Girls

What about the movies that don't make the Top 100 or even the Top 1000, the less than stunning, sometimes stunningly bad movies that you select for a quick, easy first date or watch on tv when nothing else is on or pick up at the video store for no other reason than the shirtless man on the DVD cover? Every year, over 300 feature-length films were produced in the United States. If you watched them all, one after the other, eight hours per day, with weekends and holidays off, you would spend twelve weeks in the theater.

You would see an average of two pairs of men and women kissing every hour, and one same-sex pair kissing *every week.*

You would see an average of five pairs of men and women falling in love every day, and a *total* of four or five same-sex pairs falling in love.[3]

But no one would see even that miniscule bit of representation at the Sunrise Cinema 8 in Boca del Gato or anywhere else in Kansas, since it would only in movies in "limited release," that is, on fewer than 300 screens, usually far fewer, usually only in Oz. Moviegoers in Kansas had no choice: in a year, or five years, or ten years of movie viewing, they would never see two men or two women falling in love.

They would, however, see gay "girls." Lots of them. Lots of them. During the fall of Joe's first year in Boca del Gato, moviegoers at the Sunrise Cinema 8 could see a dance contest between Stiffler and a simpering queen in *American Wedding;* an effeminate college boy in a gold lamé bathrobe in *National Lampoon Presents Dorm Days;* Jack Black horrified by the gayness of one of his prep school charges in *School of Rock,* and a dozen or so limp-wristed male secretaries, receptionists, interior designers, and unidentified fops, all doing their nails, shopping for skin care products, lip-synching to Barbra Streisand, and saying "fabulous."

Of course, movies were not alone in their insistence that gay men, if they exist at all, are really girls. That particular stereotype had been appearing in novels, short stories, radio and television, and the popular imagination since 1895, when world was horrified to discover that flamboyantly feminine Oscar Wilde was gay, and it showed no sign of disappearing. No one would dream of going to a picnic, peering at a black person's plate, and chiming, "You didn't take any fried chicken. Are you sure you're black?", yet when he mentions disliking Broadway musicals, straights invariably state, "Are you sure you're gay?"

But contemporary movies in Kansas seemed absurdly invested in promoting the myth. Every career women in search of Mr. Right had a swishy gay best friend; every horny teenager had a pink-clad gay drama teacher; every buddy comedy sent its hapless heroes into a gay bar to be accosted by an army of queens; every action movie had an effete British-accented gay villain. When there were no actual gay "girls," there are bound to be allusions to them, or jokes about them, or at least accusations.

At some point in the movie a straight man might momentarily transgress the standards of machismo – eat a salad, wear pink, carry a handbag – and be ridiculed with an anti-gay slur An enemy or a wise-cracking friend thus "questioned his masculinity."

He may try to avenge his honor, or he may counter that he is "secure in his masculinity," certain that he is not gay. Either way, to be man is by definition to be straight. Gay men exist, but by definition they are girls.

Writers who script scenes with "girls" and dialogues about straight men questioning their "masculinity," the directors who supervise them, and the actors who portray them had certainly seen gay men before, realized that the vast majority of gay men are conventionally masculine in intonation and affect, in interests and pastimes. Some were gay themselves. Why, then, did they always present gay men as girls?

Because that was the only way they would not contradict the goal of film, to offer visual "proof" of the universality of straight romance, to convince viewers, especially male viewers, that they will never be happy until they have found and married their one true opposite-sex beloved.

If even a few boys exist who desire other boys or fall in love with other boys, then straight romance cannot be universal, everyone's story *cannot* be about a boy meeting a girl.

But what if those boys are not really boys?

What if they are not strong, hard, forceful, and assertive?

What if their wrists and fingers flutter, if their voices are heavily modulated, if they are obsessed with their appearance, if they are knowledgeable about fashion, if they act like girls, if they accept being treated as girls by all of the other characters, if they in fact believe that they *are* girls? Then if they happen to gaze longingly at boys, they are merely experiencing straight desire, like every other "girl." If they happen to fall in love, their love is straight.

Kissing Jessica Stein

If movies in Kansas erased the gayness from gay men by making them "girls," so their desire was straight desire, they erase the gayness from lesbians by having them desire *both* women and men. Joe found that most commonly, no lesbians exist at all; even the beer-chugging, sports-obsessed "one of the guys" longs for men.

In the horror movie *Mortuary*, Jonathan, a straight city boy, relocates to a redneck town, goes to work at the local diner, and gets a crush on waitress Liz. He is jealous of her chummy intimacy with classmate Grady, until he discovers that Grady is gay, "one of the girls." But he never for a moment wonders if Liz is a lesbian; straightness is the female condition.

When women who do self-identify as lesbian appear in film, they demonstrate that everyone's story is about a boy and a girl by melting into the arms of a man. They may be attracted to women – "who wouldn't be?" the filmmakers reason – but they do not fall in love with women. At most they confuse friendship, warmth, and emotional intimacy with the "true love" that fills "the hearts of boy and girl with mutual flame," as Lord Alfred Douglas wrote.

In *Kissing Jessica Stein*, ultra-sophisticated Jessica lives and works in midtown Manhattan, a straight enclave only a few subway stops from Oz. She works as a journalist and hangs out with artistic types, so surely, one concludes, some of her friends and coworkers are gay, or at least know gay people.

But no, she lives in a gay-free artistic world.

When Jessica begins dating Helen, her friends all want to know "What's *his* name?" and "Who's the *guy*?", absolutely certain that no woman ever dates a woman. When they run into Jessica and Helen on what is obviously a date, they invariably assume that it is *not* a date.

Near the end of the movie, Jessica's boss-best friend Josh asks her out to dinner. She says "I can't. I'm with Helen," but he is still oblivious. Why should she be reluctant to drop the buddy for a romantic date?

Jessica tries "We're together," emphasizing the *together*, and now, finally, Josh catches on. But he is utterly shocked. He had no idea that any lesbians exist, certainly not in the artsy community of midtown Manhattan.

Of course, by the end of the movie Jessica decides that she's not a lesbian after all. She may desire women, but she falls in love only with men, so perhaps Josh's surprise was justified. *Kissing Jessica Stein* won a GLAAD media award for its positive portray of a lesbian, albeit a temporary one.

Someone Special

Erasing gay people from movies requires more than merely shouting the praises of heterosexual love 600 times a year while eight g-word stereotypes and temporary lesbians sit on the back of the bus. Dialogue and stage business in movie after movie reveals an absolute assurance that no gay people exist.

Shortly after *28 Days Later* and *Love, Actually*, Joe rented the science fiction thriller *Lathe of Heaven*, about a man whose dreams change reality. Ursula K. Leguin, author of the original novel, often created gay characters, and the star, Lukas Haas, played a gay hustler in *Johns*, so naturally Joe expected his George Orr to be gay, or at least for the script to be inclusive.

No such luck.

Early on, George tells his psychiatrist, Dr. Haber, about losing "someone special" during the reality-shifts that occur every time he goes to sleep. Dr. Haber instantly refers to the "someone special" as "Ir."

"How did you know he was talking about a 'her'?" George asks. Evidently he is aware that gay people exist.

But Dr. Haber is not aware. In all of his years of schooling and all of his years of private practice, he has never once encountered anyone gay.

In order to establish that every story is about a boy meeting a girl, your movies needs more than a fade out boy-girl kiss. It needs more than a gay "girl" doing his nails, or a straight man who is "secure in his masculinity." The tiniest details of dialogue and stage business must reveal an absolute assurance that even if gay male "girls" and temporary lesbians exist, same-sex desire and romance do not.

When filmmakers are gay themselves, one would expect an acknowledgement that sometimes boy meets boy and girl meets girl, if not often than at least once in a lifetime, or once in a millennium, or once in human history. But usually the opposite happens; they work much harder than the straights, scanning every shot to ensure no one betrays the slightest awareness of the possibility of same-sex love.

The musical comedy *Hairspray* was written by John Waters, who is gay, and directed by Adam Shankman, who is gay. Many other members of the cast and crew are gay. Nevertheless, there are no gay characters anywhere, not even in crowd scenes, not even by allusion, just three straight romances and a show-stopping finale that jubilantly proclaims the universality of straight desire:

> Ever since this old world began
> A woman found that if she shook it,
> She could shake up a man.

Even when straight romance is minimal or absent, movies still must point out that all of the major characters are straight.

In *Be Kind, Rewind*, the two slacker-buddies who re-invigorate a failing New Jersey video store do not date girls or get girlfriends; indeed, it is obvious that they are blatantly, painfully in love with each other.

Nevertheless, to be certain no one gets "the wrong idea," the filmmakers devote the opening scene to Mr. Fletcher, the video store's owner, reminiscing about the "girl that got away" and interrogating the boys about why they don't have girlfriends. Not to worry, they explain, they aren't gay, just inept around women. The heterosexuality of the three main characters proclaimed, we can get on with the story.

The Girl of Your Dreams

The assurance that every story is about straight desire or romance begins before the movie begins, before you even set foot in the theater, when the trailers play on tv a dozen times a day. Most movie trailers devote some portion of their twenty or thirty seconds to shots of a man and a woman kissing, preparing for sex, or resting up afterwards, regardless of what the movie is "really" about. Just one day of television watching during Joe's first semester in Florida revealed eight movie trailers, six with straight effusions:

The trailer for *The Black Dahlia,* about the famous murder case in noir 1940s Los Angeles, consists entirely of a man and a woman cuddling in bed after sex. The movie itself is not about romance, and contains only one sex scene.

The trailer for *The Covenant* shows a teenage boy and girl literally leaping into each other's faces to kiss – surely one of them broke a tooth. The voiceover tells us, "Imagine having the power to do whatever you want!" Apparently "whatever you want" is always straight kissing.

Pirates of the Caribbean: Dead Man's Chest stars Johnny Depp, who doesn't kiss anyone. However, the trailer ignores him shows secondary characters Orlando Bloom and Keira Knightley kissing, twice.

The amount of heterosexual practice portrayed in the movie itself is irrelevant. *Talladega Nights* contains only three straight kisses, two brief and one rather energetic (but portrayed humorously). The trailer shows all of them, implying that there are dozens more.

World Trade Center is about the 9-11 terrorist attacks, but the trailer shows a man and a woman, naked in bed, sliding toward each other, as the voiceover promises that the movie is about "the best in all of us." There is little question that "the best in all of us" means straight practice.

Other forms of advertising, such as the DVD cover art and liner notes, were just as eager to imply that the movie consists of 90 minutes of straights kissing, regardless of what it is really about.

In *Motorama*, ten-year old Gus embarks on a surreal life-long road trip in order to win a contest. Drew Barrymore advertises the prize, but Gus expresses no interest in her, or in any girl at any time during the movie. Yet the DVD cover proclaims, "The way to the girl of your dreams. . . ."

If they are not obsessing over the importance of straight desire or romance in the movie, cover art and liner notes are denying that same-sex desire or romance exists. Their most important strategy is Every Woman's Fantasy, the proclamation that *every woman* on Earth swoons over this male actor (or men in general), but no man on Earth could ever possibly feel anything, except maybe envy. Every Man's Fantasy is the proclamation that *every man* on Earth longs for a glimpse of this female actor (or women in general), but no woman could ever possibly feel even a glimmer of attraction.

In *Psycho Beach Party*, the hunky Andrew Levitas plays a surfer dude named Provolone, who is attracted to his surfer buddy. In the last scene, they kiss. But according to the DVD liner notes, this would be impossible, since "Andrew Levitas first began to melt female hearts. . . ." No male hearts, even though the filmmakers obviously know that gay men exist!

Driving Lessons stars Julie Waters as a flamboyant Auntie Mame-style actress who takes an interest in the shy Ben (Rupert Grint). Her character originally believes that Ben is gay, so Waters must know that gay teenagers exist. But on the DVD commentary, she gushes about her muscular costar: "Those biceps! The girls will be going mad!" Suddenly she has become convinced that gay teenagers do not exist, that every girl and no boy will go mad over Rupert Grint's biceps.

What Girls Want to See

Online movie reviews, whether they were submitted by fans or professionals, were very likely to express Every Woman's Fantasy or Every Man's Fantasy. The reviewers seemed absurdly eager to press the point, even when the movies they were reviewing themselves contradicted it with characters who are attracted to the members of the same sex or fall in love with members of the same sex, or actors who are gay in real life.

Zapped! stars Scott Baio as a high school boy with telekinetic powers that he uses primarily to divest girls of their bras. A reviewer on Amazon.com helpfully states that this is a wish-fulfillment fantasy: "What high school boy wouldn't want to see girls with their clothes off!" No gay high school boys exist, or if they do, they are "girls," their desire still straight.

Top Secret stars Val Kilmer as a hunky secret agent, but a reviewer on the Internet Movie Database believes that guys looked only at costar Lucy Gutteridge: she "made any adolescent boy very happy." Any and all of them, with not a single exception, and not a single adolescent girl.

Arrow in the Head gives *Silent Night, Deadly Night* a low T&A rating. That is, few girls take their clothes off. But at least "the ladies get [to see] pumped-up Robert Brian Wilson shirtless." Every lady is ecstatic, and no man cares.

It also tells us that *Voodoo Academy* is "a horror movie for girls," because there are a lot of hot guys with their shirts off; obviously all girls and no boys are interested in such a thing.

In *Swimfan*, Jesse Bradford "goes shirtless for the ladies." Why shouldn't Jesse Bradford, who played gay in *Speedway Junky* and knows that he has gay fans, go shirtless for anyone who cares to look? Because there is no such thing as a man who finds him attractive, or a woman who fails to find him attractive.

A reviewer on the Barnes and Noble website gushes that Gerard Butler, star of *Attila*, is "beautiful enough for the women to want him" and "real enough that the men want to be him."[4] No men want him.

Another Barnes and Noble reviewer tells us that *2 Fast 2 Furious*, starring Paul Walker, is "a movie any girl should rent, and don't forget to kick your boyfriend out so he doesn't get intimidated by Paul and his dreamy voice." The reviewer believes that all girls are straight, since they all have boyfriends and swoon over Paul's dreamy voice, and no boys are gay, since they never find Paul more than intimidating.

Be Cool gets an interesting review on Amazon.com. First we are told that star Uma Thurman, wearing a bikini, "is sure to arouse any man with a pulse." A moment later we hear about a gay character, a bodyguard played by the Rock. The reviewer is therefore aware that gay men exist. Does he believe that they are also aroused by Uma Thurman, or that they do not have a pulse?

Or did the presence of a gay character in the movie not detract from his confidence that, gay or straight, same-sex desire does not exist?[5]

It's Just You and Me Now

Novels are the product of a single artist's imagination, but a film is not the solitary vision of the director, in spite of what the auteur theory in film school teaches. Actors, cinematographers, editors, and dozens of supporting personnel each make their own decisions and incorporate their own dreams and desires. A movie aspiring for more than "limited release" must not make gayness visible, or at most may include "one of the girls" to demonstrate that all romance is straight romance, but not everyone in the cast and crew, easily a hundred people, can enforce such a mandate, or wants to. There will be slippages, many more than in a novel: tacitly homoerotic gestures, statements that can be "misread" as homoromantic, same-sex friendships of particular intensity, moments that subtly satirize or even reject the assertion that all people everywhere, male or female, gay or straight, are straight.

Some slippage is deliberate, a form of subtle political activism. Some is unconscious, as writers, actors, and directors struggle to portray complex characters and interesting situations. Some is even accidental, errors popping in as different crew members try, in different ways, to maintain the myth of universal heterosexual desire. No doubt *Rebel without a Cause* depicts a homoerotic bond between Sal Mineo and James Dean because the actors were actually in love at the time, and incorporated their real-life desire into the stage business. But when that bastion of hetero-romance, *Casablanca*, fades out not with Humphrey Bogart walking into the night with Claude Raines, "This looks like the beginning of a beautiful friendship," surely the homoerotic import is accidental.

During his first year in Florida, Joe went to a "wide release" matinee at the Sunrise Cinema 8 almost every Friday afternoon, and nearly every movie he saw was easily queerable, in spite of its purported goal of showing men and women falling into each other's arms.

Second-Hand Lions is a "coming of age" story that gives Haley Joe Osment no girl to smooch, and features his two "uncles" a lifelong same-sex partnership.

The animated *Teacher's Pet* is about a dog (voiced by gay actor Nathan Lane) who gets the chance to become a human being, but decides to remain a dog so he won't lose his buddy-romance; "I love you, and I want to be with you," he says in a moment of eye-gleaming tenderness.

The 1970s cop partners *Starsky and Hutch* get girls but also share an eye-bulging buddy-romance.

Around the World in Eighty Days, a humorous remake of the classic Jules Verne novel, gives Passepartout no interest whatever in girls, but an arguably romantic attraction to Phineas Fogg.

But in Kansas, most viewers leave the theater with no idea that they have just seen two men or two women falling in love. Some reject all evidence and stubbornly insist that all movie characters are to be read as straight unless they specifically use the word "gay." But most often they are simply unable to see the evidence in the first place.

The Lost Boys was directed by Joe Schumacher, who is gay, and starred teen idol Corey Haim, who was widely rumored to be gay at the time. The plot, about a high schooler named Sam suspecting that his older brother has become a vampire, is overloaded with homoerotic relationships. There are endless beefcake scenes and vows of same-sex commitment, but only one act of heterosexual intercourse, with the man's nude body on display and the woman hidden from view (instead of the usual scenes of a nude woman atop a fully-clothed man). Surely even the most oblivious straight could queer a film when the clues were drawn so blatantly, Joe thought.

But not one of the nearly 200 user reviews on the Internet Movie Database and nearly 500 fans on a *Lost Boys* fansite noticed the beefcake, the lack of attention to girls, or the many homoerotic bonds.

One thread did ask if Sam might be gay, and as evidence, pointed out that he has a poster of heartthrob Rob Lowe on his bedroom wall, he wears a "Born to Shop" T-shirt, he takes bubble baths, and he sings an old novelty song with lines like "I'm a lonely girl."[6] Could such feminine behavior indicate that Sam is "one of the girls"?

Even such broad, blatant, stereotypic evidence was lost on most fans, who stated in bewilderment that they "never noticed." "I've seen that movie probably somewhere around fifty times, and never once stopped to think that [Sam] was supposed to be gay." They immediately marked him as "straight" and ignored all evidence to the contrary, just as Joe's straight friends did in real life.

Some spent a good deal of energy trying to "disprove" Sam's gayness:

"He's fifteen years old, too young to be gay!"

"He hasn't noticed girls yet, it doesn't mean he's gay!"

About the beefcake poster: "It was his grandfather's idea, to give him a manly role model! It has nothing to do with being gay!"

About the "Born to Shop" t-shirt: "It was the fashion in 1987! It has nothing to do with being gay!"

And, most emblematic: "This is ridiculous! You can read anything into a movie if you try hard enough!"

Finding same-sex desire is ridiculous. Finding gay characters is ridiculous. Movies contain only straight characters, only depictions of straight desire, period. Nothing else is possible.[7]

In *Lake Placid,* about a team of scientists investigating a giant crocodile in an isolated lake in Maine, foppish bon vivant Hector bicker-bonds with stick-in-the-mud Sheriff Hank. They bond so passionately, and with so many homoerotic double-entendres, that one expects them to kiss at any moment. In the last scene, as Hector is taken to the hospital after a minor injury, Sheriff Hank offers to ride along in the ambulance with him.

But of over 100 reviewers on Amazon.com, only one mentions the homoromance: he complains about the "suppressed homoerotic dialogue between two adult men," as if same-sex desire is appropriate only for "confused" adolescents, as if adults must always be straight. The others apparently did not notice.

Orange County is not strictly subject to queering, since it contains an explicit homoromantic pair. Throughout the movie, the protagonist's slacker buddies, Arlo and Chad, behave like bickering long-term partners, yet they also flirt with girls. One concludes that they are standard movie buddies, presented as straight but with an unstated homoerotic attraction. Then, in the penultimate scene, they make an announcement:

> Chad: "Last night we're at this party, little Arlo here
> decides to profess his undying love for me.
> Didn't I tell you he was a fruitcake?"
>
> Arlo: "That's not true, Bro. . .Chad crashed at my
> house, right, and I woke up in the night, he
> was fondling my. . . ."
>
> Chad: "Dude, I lost my keys. I was looking for 'em."

Though they use the homophobic term "fruitcake" and fail to agree precisely on the events of the previous evening, they are sitting in their car in a position of quiet intimacy, at peace with each other. They seem delighted that there is no longer any doubt about the romantic nature of their relationship. Their friends respond with approving grins, not with surprise, since they have been aware that the two were a couple all along. The revelation resonates strongly with the theme of the movie, about searching everywhere for happiness and then realizing that it's right in front of you, in Orange County.

Most fan reviews of *Orange County* on Amazon.com and the Internet Movie Database omit all references to Arlo and Chad. Those who mention them are confused: "What the heck does the last scene mean?"; "Weird last scene"; "It's a joke, right?"; "Are they supposed to be gay, or what?"

Why are viewers baffled by an explicit statement that the two are romantic partners? They are trying so hard to be unaware that gay people exist that, unless someone actually states "I am gay," they will remain unaware.

Arlo has never said "I am gay," so why would he profess his "undying love" to another guy?

Chad has never said "I am gay," so why would he fondle another guy? I

Even when you give them the tools they need to see, most straights and many gay people still will not.

In his *Popular Culture* class in Florida, Joe explained about queering, how it reveals same-sex desire or same-sex romance in characters who are not specifically portrayed as gay, often without the conscious intent of the actors or directors, often within a heterosexist plotline. He told the students exactly what to look for: absent or minimal straight interest, extraordinary intimacy between the same-sex characters, a "falling in love" scene, quarrels and breakups, and a resolution involving a same-sex bond.

Then he showed them an easy example, *Hair*, about young army draftee Claude, who arrives in New York in 1969 for his induction and befriends a tribe of hippies. The hippie leader, Berger never expresses any interest in women, but he is obviously quite taken with Claude.

He walked the class, beat by beat, through a scene in which Claude has a bad LSD trip and gets lost in Central Park. Berger searches for him all night, and when he sees him, he rushes up, grabs him, hugs him, touches his face.

Then Sheila, who has been helping Berger search, calls out. She seems decidedly jealous; she wants Berger to choose her over Claude.

Berger ignores her. He is not interested in Sheila in that way. He is busy reconciling with his boyfriend.

The class objected. Wait – surely anyone who acknowledges the presence of a member of the other sex is to be taken as straight!

One student said, "Claude can't be gay. He's interested in Sheila. That's why he stays with the hippies: Berger offers to help him get into the party to see her."

Another agreed. "Berger can't be gay. He flirts with Sheila. He puts his hand on her leg, in the car scene. Why would a gay guy do that?"

Others insisted that no male character can be read as gay unless he is portrayed as "one of the girls":

"Claude can't be gay. He's not fruity at all."

"Berger doesn't act gay, either. I'm not saying that all gays are effeminate, but when this movie was made, an actor who was trying to portray someone gay would act all fruity, and Treat Williams acts completely masculine."

Some returned to the scene that he had walked them through, and struggled hard to find any explanation that would allow them to avoid thinking that Berger might be in love with Claude.

Why does Berger touch Claude's face? "To see if his eyes are dilated. He just wants to know if his friend is still high. It has nothing to do with being gay."

Why does Berger reject Sheila? "Because he's tired. Wouldn't you be tired, if you were up all night looking for your friend? Sometimes you're just not in the mood. Every time you turn down a girl, it doesn't mean you're gay."

Why does Sheila seem jealous of Berger? "She's tired, too. She's been up all night, and she just wants to go home. So she comes off as a little bitchy. She doesn't think that Claude and Berger are lovers."

Perhaps the most conclusive objection came from a student who rarely participated in class, who seemed embarrassed by how easily he – and many of her classmates – bandied around words like "gay" and "lesbian" and "queer." During yesterday's discussion of queering, her face reddened, she stared savagely into space, and she clenched her pen so tightly that he thought it would break. Today she raised her hand and said simply, "I don't think they're gay."

"Why not?" he asked.

"I just don't."

Who could argue with that?

Was It a Screen?

A jaw-dropping instance of willful ignorance occurred in March of Joe's first year in Florida. Todd, his upstairs neighbor, had shoulder-length blond hair and a soft, androgynous face, slim and fragile and wounded; he always looked like he needed a hug. He worked at the Thai restaurant downtown, but he really wanted to be a musician: every

Saturday night he played the saxophone in a club in Fort Lauderdale.

Todd dated girls, and frequently invited them to spend the night (you could hear the bed squeaking directly above his head), so naturally Joe assessed him as "straight." Surely, since Joe dated men, and frequently invited them to spend the night, Todd assessed him as gay!

Around Valentine's Day, Joe began dating Jan, a blond giant from one of the Baltic republics, a new Ph.D. in Russian from the University of Wisconsin who had a one-year at a college about thirty miles away.

Todd never met Jan, but Joe was not shy about telling him every detail of his romance: the movies they saw, the dance clubs they visited, the gifts they exchanged, our arguments and reconciliations. Granted, the foreign-sounding name did not make his boyfriend's gender obvious, but surely Todd could not fail to notice the constant "I" and "him," not to mention his detailed descriptions of Jan's biceps, chest, and so on.

Evidently Todd *could* fail to notice. In March, in the midst of some conversation or other, Todd turned to him, a look of utter shock on his fragile, wounded face, and said "Wait. . .are you trying to tell me that you're gay?"

Now it was Joe's turn to be shocked. "No.. . .how could you not know that? I've been telling you about my boyfriend for a month now."

"You mean your girlfriend?"

"Boyfriend," Joe repeated.

"Well, maybe it's your boyfriend, but you definitely told him she was a girl. Was that a screen?"

They sat around for twenty minutes trying to figure it out. Todd recalled Joe using the words "girl" and "girlfriend." He could remember the expression on his face, the intonation of his voice, as he said: "She was flirting with other guys last night," "I gave her a romantic birthday card," or "I'm inviting her home to meet my parents."

But Joe told him that he found passing abhorrent; he would never dream of transforming "He" into "She," or even of using vague terms that left one with the impression of straightness without actually saying it.

Todd was switching the pronouns himself. Without even realizing it, he had been making mental adjustments, hearing "girl" instead of "boy," "she" instead of "he," "her" instead of 'him."

What about the descriptions of Jan's hot body, chest, abs, biceps? Able to bench press 280 pounds?

In those cases, Joe had obviously switched, in mid-sentence, to describing a non-romantic male buddy – who, coincidentally, had the same name as his girlfriend.

---

[1] American Film Institute, http://www.afi.com/.

[2] *Time Magazine,* http://www.time.com; *Empire Magazine* Film Site, http://www.filmsite.org/empireuk100.html; *Premiere Magazine,* http://www.premiere.com

[3] It was estimated that 85% of movies contain a straight romance, with an average of three straight kisses and two straight sex scenes apiece.

[4] http://video.barnesandnoble.com/search/ product.asp?ean=25192266027&pwb=1&z=y

[5] Amazon.com, http://www.amazon.com; Barnes and Noble, http://www.barnesandnoble.com; Internet Movie Database, http://www.imdb.com; Arrow in the Head Reviews, http://www.arrowinthehead.com

[6] "Ain't Got No Home," words and music by Clarence Frogman Henry.

[7] Gay Lost Boys Thread, http://ask.metafilter.com/mefi/32644

Chapter Six
Dinner for Two

Since his job in Florida was in Sociology of Culture, Joe modified his research on gay teenagers slightly, looking at media representation instead of real life: homoromantic subtexts in children's cartoons, television sitcoms, Disney movies, and Archie comics, culminating in a book. Then he began another book. Since he was hired with a resume full of gay-themed research, he assumed that the Dean would not object to more gay-themed research, even if some of the students and faculty happened to be homophobic.

She did object.

Only two months after Joe arrived in Florida, he received a telephone call from the Dean at 7:00 pm on a Saturday night – never a good sign. "The President wouldn't understand your research on gay teenagers. Better pick something less controversial."

In February, she denied his request for funding to go to a conference on LGBT studies, where he would be the keynote speaker.

Joe co-founded a committee to add a Gay Studies minor to the curriculum, but in March the Dean disbanded it. "Too controversial."

At his first year end review in May, Joe got high marks for teaching and service, but "unsatisfactory" for publications, even though he had published three articles and gotten a book contract. The Dean complained that his re-search "exceeded the boundaries of traditional sociology." If he wanted to stay at Florida University, he would have to select more "appropriate" research topics.

To enforce his exclusion, during his second year Joe was given a new office, far from the rest of the department, and his teaching rotation contained no course in Gay Studies, or Gender, or even the Sociology of Culture. Instead, he got *Research Methods, Sociology of Religion,* and *Sociology of the Family.*

He could hear the Dean snickering, "Let's see him try to include gay people in those courses!"

Joe had had enough. In the spring of his second year in Florida, he officially resigned his position – no doubt to sighs of relief from the administration – found some allies among the faculty to write him letters of recommendation, and went back on the job market.

But the ultra-conservative political climate of the post- 9/11 world had made gay-themed research "controversial" everywhere, and resigning from a tenure-track position was always a fatal red mark on a job application, so Joe received no interviews from any college within commuting distance of Oz.

As recruitment season wore on, he started applying for everything, everywhere. He interviewed in the mangrove swamps of South Carolina, in the pine lakes of Minnesota, in the Black Hills of South Dakota, 300, 400, and 500 miles from Oz.

In June, when Joe was almost ready to give up, go back to West Hollywood, and get a job in retail, he saw an ad for a visiting position with possible upgrade to tenure-track, at Wesley College. It looked perfect, except for three little details:

The job was in criminology. Joe had taken some courses in criminology in grad school, when his advisor suggested he have something to "fall back on" in case he couldn't find a job in Gay Studies, but he hadn't published anything in criminology.

Wesley College was religious, affiliated with the United Church of Christ, with chapel every Wednesday and prayer before faculty meetings.

And it was in central Wisconsin, seventy miles from Oz.

But the Admissions Office stated that it did not discriminate against gay and lesbian students, the Human Resources Office stated that same-sex partners were included in the benefits package, and the search committee listened to his jobtalk without raising any eyebrows. Besides it couldn't be worse than Derry, Maine.

It was certainly more isolated. You started in Walker's Point in Milwaukee and drove through sixty miles of rolling farmland, then the tiny town of Northland, famous mostly for frozen custard, taco pizza, and Kohler bathroom fixtures. then more fields. You turned right at County Road M (look for the feed sign) and arrived at Wesley College, six red-brick buildings amid a wind-whistling silence.

Joe found an extremely upscale apartment for a very low price in Northland, probably because there were only a few upscale professionals around. Everyone was proudly working class, conservative, religious, overweight, and straight or pretending to be.

There were no gay organizations in Northland, and only one gay bar, the Blu Light, which, like Somewhere in Derry, you entered through the alley in back.

Still, Joe was determined to stick it out; he was going to make friends, find a partner after his romance with Jan fizzled out, get the tenure-track position, and stay in rural central Wisconsin forever.

The Name of Your Soul Mate

Dating proved to be a problem. The men he met in Oz tended to walk off, shaking their heads in amazement, when he admitted that he lived seventy miles away.

The men he met in Northland were as devoted to passing as those in Derry, throwing about terms like "discrete" and "straight-acting." So Joe decided to look for love online.

On daytime television, several times an hour, he saw a series of commercials in which ecstatic male-female couples gushed about how they completed each other, two halves making a whole. Then a white-haired, grinning televangelist type appeared to assure viewers that eternal happiness was just a mouse click away, in the arms of the soul mate they would surely discover at Eharmony.com.

But when he visited the website, the gender of his potential soul mate was not requested. He thought this a curious oversight: he certainly would never find a soul mate if he could only be paired women.

He emailed Eharmony, and was told, succinctly, "We do not perform matches for homosexuals." Like the Boy Scouts, Eharmony disapproved of gay people, but did not express any overt homophobia; it simply assumed that gay people do not exist. No doubt very few of the straights who joined noticed.[1]

Two other online dating services, Jdate (for Jewish singles) and Christian Café (for Christian singles), also prohibited same-sex matches due to homophobic bias, the assumption that God hates gay people. However, they never state that straights only need apply; the websites gave no indication that gay matches are even possible. At least the Book of Matches was aware that it is excluding someone: it was a "matchmaking and friendship service for heterosexual adults."

The rest of the online dating services that Joe checked, Chemistry.com, Cupid Junction, Search Your Love, Date.com, Match.com, and Yahoo Personals, asked for the customer's gender and the gender of his or her potential partner, to allow for the possibility that some people may want to date members of the same sex.

Still, pictures displayed only men and women hanging on each other, and the advertising copy bragged endlessly about the millions of hetero-marriages that resulted from the service.

Date.com required that he select as a goal "Marriage, Serious Relationship, or Dating," either unaware that gay people are not permitted to marry, or assuming that all participants are straight.

Match.com asked "Married, Single, Divorced, Separated," and would not let him leave the question blank.

SearchYourLove.com asked him to designate his gender and his match's gender by selecting the appropriate partner of a male-female couple in bridal gown and tuxedo, emphasizing that "real" romance was always straight.

When the online dating services moved from making matches to offering dating tips, the inclusion of gay people quickly faded away.

SearchYourLove.com guided the eager participant through the art of flirting, "an essential element in meeting and making contact with the opposite sex," and offered men tips on "Finding Miss Right," with no hint that any man might want to find Mr. Right.

RomanceClass.com offered thousands of tips for daters in many different categories, "newly single," "dating after fifty," and so on, all assuming straight dates. For instance, "young guys" were advised to "choose your own girl, don't let your friends do it for you"' and "Talk to all of the girls in a group."

A search for "gay" in the advice forum yielded twelve entries, all framing gay men as a threat to the straight relationship: "I think his boyfriend is gay" and "My gay friend keeps hitting on his girlfriend."[2]

Straight Guys on the Prowl

In spite of the tacit erasure, online dating services worked; during his first year in central Wisconsin, Joe found nine men living in or near Northland who were the right age, adequately attractive, not passing, and willing to date rather than "hook up." The only problem they faced was where to go on the date.

In West Hollywood, the first date always took place within a few block's radius of Santa Monica Boulevard and San Vicente -- movie at the AMC Century City, dinner at the Café Etoile, dancing at the Rage – so if at any point one of them decided to shout "Next!", they could be home in no time, eating Haagen-Dazs and complaining to their respective roommates.

In the West Village, Joe never accepted a date with a man who lived more than a ten-minute subway ride away, for the same reason.

But in rural central Wisconsin, going to Oz meant an hour of painful first-date small talk on the way there, and another on the way back. So Joe and his dates ended up going to movies, restaurants, and dance clubs in Kansas.

The classic first date has four parts: movie, dinner, dancing, and kiss on the doorstep.

No gay-themed movies ever played in Northland, and they didn't want to spend a first date watching naked ladies emerging from showers or groaning and writhing atop men. A kid's movie like *Peter Pan* would omit the most graphic of the straight hijinks, but straight people, even the most enlightened, always seemed to suffer from a nagging suspicion that gay men are pedophiles, and they didn't want to fan any flames by watching movies about prepubescent boys. So they decided on animated features, like *Finding Nemo* or *Rugrats Go Wild!*, or G-rated features starring teenagers or adults, like *Holes* or *Cheaper by the Dozen*. There were still a few odd looks from patrons, as they wondered why we didn't sit with a seat between us like most straight men who attend movies without women, but if the theater was crowded or if they arrived during the previews, no one noticed.

The erasure began in the second part, dinner: not once did anyone in Northland ever realize that they were on a date. They were always the only same-sex pair amid tables of men and women stretching out to infinity in all directions, and they were constantly assumed two straight guys on the prowl.

At Il Retrovo, the host repeated "How many in your party?" twice, as if not sure he had heard them properly the first time, that their wives or girlfriends must be on the way. The waitress met them with momentary hesitation and a questioning frown.

The waitress at the Mucky Duck Shanty looked behind them, searching for the women who must be taking up the rear.

At Legend Larry's Wings and Things, as they sat in the bar waiting for their table to be ready, two ladies approached and asked to join them, assuming that two men together were necessarily available.

On another night, a lady in the next booth sent Joe's date a drink.

After they were seated, diners at other tables often looked over, then nudged their companions so they could look as well. Joe could imagine their conversations: Two guys together! Could they be brothers? College buddies? Father and son? Waiting for their dates? Dumped by their dates?

When they made our relationship obvious by holding hands or cuddling against each other in the booth, there was no homophobic harassment, just some embarrassed attempts not to look.

Joe and his date were ignoring what Kenji Yoshino call "the demand to cover," the demand that people with stigmatized identities go incognito, erase as much of their stigma – and as much of their identity – as possible.[3] Ethnic minorities must "act white," religious minorities must avoid the dress and symbols of their faith, and gay people must behave as if they are straight. Two gay men on a date must be indistinguishable from two straight men on a non-romantic outing.

Boys Dance with Girls

In the third segment of the date, dancing, observers could no longer maintain the pretense that no gay people exist. Thinking hard, they could come up with reasons why two straight men might go to a movie together, even on a Saturday night, or dine together, even at a romantic restaurant. But they could come up with no reason for two straight men to dance together, alone, with no female partners in sight.

For thousands of years, dancing occurred in unpartnered groups, usually of the same sex, but during the 16th and 17th centuries, in the royal courts of Europe, men and women began to dance with each other. Upper-class society was gradually allowing people to select their own marital partners (as long as they were of the "opposite" sex) rather than being bound by their parents' choices, and the closeness of a dance provided an ideal means of evaluating each other's physical attributes without illicit groping and fondling. Eventually the lower classes developed their own styles of male-female dancing, and by the early years of the 20th century, most successful straight courtships required expertise in the Charleston, the Lindy Hop, the Turkey Trot, or the Big Apple.

In the 1960s, discothèque-style dancing came into style, with free-form moves that did not require touching one's partner, yet still every dance paired a man and a woman. Women were permitted to select each other as partners when no man had asked, but men were never permitted to dance together under any circumstances. In fact, most cities had ordinances allowing the police to raid establishments that permitted same-sex dancing.

Today, few such ordinances remain, struck down, say legislators, by the many straights who want to dance in groups-- but every venue is free to set its own standards of conduct, and many "standards" mandate that the dancing must be "clean," that is, straight.[4]

Joe checked several online dating sites.

Rick Archer, owner of a large dance studio in Houston, insisted, "We are not bigots. People who are gay are more than welcome here as long as they accept a simple rule:

boys dance with girls." (Similarly, a restaurateur might say "Jewish people are more than welcome here as long as they eat shellfish.")[5]

The United Country-Western Dance Council required that all couples "consist of a man and a woman."

The World Swing Dance Council did not own up to its homophobia on its website, but the application form for the U.S. Open Swing Dance Championship, held Thanksgiving Weekend in Anaheim, California, asked for the "Male/Leader" and "Female/Follower."[6]

The American Ballroom Dance Association did not mention gay people in its bylaws, but when the Starlight Ballroom, the largest venue for ballroom dancing in the United States, held classes, it referred only to "the man" and "the woman," certain that no other configurations are possible.[7]

Dancing in Kansas would require Joe and his date to "flaunt it" at a club where they were not supposed to exist, where they could be physically ejected or worse, which certainly would put a damper on any dating experience. So they had to skip the dance segment of the date, or go to the Blu Light, or drive into Milwaukee.

It's Raining Men

Of the Billboard Top 100 Singles for his year in Wisconsin, 80 were about attraction, sex, or love specified as exclusively straight:

"You're the type of woman deserves good thangs" (Mario, "Let Me Love You").

"You should see the way she wind her hips in slo-mo on the floor" (50 Cent, "Candy Shop").

"I shake it like jello, make the boys say hello" (Ciara, "1, 2 Step").

In Oz, the music playing at dance was about gay romance, gay sex, or how much a male singer liked men. But at the Blu Light in Northland, songs were overwhelmingly about straight desire or romance:

The Pussycat Dolls don't care to share their man with other girls ("Don't Cha").

"All the boys" enjoy looking at the breasts of the Black Eyed Peas ("My Humps").

Some songs did not specify the gender of the beloved:

Kelly Clarkson has broken up with someone and is moving on ("Since U Been Gone").

Mariah Carey wants to hug and kiss her lover ("We Belong Together").

However, their videos showed their squirming, mostly-naked bodies so intimately that there was no question that they are aimed at an audience of either lesbians or straight men. Why were gay men watching, and listening?

Every recording artist to ever crack a Billboard Top 100 list for the first time was straight or pretending, though some, like Elton John and George Michael, reveal their "secret" after fame hit.[8] But there were hundreds of gay and lesbian artists, working for independent labels or self-producing: Justin Tranter, Eric Himan, Daniel Cartier, Acoustic Souls.[9] They came in every genre, every mix. But where could you find them for your playlist or CD collection? Not at a straight world record store. Tower Records. com, Amazon.com, and Barnesandnoble.com had no categories for "gay music."

Unless they stick to classical music, gay people in Kansas had to find meaning where none was consciously intended, placing themselves in songs written for someone else. Men must pretend to be Kelly Clarkson as she awaits her male lover, and women must pretend that they are the male lover. Their desire must be arguably straight.

Kiss on the Doorstep

In rural central Wisconsin, the last part of the date, the kiss on the doorstep, was simply out of the question. Joe saw straights kissing each other constantly, on doorsteps, in hallways, on sidewalks, at bus stops, at the movies, at the bank, even in church, never thinking for a moment that anyone who saw them would fail to swoon with utter delight at this evidence of "their love."

But same-sex kisses must be conscious, deliberate, both partners aware of their surroundings and prepared for possible violent confrontation. His dates always rushed him inside for a closeted goodnight kiss, leaving passing straights secure in their knowledge that no one in their neighborhood, in their town, in their world was gay.

The Facts of Life

Joe moved to West Hollywood during the height of the AIDS epidemic, and the sexual hedonism of the 1970s had vanished. A few first dates still culminated with "How do you like your coffee in the morning?" but generally sex didn't happen until the second, third, or fourth date, and casual one-night stands were unthinkable. Everyone knew people who "tricked," picking up men in bars as a form of recreation, but they looked down on them and didn't invite them to parties.

But in Northland, one of the men Joe dated declared that he would like to "get the sex out of the way" before they left for dinner, so his horniness would not blind him to the quality of the conversation.

Another responded to Joe's introductory email with the question "Size?" to make sure that he would not be wasting his time with further contact.

One man Joe contacted wanted sex without dating, a "sex buddy" who would never stick around for coffee.

Another wanted dating without sex, saying "Why would you debase a boyfriend by treating him like a trick?"

It was not surprising that gay men in Kansas would have conflicting ideas about what sex is for, since they were told, over and over, that if gay people exist at all, they do not have sex.

The term "facts of life" used to refer to any of the harsh realities of life, such as death and taxes, but since World War II it has meant only the details of straight intercourse. The information is traditionally conveyed to wide-eyed children by their fathers or mothers, who "know," with no uncertainty whatever, that they will engaging in such intimacies soon, when they march down the aisle to marry. More recently, the information has become the parvenu of middle school health or sex education teachers, who again are absolutely certain that all students, with no exceptions, will be engaging in such intimacies soon, if they haven't begun already.

Only a tiny percentage of sex education classes mention gay people, and always as aliens, beings far removed from the everyday experiences of the indefatigably straight adolescents (and their sexual activities are not mentioned at all).

Until college Joe thought it an undisputed fact that gay people never had sex; they might hold hands, they might even kiss, but they lacked the proper anatomy to participate in "the facts of life" as explained by his father and middle-school health teacher.

Twenty years later, Joe found that most residents of Kansas still believed that gay people, if they existed, were unable to engage in sexual activity, or had no interest in trying. On the tv sitcom *Seinfeld,* Jerry announces that "sex is about love between a man and a woman," certain that no other possibility exists.[10]

The snopes.com website, which debunks urban myths, didn't bother with debunking the myth that gay people do not have sex: "We engage in sex because we have a powerful biological urge to do so: it's nature's way of ensuring that we reproduce."[11]

This notion comes from sociobiology, a mesh of outdated structural-functional sociology and outdated Darwinian biology that hopes to explain all human behavior, including physical attraction, as the result of "powerful biological urges."[12] For instance, all men are attracted to women with large breasts because they nourish infants more efficiently than women with small breasts, and their children will therefore be more likely to survive. Though it still pops up from time to time – students love it – sociobiology has been completely discredited, mostly because mystic urges are impossible to prove (one might as well say that Cupid causes physical attraction by shooting magic arrows, and big breasts are an easier target to hit).

Joe encountered sociobiology at a sociology conference in Milwaukee during his second semester at Northland. The presenter examined personal ads to see if all men really want women with big breasts? Did all women really want men with big muscles?

He asked her why she didn't include any gay personal ads. She stared – obviously she was not aware that gay personal ads existed – and finally said, "Well. . .you know. . .we just looked at men and women."

That didn't answer the question, so Joe asked what sociobiology thought of gay people. She hesitated and fumbled some more, until someone in the audience chimed in: "They're freaks!"

Sociobiology actually explains them as an evolutionary misfire, a regrettable waste of genetic material.

Scholars in Kansas, especially those who research sexuality, should be aware that gay people have sex, but Joe found that they often are not.

An article in *The Journal of Sex Research* looks at instances of casual sex among college students, and defines "sex" as "the penis entering the vagina," unaware – or pretending to be unaware -- that any college student is gay.[13]

An article in the prestigious *American Sociological Review* argues that parental advice and neighborhood monitoring play a role in the "timing of first intercourse" for adolescents.[14] Intercourse is not defined, but since gay people do not use that term for their sexual activity, it presumably means heterosexual intercourse. There is no hint that anyone might not participate in a "first intercourse," and a second, and a third, ad infinitum, or that anyone might participate in a sexual act involving two penises or two vaginas. There is no hint that gay adolescents exist.

In *Law in America,* prolific legal scholar Lawrence M. Friedman notes that because the age of consent is usually seventeen or eighteen, when two sixteen-year-olds have sex, "the male" is technically a rapist, and "the female" a victim. Joe wondered how Friedman managed to become a professor of law at Stanford University and publish 23 books without ever once hearing that some sexual acts occur between two men, or between two women.[15]

When sexual practices other than "intercourse" are mentioned, they still occur only in the context of men and women together. Where did we get the expression "that sucks," for something bad? Criminologist Jack Katz knows: it denigrates "the woman's position in fellatio."[16] Katz is not aware, or does not want to be aware, that men are perfectly capable of performing fellatio.

The only gay sexual activity that residents of Kansas would grudgingly acknowledge was anal sex. Of course, many lesbians, and straights themselves, engage in this activity, and many gay men do not, but still, the association is so strong that before they were invalidated by the Supreme Court in 2003, sodomy laws were often applied only to gay men.

In the first session of *The Sociology of Sexuality* at Wesley College, Joe began, as usual, by fielding open questions from the students. One of the back-of-the-classroom jocks asked, "Why do homos do that sex thing?"

He answered with his set piece: why does anyone have sex? To express love; to express an identity; to express dominance; because they are lonely; because they are horny; because it is fun.

"No," the jock persisted, "That. . .that butthole thing! It's nasty!"

In "Is the Rectum a Grave," Berkeley professor Leo Bersani, who has written scholarly studies of Proust and Mallarmé, offers a strikingly homophobic (and, for that matter, sexist) denigration of the passive partner in gay anal sex: "the infinitely seductive and intolerable image of a grown man, legs high in the air, unable to refuse the suicidal ecstasy of being a woman."[17]

That particular position is not common, since it requires a great deal of flexibility and no belly bulge, but Bersani insists that this is what *all* gay sex is, so he can critique it as a mirror of "normal" straight intercourse: the butt instead of the vagina, leading to human waste instead of ova, to death instead of life. He only omits a mention of Satan presiding over the activity.

The image of the rectum as something gay, and therefore off-limits to "normal" people, may have some negative consequences for straights. A regular check of the prostate gland, called the DRE (Digital Rectal Exam), is essential for men over 40, but many straights are refusing it with a shudder of disgust.

An article in *Time Magazine* states that fear of the DRE is the "single leading reason" why many middle-aged men do not go to the doctor at all.[18] Why is the exam so dreaded? The physician inserts a gloved finger into the anus to check for any prostate enlargement; it is less painful than checking your blood pressure, and it takes less time. Could it be that the straight men are humiliated by a procedure that they believe feels like anal sex, hence like being gay?

For Her Pleasure

If a man has the slightest inkling that the date will end in a bedroom, he will certainly go shopping for condoms. Durex, Crown, Pleasure Plus, and Trustex brands are aware that gay men exist, so they avoid specifying the sexual orientation of potential customers: the condom boxes feature graphic designs instead of a hetero-couple, and there are no instructions on "how to please a woman" in the advertising copy. An article-length advertisement from Durex extolling custom-fit condoms for men of different sizes repeatedly talks about the man and "his partner," never suggesting that men always have sex with woman.[19]

But these brands were not widely available in Kansas. At the Walgreen's in Northland, Joe had a single choice: Trojan Condoms, designed "for her pleasure," with a man and a woman about to kiss on the cover of every box, and of course a sales clerk who consequently believed Joe to be straight.

The official Trojan website started off with an inclusive announcement about people with HIV informing their "partners," but went on to talk about, and depict, nothing but straight couples, as if gay men did not purchase condoms, as if gay men did not have sex, or did not exist at all.[20]

Gentlemen's Clubs

Most small and medium-sized towns feature "adult bookstores," a misnomer, since they do not sell books at all; they sell erotic magazines, videos, games, and toys. In West Hollywood, Joel sometimes went to the Pleasure Chest, a few blocks east of the French Quarter, his favorite Sunday brunch spot. It was egalitarian, with sections entitled "For Him and Her," "For Her and Her," and "For Him and Him."[21]

But Northland offered only Private Pleasures, on a sleazy stretch of State Highway 42 that also featured Happy Times Costumes, a tattoo parlor, and a tavern called Shuff's Last Resort.

The video section did stock gay titles, but to get to them, you had to sort through endless racks of *Big Bubble Butt Brazilian Orgy* and *Brooke's Bitches*.

The magazine section was all straight (or lesbian-straight).

There was also a poker deck "for him" (with pictures of naked ladies), a "Down and Dirty" card game (with pictures of naked ladies), and an Oral Sex game (gender not specified, but shaped like female lips).

Oddly, CruisingforSex.com, a directory of popular spots for anonymous sex, listed Private Pleasures. Evidently men can have sex there, hidden away in the video preview booths, while on screen naked women gyrate atop men, and out on the street, straights come and go, secure in their belief that gay people do not exist.

If you would prefer to see real people rather than videos, many cities and medium-sized towns offer "gentlemen's clubs," usually on the same deserted street as the adult bookstore, but "gentlemen" means "straight gentlemen": the clubs feature semi-naked ladies gyrating on poles. There are clubs with male dancers as well, but most assume that only women are interested.

Joe thought of inviting a date to spend the weekend in Chicago, and taking him to see the famous Chippendale Dancers, but he was informed that performances were for "ladies only." The official website did not explain the policy, but in the online forum, fans usually expressed their appreciation: when tagalong "boyfriends and husbands" are excluded, the women can be more uninhibited. No one betrayed the slightest awareness that any man could want to see male dancers.[22]

If you would prefer to stay home, many agencies will send over a male stripper or even a whole "all-male revue," but only if you and your guests are all female. In Northland, one could hire Wisconsin Hunks and Babes, but the hunks would only go to babes' houses, and the babes to hunks' houses. Mixed parties were ok, as long as 51% or more of the guests were of "the opposite sex of the entertainer."

This seemed to indicate an awareness of – and disdain for – gay people, but nothing on the website suggested that any customer could actually be interested in a same-sex hunk or babe.

Wisconsin Strippers offered "Bachelorette Party Fun" (in pink letters) and yelled "Ladies! Give the gift that unwraps itself." Their website stated no policy about "51% opposite sex," but when Joe called to inquire, the agent said "Ha, ha, big joke!" and hung up.

Love Between a Man and a Woman

Over a century ago, Lord Alfred Douglas, lover of Oscar Wilde, distinguished between "true love" between boys and girls, and same-sex love, "sad and sweet," but too afraid, too ashamed to speak its name.[23] In Kansas, Joe found that the problem was not fear of speaking the name, but no one hearing it when it is spoken, yelling the name to an audience deafened by their belief that no boy has ever loved a boy, and no girl has ever loved a girl.

In *Queen of Outer Space* (1958), two American astronauts and a scientist are stranded on a planet Venus populated entirely by women. How is an all-female world possible? How do they reproduce? Professor Konrad (Paul Birch) suggests: "Perhaps they've learned to live without love." He is the term "love" as a euphemism for heterosexual intercourse – perhaps the women have the technology for reproduction by parthenogenesis.

But his astronaut chum quips, "You call that living?", suggesting that *he* means falling in love, the theme of everybody's dreaming, which only ever occurs between women and men.

Ten years later (1967), *Star Trek* tells us of explorer Zefram Cochraine, who has been stranded on an alien planet for many years with no company except a sentient energy cloud. The Starship *Enterprise* comes to the rescue with a translation device that allows it to speak. It states that it is in love with Cochraine – in a female voice. Why a female voice?

"The idea of male and female are universal constants," Captain Kirk helpfully informs us.

Thirty years later (1997), the townsfolk of *The Simpsons* mistake a sedated Mr. Burns for a space alien. He proclaims, "I bring you love!"

Dr. Hibbert asks for clarification: "Is that the love between a man and a woman or the love between a man and a fine Cuban cigar?"

A century after Lord Alfred Douglas, we hear again about two loves, but now the object of a man's desire can only be a woman or an inanimate object. The love "that dares not speak its name" has ceased to exist.

My Girlfriend Doesn't Like My Boyfriend

When you are dating someone steady but have not yet made a permanent commitment, you have a "boyfriend" or a "girlfriend." Technically, either term can be used to proclaim that no gay people exist. Though most people in Kansas asserted Joe's straightness by referring to his "wife," some said "girlfriend," when they thought he was a young adult in spite of the balding.

For men, however, the erasure ends there. "Girlfriend" and "boyfriend" both refer to someone they are currently dating, in love with, or sleeping with, so gay or straight, the meaning is clear.

However, lesbians are doubly erased. For women, the term "girlfriend" has two possible meanings: someone they are dating, and someone they are not.

Someone they are sleeping with, and someone they are not.

A romantic partner, and a non-romantic buddy.

One would expect confusion to arise when women make statements like "My mother doesn't like his girlfriend"; "My girlfriend and he went to a movie last night"; "I asked his girlfriend's advice about which car to

buy." But in Kansas, confusion does not arise. Since no lesbians exist, no woman has ever had a romantic relationship
with a woman in all the history of the world. Therefore a
woman's "girlfriend" can only be a friend.

In November of his year in Wisconsin, Joe conducted
an experiment: he asked ten faculty members, either straight
or passing, to identify whether a man or a woman made
these statements:

A)   My girlfriend got upset when she caught him
      flirting with another girl.
B)   he gave duplicate apartment keys to his best
      friend and his girlfriend
C)   After we broke up, he cried on his girlfriend's
      shoulder for three hours.

Only one answered, "I can't tell. A and B could be either men or women, and C makes no sense. Why would you
cry on your girlfriend's shoulder after you broke up with
her?"

The others all answered "That's easy. Obviously, A
and B were made by a man, and C by a woman." They could
not conceive of the possibility that a woman's girlfriend
might really be a girlfriend.

In Maine, Florida, and Wisconsin, Joe always asked
for clarification from women who used "girlfriend" without
specifying friend or romantic partner, usually students who
wrote in their papers that "I asked his girlfriend about the
problem" or "I invited his girlfriend to the party."

But when the professor who would be completing his
year-end review told him that she had spent the weekend
"in Chicago with a girlfriend," Joe chickened out. He knew
she was married to a man; he knew that she was erasing les-

bians from the world; but he did not want to be labeled clannish, argumentative, or uncollegial.

Renting a U-Haul

When straights decide that they want to make their relationship permanent, they have two choices. They can rent a U-Haul and move in together. Or they can buy rings and publish an announcement in the newspaper, then spend a year deciding on a minister, a band, a caterer, a photographer, and a florist, renting a church and a reception hall, registering with the state, and buying new rings, tuxedos, and gowns. At the end of the year, they can invite 200 of their closest friends and relatives to several days' worth of ceremonies, dinners, and parties, with another announcement in the newspaper, 200 gifts to unwrap, a vacation trip, and a final price tag of $20,000, usually paid for by one or both sets of parents.[24] They are now "one flesh" in the eyes of God and a legal partnership in the eyes of the state.

Four times during his life, Joel decided to make a relationship permanent, and four times, his only option was the U-Haul. Some Protestant denominations will perform commitment ceremonies for gay people, but most refuse, believing that God hates them.

Some states will allow gay people to register as domestic partners, with some of the rights of straights, but most refuse, believing that the law hates them.

Surveys show that most American straights are perfectly happy with the idea of a gay domestic partnership, but start screaming at the idea of gay marriage.

Why do straights want to keep the flowers, the rings, the photographers, the announcement in newspapers, the tuxedos, the gowns, the catering, and the presents all to themselves? Is it pure selfishness – I get a lot of stuff, and you don't? Is it homophobia – weddings are suitable only for "true" straight love, not perversion? Or is it that the wedding is the one place where their triumph is complete?

Judith Butler tells us that the wedding ceremony is central to the "Heterosexualization of the social bond," [25] the one place where one can be absolutely "certain" that every story is about a boy and a girl. How dare gay people force us to admit that they desire each other and fall in love with each other? So give them all of the rights of marriage, give them separate but equal domestic partnerships and commitment ceremonies, but never, ever let them marry.

For this reason, the multibillion dollar wedding industry has barely acknowledged the money to be made in planning gay weddings. Joe checked five websites of wedding planners and found no concession for same-sex couples, whether they are to be married or simply committed. The Association of Bridal Consultants had a director of ethnic diversity, but did not mention sexual orientation. Nor did the Association of Professional Wedding Planners.

Not that they are necessarily homophobic. When Richard Martel, president of the Association for Wedding Professionals International, surveyed industry members concerning their views on gay marriage, only three of 1,500 responses expressed opposition. The others may not oppose gay marriage as a theoretical case, but their daily lives are so thoroughly immersed in straight coupling that they can easily forget that gay people exist. The AWPI's Bridal Directory lists services in 90 categories, from "Dove Releases" to "Veils and Tiaras," but nothing for gay weddings. [26]

The most recent edition of *Emily Post's Wedding Etiquette* mentioned gay couples five times, and even included a few suggestions for them (for instance, a reading of the Biblical story of Ruth and Naomi). [27] *Wedding Planning for*

Dummies included gay weddings in a chapter called "Creative Celebrations," along with military weddings, renewing your vows, and bachelor/bachelorette parties.

But there was no hint of same-sex ceremonies in *The Best of Martha Stewart Living Weddings, Intimate Weddings, The Complete Outdoor Wedding Planner,* or *The Knot Ultimate Wedding Planner. Wedding Cakes You Can Make* did not envision the possibility that there ever might be two grooms or two brides atop the cake. *Digital Wedding Photography* did not envision the possibility that there ever might be two grooms or two brides in the photograph.[28]

Yet gay people are sought after to participate in these straight weddings. If you have straight coworkers, neighbors, or acquaintances, you will probably be invited to a dozen every year. The florists, photographers, jewelers, caterers, and entertainers are often gay. The wedding planners are often gay. The triumph cannot be complete unless gay people are complicit in their own erasure, grinning their approval as the straights stand alone at the altar or under the chuppa, proclaiming as loudly as anyone else that all desire is straight desire, all love is straight love.

---

[1] Eharmony, http://www.eharmony.com

[2] Romance Class.com, http://www.romanceclass.com

[3] Yoshino, Kenji. *Covering: The Hidden Assault on our Civil Rights.* New York: Random House, 2006.

[4] "History of Same-Sex Dance," Fred Astaire Dance Studio, http://www.fadsboston.com

[5] http://www.ssqq.com/information/samesex.htm

[6] World Swing Dance Council, http://www.usopen swingdc.com/compete.html

[7] Starlite Dance Club, http://www.starlitedanceclub.com /faqs.php#Anchor-Do-14210

[8] Smith, Richard. *Other Voices: A History of Homosexuality and Popular Music*. Cassell, 1997.

[9] Directory of GLBTI Musicians, Stonewall Society, http://www.stonewallsociety.com/GLBTArtists/glbtmusicians.htm

[10] Original airdate October 16, 1997.

[11] Urban Legends Reference Page: Risque Business, http://www.snopes.com/risque/risque.asp

[12] Ridely, Matt, *The Red Queen: Sex and the Evolution of Human Nature*. San Francisco: Harper Perennial, 2003; Buss, David. *The Evolution of Desire: Strategies of Human Mating.* New York: Basic Books, 2003.

[13] Grello, Catherine M., Deborah P. Theylsh, and Melinda S. Harper, "No Strings Attached: The Nature of Casual Sex in College Students." *Journal of Sex Research* 43.3 (August 2006): 255-267.

[14] Browning, Christopher R., Tama Leventhal, and Jeanne Brooks-Gunn, "Sexual Initiation in Early Adolescence: The Nexus of Parental and Community Control." *American Sociological Review* 70.5 (October 2005): 758-778.

[15] Friedman, Lawrence M. *Law in America*. New York: Modern Library, 2002: 100.

[16] Katz, Jack. *Seductions of Crime*. Basic Books, 1990.

[17] Bersani, Leo. "Is the Rectum a Grave?" pp. 249-264 in *Reclaiming Sodom*, ed. Jonathan Goldberg. NY: Routledge: 251.

[18] Gorman, Christine. "The Private Pain of Prostate Cancer." *Time Magazine*, October 5, 1992.

[19] Glickman, Adam. "The Next Big (or Not So Big) Thing: Why Condom Size Matters." http://secure. condomania.com/TheyFit/Media/NextBigThing/

[20] Trojan Website, http://www.trojan.com

[21] The Pleasure Chest, http://www.thepleasurechest.com.

[22] Chippendales Online, http://www.chippendales.com

[23] Lord Alfred Douglas, "The Two Loves" (1894). Originally published in *The Chameleon*, and quoted during the trial of Oscar Wilde. http://www.law.umkc.edu/faculty/projects/ftrials/wilde/poemsofdouglas.htm

[24]Statistics taken from the National Council of Wedding Ministers, http://www.aweddingministers.com/wedding/statistics.htm.

[25] Butler, Judith. *Bodies that Matter: On the Discursive Limits of Sex*. New York: Routledge, 1993.

[26] Finer, Jonathan. "At Expo, Few Disagreements on Gay Marriage." *Washington Post,* May 4, 2004.

[27] Post, Peggy. *Emily Post's Wedding Etiquette*, 5th edition. New York: Collins, 2005.

[28] Blum, Marcy, & Laura K. Kaiser. *Wedding Planning for Dummies*. New York: For Dummies Books, 2004; Stewart, Martha. *The Best of Martha Stewart Living: Weddings* (Clarkson Potter, 1999); Friedrichsen, Christina, *Intimate Weddings* (North Light Books, 2004); Naylor, Sharon. *The Complete Wedding Planner* (Three Rivers Press, 2001); Roney, Carley, *The Knot Ultimate Wedding Planner* (Broadway Books, 1999); Wilson, Dede, *Wedding Cakes You Can Make* (John Wiley & Sons, 2005); Johnson, Glen. *Digital Wedding Photography* (John Wiley & Sons, 2006).

Chapter Seven
Sunday Morning in Milwaukee

When he first moved to West Hollywood, Joe dated a film archivist named Aaron, who worked deep in a vault inside NBC Studios and boasted about the many tv stars he could introduce him to. Aaron grew up in the Orthodox Jewish enclave of "Beverly Hills Adjacent," and he was still deeply observant.

He would not work, play, or have sex between sundown Friday and sundown Saturday.

He refused cheeseburgers, ham, and shrimp.

His apartment was cluttered with thick, heavy Hebrew tomes, photographs of dour ancestors, glittering menorahs, Passover plates, and mezuzot.

In his sheltered Midwestern childhood Joe had barely met a Jewish person, and he was mesmerized by this new culture. Soon Aaron was taking him to picnics, potlucks, special events, and sometimes Friday night services at Beth Chaim Chadashim, the gay synagogue on Pico Boulevard.

At the time, most of Joe's social life revolved around All Saints Metropolitan Community Church in West Hollywood, so naturally he invited Aaron to their parties, potlucks, and special events. But Aaron always had other plans. When our Saturday night dates lasted until Sunday morning, Joe naturally invited him to church. He was always too tired, or he had nothing to wear, or he was dying to try that new place for Sunday brunch. Joe found this evasion troubling. If he had no difficulty with Aaron being Jewish, why should Aaron object to him being Christian?

It took a little prying, but finally Aaron admitted that he was terrified of Christian churches. He believed that every Sunday morning, millions of Catholics, Methodists, Presbyterians, and Pentecostals filed into their white-spired churches to hear preachers rant about how the Jews were poisoning wells, killing children, and otherwise trying to destroy society, followed by an exhortation to drag all of the Jews in town to the nearest baptismal font, or kill them.

Joe told Aaron that he had never heard any of those accusations against Jews, or any exhortations to convert or kill them, in all of his years of regular church attendance. He couldn't quite believe it. Actually, a preacher in the fundamentalist church of his childhood once mused on the irony of Jews rejecting Christ during his first appearance, when they would eagerly embrace the Antichrist. Still, assuming that he began paying attention at age seven and listened to two sermons, a Sunday school lesson, and a youth group lesson every week until he left the church at age twenty, he had over 4,000 opportunities to hear anti-Semitic utterances. One hardly suggests an obsession.

In Kansas, Joe found that most people associated Christianity with homophobia rather than anti-Semitism. They believed that every Sunday morning, millions of Catholics, Methodists, Presbyterians, and Pentecostals filed into their white-spired churches to hear preachers rant about how gay people were spreading disease, molesting children, and otherwise trying to destroy society, followed by an exhortation to drag all of the gay people in town to the nearest baptismal font, or kill them. All Christians were antigay and all gay people anti-Christian, two opposing camps like the

Axis and the Allies during World War II, each loathing the other, each trying to destroy the other.

Often they did not limit their sense of contradiction to gay people and Christianity. They thought that that Buddhism, Hinduism, Judaism, Islam, all religions were antigay and gay people anti-religion, as if gay people were constitutionally incapable of seeing anything beyond the material realm, as if belief itself required straight intercourse

Shortly after he arrived at Wesley College, a colleague told Joe that students would resist hearing about gay people from a gay person, thinking that they were being "brainwashed" into accepting a secret "homosexual agenda." So he should throw out a casual comment about something that happened in church last Sunday. It could also be at temple Friday night – it didn't matter, any religion would do. The students would conclude that since he was religious, he must be straight. They would then be as docile as lambs.

.   On the final exam in *Drugs and Society,* Joe asked: "Why are self-help addiction recovery organizations like Alcoholics Anonymous less effective with gay and lesbian clients?"

Most students answered correctly, with essays about closeting and heterosexism, but more than one wrote something like: "Alcoholics Anonymous requires belief in a Higher Power, and gays and lesbians do not believe in God."

Gay people were indeed slightly more likely than straights to be atheists, but only slightly; the vast majority believed in God. Many were drawn to the spiritual realm to find relief from the oppression they faced in their everyday lives. There were gay Buddhists, Hindus, Muslims, Jews, Wiccans, and Christians. Every Sunday morning, gay Catholics, Methodists, Presbyterians, and Pentecostals filled church pews, and conducted the services: gay people was especially drawn to roles in church leadership, since preachers need not be gender-polarized macho men or quiet, demur ladies, and priests need not express any straight interest at all.

Far from being innately homophobic, religion was the first social institution to champion the humanity of gay people. Long before the government started decriminalizing gay relationships and psychiatrists were starting to admit that maybe gay people weren't psychotic after all, the Quakers were admitting gay members and the Council on Religion and the Homosexual was protesting antigay police harassment in San Francisco. The first gay-specific Christian church was founded in 1968, a year before Stonewall.

Why did Joe find so many people in Kansas convinced that religion is by definition homophobic? Because they never heard that some religions and Christian denominations welcome gay people, even if they belonged to one. Because they never heard about gay believers. In the everyday life of their church or religion, gay people were never acknowledged, they were never permitted to exist.

The Truth about Sexuality

Members of homophobic denominations may scream at a Gay Pride Parade, or sign a petition promoting the removal of this or that bit of gay freedom, but in everyday life, in sermons, Sunday school lessons, Bible studies, and miscellaneous meetings week after week, year after year, they rarely if ever hear anyone say "Adam and Eve, not Adam and Steve!"

If asked, they would certainly agree that gay people are monstrous, demon possessed, abominations in the eyes of God, destined for the lake of fire, and so forth. But in ninety-nine Sundays out of a hundred, the subject simply doesn't come up.

The Church of the Nazarene, Joe's childhood denomination believes that many common practices of "the world" anger God: drinking, dancing, playing cards, going to movies, buying on Sunday, men wearing long hair, women wearing pants; but the worst abomination of all is same-sex desire. The most recent version of the *Manual,* the ubiquitous black-bound Nazarene rule book, lamented "the depth of perversion that causes homosexuality." Gay people have strayed so far from God that most do not even recognize how evil they are, and many actively try to recruit others, especially children, into their ranks.[1]

But when he checked the online text of 200 sermons delivered at the local Church of the Nazarene in Newark, Ohio, Joe found only two expressions of hatred of gay people.

Evidently the minister considered this particular "sin" far too alien to everyday experience to bother condemning regularly; surely no one in the congregation was gay, or knew anyone gay.

Fox Valley Christian Church in the Chicago suburb of Batavia, Illinois offered a more hip style of fundamentalism: casual attire was suggested, there is no lengthy list of prohibitions, and worship services used cutting edge multimedia technology rather than a staid piano and organ. Of course only straights were welcome. But in online archive of 44 sermons preached over a period of two years, gay people were not mentioned at all, except perhaps once by implication: Pastor Dan Fields notes that American public schools do not always teach our children the truth "about human nature, sexuality, or theories of origins."

Otherwise the pastor simply assumes that everyone on Earth is straight.

Every seminary student learns that the Greeks recognized three types of love, *eros* (between romantic partners), *phileo* (between friends), and *agape* (between God and humanity), so Joe expected that the sermon on "Find a Buddy!" would be about *phileo*. Actually, it is about *eros,* or more precisely straight marriage, which God instituted because he wanted you to have a "buddy." Why this marital "buddy" could not be of the same sex was never explained, since presumably the question never occurred to the pastor or to anyone in the congregation.[2]

Christ Episcopal Church in Portland, Oregon was not affiliated with the pro-gay denomination, but with the Reformed Episcopal Church, tiny, fundamentalist, and homophobic: it taught that "homosexual acts are sinful in all circumstances." [3]

But in an online database of over 100 sermons preached over a period of three years, "homosexual acts" are never explicitly condemned. There was no need, since everyone on Earth was straight. In a sermon entitled "Filling the Void," Pastor William Kloeck tells us: "human beings find the image of God in ourselves through the relationship between man and woman. When we see this, it should point us to the prototype of the image in us – the plurality of our Trinitarian God." He doesn't explain why the two people have to be of different sexes, because he doesn't need to: no one has asked.

Are You a Whosoever?

Not every fundamentalist church is homophobic, or comprised mainly of straights. Over two hundred gay churches in the United States are fundamentalist, "Bible-believing and spirit-filled," preaching the "whole truth" and the "full gospel." Yet when they are in Kansas, their websites tend to pretend that there are no gay members at all, or that the gay members are a tiny minority in an overwhelmingly straight congregation. Most refrain from using the word "gay" anywhere on their websites.   Instead, they merely state that "everyone is welcome," and put the "everyone" in capitals, boldface, red or purple, or several font-sizes larger than the rest of the sentence.

The Casa de Cristo Evangelical Church announces that "we are a church where EVERYONE is welcomed and affirmed."

Christ the Cornerstone Church offers "God's love and acceptance to ALL."

Or the website will refer to John 3:16, a key text in the evangelical doctrine of personal salvation: "For God so loved the world that he gave his only begotten son, that whosoever believeth in him shall not perish, but have everlasting life."

World Harvesters Church puts the WHOSOEVER in boldface.

Central Community Chapel asks "Are you a WHO-SOEVER?"

Readers are expected to interpret EVERYONE, ALL PEOPLE, and WHOSOEVER as code for "gay men and lesbians."

Some churches use a nondiscrimination statement in lieu of WHOSOEVER, and place sexual orientation near the end of an unusually long list, to "hide" in plain site by suggesting that gay people are welcome but a small minority in the congregation.

The Calvary Open Door Center welcomes everyone "regardless of race, color, national origin, religious affiliation, or sexual orientation."

St. Gabriel Community Church is open to "Black, White, Hispanic, married, divorced, single, widowed, straight, gay, lesbian, etc."

The Casa de Cristo Evangelical Church places sexual orientation between race and age in an extraordinarily long list: "We have and love people of all types: Native American, African American, Asian, Caucasian, Hispanic, Multi-Racial, Lesbian, Straight, Transgendered, Gay, Transsexual, Young, and Old to name a few."

Several gay fundamentalist websites use visual images to avoid identifying as gay: they publish photographs, purportedly of members of the congregation, but so young, attractive, and "picture-perfect" that they must be stock, to give the impression that the congregation is all young, attractive, picture-perfect, and most importantly, straight.

The website of the Open Door Community Church displays eight photographs, five of male-female couples and three of mixed-gender groups. No same-sex couples appear, and no individual displays any iconic sign of gay identity, such as a rainbow flag or a gay pride banner.

The website of the Jubilee Apostolic Christian Center contains fifteen photos, about half male-female couples with children, a third male-female couples without children, and a third unpartnered people. One of fifteen does depict two intense-looking young men, professionally posed in stylish outfits; a viewer trying desperately to find signals of gay identity might possibly conclude that they are a gay couple, but they are not embracing or even standing side by side to signify their romantic commitment.

Emmanuel Fellowship Church displays two photographs, one an interracial male-female couple, and the other a white woman holding a mixed-race baby, as if the primary focus of the church is on decreasing the stigma attached to interracial relations rather than gay/lesbian identity. There is no hint that any of the congregants are gay men or lesbians of any race.

Welcoming Churches

The Episcopal Church, the Presbyterian Church, and a number of other Protestant denominations have made official policy decisions stating that God is not homophobic. Gay people are to be fully accepted as members, and their relationships are to be deemed just as valid as those of the straights. Several thousand local congregations, including some from denominations that do not have official pro-gay policies, have gone even further, announcing that they are "welcoming" or "open and affirming," ready to include gay individuals and couples not only as a theoretical category but as part of the everyday life of the church. Yet still, in the everyday life of the church, gay people are mostly absent.

The United Church of Gainesville, Florida, "values the diversity each individual brings to the congregation, including racial identity, ethnicity, sexual orientation, and religious background."[4] However, in an online database of 152 sermons preached over a period of four years, gay people are mentioned only twice, and are central only once, in a sermon about homophobia.

But straight husbands and wives appear constantly, in anecdotes about the pastor's own relationships, in illustrations, in asides. Even when they are absent, countless snide comments assume universal straight desire and practice. For instance, in "Lost Relatives," the pastor tells us that "Women and men need each other's qualities to be who God created us to be." But surely, since he pastors a "welcoming church," he believes that gay people can be who God created them to be, even without a man or a woman by their side. Clearly he forgot that gay people exist.

Trinity Lutheran Church in Norton, Ohio belongs to the pro-gay ELCA (Evangelical Lutheran Church in America), which states: "Gay and lesbian people, as individuals created by God, are welcome to participate fully in the life of the congregations."[5] But in one sermon, Pastor Dee Miklos told congregants all about marriage: "The husband helps the woman to be more fully herself and the wife helps the husband to become more fully himself. . .That is God's design for marriage."

Maybe Pastor Miklos is homophobic, in spite of her pro-gay denomination, and believes that gay people are alien to God's plan. But Lutherans are hierarchical, and surely she would receive censure form her bishop for not preaching official doctrines. It is more likely that she momentarily forgot that gay people exist.[6]

Liberal theologians are eager to decrease sexism by imagining God as androgynous or female rather than a patriarchal Father, but they still talk about a God who *creates* the world in a myth of straight fecundity nearly as blatant as that of the ancient Egyptian gods who fashioned men from their semen, and who *loves* the world with an biological, reproductive urge that sounds suspiciously like heterosexual romance.

In her *Models of God,* Sallie McFague discusses various types of love, *eros, phileo,* and *agape,* and then gushes that the highest type of love "engenders new life," that is, makes babies.[7] She appears to be unaware that a man and a woman can engender new life when they don't like each other, and even when they don't know each other. A woman who is raped can get pregnant; what does love have to do with it?

Surely McFague does not believe that every act of straight coitus, however sordid, represents "the highest love," and no same-sex act ever approaches that pinnacle, regardless of the circumstances. Mostly likely she is unaware that gay people have sex, or, like the pastors of Trinity Lutheran and the United Church of Gainesville, she has forgotten that they exist at all.

Jesus was Straight

Joe liked to suggest, that Jesus might possibly have been gay, to see how his straight-world acquaintances would react.

The liberal, welcoming Christians always issued a stern, livid denial – "Absolutely not! Don't be ridiculous!" – and refused further conversation on the topic.

Christians who were slightly less liberal and welcoming shrank back in horror and stopped returning his telephone messages.

He only tried it on a conservative Christian once. She literally ran from the room.

Why were Christians in Kansas, from the most liberal to the most conservative, so insistent that Jesus was straight? Surely they don't expect him to have slept with women – *The Da Vinci Code*, which postulates a sexual relationship between Jesus and Mary Magdalene, was rebuked as heretical. Catholics and fundamentalists picketed *The Last Temptation of Christ* simply because it depicts Jesus being tempted to marry and live a "normal" life.

If he wasn't sexually active, what does it matter if Jesus was attracted to men, women, both, or neither? Joe gradually began to think of the question as a litmus test for erasure. Jesus was perfect, the Son of God, the true human that all of us should be. If he was straight, then we all are – or should be – straight, then in a perfect world gay people would not exist. But if he was gay. . . .

Postponing Marriage

About 22% of the Jews in the United States are Orthodox, believing that gay people are abominations, hated by G-d, awaiting fire and brimstone in Gehenna; they may not attend Shabbat services, and any gay child who comes out to a parent must be rejected, never spoken to or spoken of again. About are Conservative, believing that gay people have failed to live up to God's straight standards, but are no more abominations than straights who divorce; they may attend Shabbat services, lead prayers, and read from the Torah. And about 38% are Reform, believing that gay is just as good as straight, so gay people may not only attend Shabbat services, they may stand with their partners under the chuppa to have their unions blessed in the eyes of God. At least one Conservative seminary and most Reform seminaries admit gay students, so a significant number of rabbis are gay.[8]

Since Jews are frequently assumed not to exist, especially around Christmastime, Joe thought that the members of a Reform synagogue might be sensitive to erasure, and avoid assuming that everyone on Earth is straight. So he visited the Emanu-El B'ne Jeshurum synagogue in Milwaukee.

Rabbi Marc Berkson favored legalizing gay marriage, but extolled "straight, monogamous procreative marriage" as "the ideal human relationship and the paradigm of our relationship to God."

He also criticized young Jewish women who go to college, pursue careers, and "postpone marriage and sometimes childbearing," as if the function of the female body is to have children, as if no young Jewish woman are ever gay.

At the coffee hour after Shabbat services, Joe heard the same old litany: "Are you married?", "Did your wife come with you?"; "Do you have a family?"

He was told about two important organizations, the Brotherhood ("leave your wife at home and do some male bonding"), and the Sisterhood ("tell your wife she should get involved in the congregation").

He was told of many opportunities to engage in a mitzvah (good deed) in the community. He could work in a soup kitchen or homeless shelter, or teach adult illiterates how to read, or visit a Jewish nursing home. But he could do nothing whatever for gay people; there were none. [9]

Becoming Deaf

Historically, Islam has been far more accepting of same-sex desire and practice than Christianity or Judaism. During the Middle Ages, Muslim poets commonly compared God to a same-sex lover, and well into the 20th century, same-sex practice gained no social disapprobation across the Maghreb and the Middle East. Western gays from Oscar Wilde and Andre Gide in the 1880s to Joe Norton and Alan Ginsburg in the 1960s traveled to North Africa to enjoy homoerotic liaisons that would cause shudders of disdain back home.

But that freedom vanished with independence. The new nationalists associated same-sex practice with European imperialism, with the decadent West, and the ulema, Muslim scholastics, followed suit, proclaiming that there had never been gay Muslims, that Islam had never approached same-sex practices with anything but utter disgust.

Today liberal Muslims believes that gay people are mentally ill and morally bankrupt, a danger to society, deserving imprisonment or psychiatric treatment or both. More conservative Muslims add the term "abomination" and suggest the death penalty. Life for gay people in the most liberal Muslim countries approximates the years before Stonewall in the United States; in the more conservative countries, it approximates the years of the witch burnings.

Gay Muslims in the West must always pass. Any family member who discovers their "secret" will never speak to them again; any straight Muslim friend will drop them, instantly, and without hesitation. And of course, they will be forcefully ejected from the Masjid. The most radical gay Muslim hopes that the faith will one day "progress" to the relative tolerance of the Southern Baptists.

The two Muslim students in Joe's *Juvenile Delinquency* class at Wesley College were determined not to learn anything about gay people other than the lies they already "knew." They skipped class the day gay people were scheduled for discussion; they skipped exam questions about gay people, or if that was impossible, scribbled quick, nonsensical answers that displayed no knowledge of the course content. When gay people were mentioned in a lecture without previous warning, they stopped taking notes and stared into space. They tried their best to not see, not hear, not remember.

Masculine and Feminine Energies

In Oz, Joe knew many Buddhists. They told him that Buddhism promoted the dignity of all people, and that sexual orientation was simply not an issue. Celibacy was the ideal, of course, since sexual desire and relationships were burdens on the path to enlightenment. But same-sex practice was no more heinous than straight practice.[10]

However, Buddhists living in Kansas were more likely to believe that no gay people existed. The Dalai Lama, in one teaching, classified same-sex behavior as a violation of one the Five Precepts that the Buddha set down for his followers, "Do not engage in sexual misconduct." However, dozens of other teachings did not mention gay people at all. Zen Buddhist stories were always about male monks resisting the temptation of women, never about the temptation of men.[11]

Few people in Asia practice Taoism alone, without mixing it with elements of Buddhism and Confucianism, but many Westerners have adopted the teachings of the *Tao Te Ching*, with its philosophy of action through inaction, as a stand alone form of spirituality. The heart of the Tao is the symbol called yin-yang, the "union of opposites" that drives all of life: dark and light, strength and weakness, activity and passivity. However, the Taoist writings that Joe researched went beyond such general philosophical concepts to specify that yin represents female, and yang male.

Thomas Cleary tells us men and women come together like the yin-yang into a "primal whole," leaving gay people forever incomplete, forever broken, if they exist at all.

Alan Watts tells us that the masculine and feminine energies of yin-yang inform every aspect of life, so the only union that could possibly exist in this or any world is between men and women.[12]

Confucianism, arguably the ground of the whole of Chinese culture, politics, and society, divides social life into five cardinal relationships: ruler and subject, father and son, older brother and younger brother, husband and wife, and

friend and friend. Gay people can fit into four of the five relationships, regardless of whether Confucius knew they exist
or not. However, they are absolutely omitted from the most
important goal in Confucian belief.

The most important task any individual has – indeed,
the only reason for existing – is to continue the family
through marriage and reproduction (with male children only). Those who marry but fail to produce male children are
viewed as disgraces to the family name. Those who refuse to
marry at all, for whatever reason, are much worse. They are
guilty of treason. Obviously gay people would be guilty of
treason, if they existed at all, but they do not; no work on
classical or contemporary Confucianism that Joe found acknowledged the possibility of same-sex desire.[13]

Contemporary India is vehemently homophobic, so it
is quite surprising that many gay people have been drawn to
Hinduism for spiritual support. The most famous was Christopher Isherwood, who wrote *My Guru and His Disciple*.
However, most sects of Hinduism that Joe researched
seemed utterly that no gay people exist.

The Vedanta Society of Southern California offered a
course in "Vedanta 101," which proclaims that marriage is
the most important human relationship because men and
women "constitute a fundamental unity," like the yin-yang
of Taoism. And, as in Taoism, gay people are destined to be
forever incomplete, forever lonely, if their existence is acknowledged at all.

The God and the Goddess

Wiccans and other neo-pagans often accept gay
members, or at least do not burn crosses on their front
lawns. The Wiccan primary rule, or rede, states: "A'in it
harm none, do what thou wilt." Do what you want on your

own time. However, neopaganism remains joyously gay-free. When Joe sat in on a Wiccan ceremony, he heard endlessly of the "Union of the God and the Goddess," masculine and feminine energy, the source of all life in the universe. On the altar he saw an atheme, or ceremonial sword, symbolizing men's sex organs, and a chalice, symbolizing women's sex organs. As in Hinduism and Taoism, they must merge in a continual replay of straight desire and release. Blessed be.

Charm the Opposite Sex

When Joe lived in West Hollywood, he could walk five blocks south and three blocks east to the Bodhi Tree, the largest New Age bookstore in the world. Nearly a hundred sections sold every book imaginable on astrology, Tarot, herbs, chanting, meditation, past-life regression, and so on. Many of the patrons were celebrities – on any given Saturday Joe might see Joyce Dewitt (formerly of *Three's Company*), Billy Connolly (then starring on *Head of the Class*), or 1970s gadabout Adam Arkin. Many other patrons were gay (and of course, some were gay celebrities).

It occurred to Joe that celebrities and gay people shared the same problem: the world had turned out to be much bigger and more complex than the small, circumscript religious systems of their childhoods taught: everyone didn't stay home, everyone didn't go to work in the factory, everyone didn't marry and have kids. Now they were looking for a spiritual path that could explain a world that was more complex, more confusing, with more potential for happiness and love but also more potential for tragedy than the doll house world of their childhood.

Astrologers have been advising people whom to hook up with for hundreds of years, and though gay people are as interested in the paranormal as anyone else, they are summarily excluded from horoscopes. Whenever romance is hinted at, it's of the "you will be attractive to the opposite sex today" sort.

Astrology books can go into more detail, specify "men" or "women" in their forecasts, so they are happy to specify that everyone on earth is straight. A browse through the Barnes and Noble in Milwaukee revealed a dozen astrology guides that tell men how to hook up with women, and women men.

Sexual Astrology: A Sign by Sign Guide to Your Sensual Stars, advised him to "Be on guard. The Aries female is hard to figure out . . .her dynamic restlessness will keep any male on the move."[14]

Linda Goodman's *Love Signs* uses "gay" to mean "happy" a few times, but the advice was all about how "the dizzy power of his manhood (or womanhood) gives Leo a sense of personal dignity and importance – through the opposite sex."[15] Why? Because we are "chemically attracted to the opposite sex."

Online astrologers are also adept at erasure.

The AOL Horoscope invited Joe to discover "what qualities make you most attractive to the opposite sex."

Astrology Online told him, "You'll find it easy to charm members of the opposite sex."[16]

Yahoo.astrology offered a "Romantic Compatibility" guide based on his sign and his potential mate's sign. All of the grinning couples pictured were straight.

What about other forms of divination? Tarot cards are a deck of 78 cards divided into four suits (swords, wands, pentacles, and coins), plus mysterious, disturbing additions, such as the Hanged Man, the Devil, and the Fool. They have been used for hundreds of years for divination of all types.

The *Oak Tarot of Love and Romance* told Joe that the four suits represented four types of love: spiritual, platonic, emotional, and "physical love between the male and the female," oblivious to the fact that gay people have sex.

Tarot d' Amour: Find Love, Sex, and Romance in the Cards, was all about finding a partner experience "the union of male and female energies."

Only *Romancing the Tarot* offered to teach both gay and straight people "how to find true love, spice up your sex life, or let go of a bad relationship."[17]

Celebmatch.com uses biorhythms to determine your romantic compatibility with celebrities, specifying the gender of your prospective match. It was an anomaly, permitting same-sex matches.

After Joe knocked a few years off his age, it matched him with gay former teen idol Lance Bass, Jesse Bradford, who has played gay several times, and Olympic swimmer Aaron Peirsol, whose sexual identity proved impossible to determine.

Joe also looked at fifteen books on dreams, divinations, spiritual journeys, channeling, chakras, and the generic term "New Age." They were all overbrimming with the success stories of people who have learned to take charge of their lives. But gay people were mentioned in only one of the books, *The Power of Now: A Guide to Spiritual Enlightenment.* The author, mystic Eckhart Tolle, is asked if being gay is a help or a hindrance in the quest for enlightenment. He answers that it can be a help, since being an outsider forces people to "wake up." However, if "you develop a sense of identity based on your gayness," you are in trouble.

This appeared to Joe to be the old "being gay is only a small part of who I am" erasure: be gay, just don't talk about it. Tolle has no problems with people developing a sense of identity based on being straight.

Female Spirits, Male Bodies

The afterlife is always straight. Joe read five books on ghosts and hauntings, and the ghosts who return to haunt us, or to communicate with us from beyond the grave, always describe husbands, wives, and children, entire heteronormative trajectories. Only Edith Fiore's *The Unquiet Dead: A Psychologist Looks at Spirit Possession* mentions gay people at all, and they are not really gay.[18]

Fiore describes the conundrum of living people accidentally being possessed by deceased spirits. They happen to pass by where someone has died recently (within the last few minutes), and that person's spirit, disoriented and confused, piggy-backs onto them. A clue that you have been possessed is a sudden new hobby, ability, interest, or entire personality. If the parasitic spirit liked classical music in life, you put your country-western cds in storage and get season tickets to the symphony. If it was an alcoholic, you suddenly spend every night at the corner bar. If it died from falling out of window, you become afraid of heights. And what if a man is possessed by a female spirit?

Fiore argues that this is the cause of "most cases of homosexuality." This is the old homophobic myth that gay men are actually "girls," except now they are possessed by the spirits of girls. All desire is straight desire, women searching for men or men for women.

On the other hand, maybe your gayness is not due to being possessed by a spirit of the other sex. Maybe you were a member of the other sex in your past lives, and now you're just confused.

According to *The Search for Past Lives,* by Bryan Jameison, we have died and been reincarnated many times, with frequent sex changes.[19] Since the soul itself has no gender, usually there is no problem: we are "naturally" drawn to the bodies of the "opposite sex," regardless of what sort of body we occupied in our last life. But if the change is abrupt, if we died suddenly last time, we are unable to adapt, so the soul may continue to "think" that it is female even though it now has a male body, and feel drawn to the same sex, thus "causing homosexuality." Fortunately, it's an adjustment problem that can be easily solved. In fact, Jameison's therapy can cure "homosexuality, birth defects, phobias, compulsions," the gamut of physical and psychological diseases. No one told him that "homosexuality" is not a disease.

Your spiritual path doesn't matter. In Wicca, in Hinduism, in Buddhism, in Christianity, except for a few small whispers of inclusion, God's story is the story of male and female. All desire is straight desire, all practice is straight practice, the spiritual realm is entirely straight.

Strategizing

In graduate school, Joe often fantasized about his future life as a professor: mornings in the stacks of a vast, ornate library, leafing through old books to uncover the hidden gay lives of the past; quiet afternoons writing in his stately, book-lined office, looking up from his desk only to gaze out at the quad below, at the frat boys tossing Frisbees or reclining with paperbacks; classes of bright-eyed gay and lesbian students gathered around small seminar tables, talking about Victorian "adhesive friendships" or the gay subcultures of prewar Berlin.

In real life, he rarely set foot in the library, and it was never vast or ornate. His office was not booklined, and the one time he had a window, it looked out onto the loading dock of the Biological Sciences Building. Most of his classes were not in Gay Studies, none were taught around small seminar tables, and every one of his students, even in *The Sociology of Sexuality*, was straight, or pretending to be.

But the most startling difference between Joe's expectations and reality was that teaching and research did not constitute 100% of his job. Not even 50%. A college is a non-profit corporation, a business, and the business of business is meetings.

During the daytime, Joe sat at a dozen small seminar tables for meetings of the Department, the College of Arts and Sciences, the Student Affairs Committee, the Recruitment Committee, and the Newsletter Committee, plus new faculty orientations, teaching workshops, and grant-writing workshops. All had typewritten agendas, powerpoint presentations, endless discussions of goals, arguments about issues that have been hashed and rehashed for decades, long-term antagonists railing on each other, old wounds being opened, feelings being hurt, and people rushing off to hyperventilate in the bathroom.

In the evening, there were more meetings, called "parties" or "receptions." he had to click wine glasses and nibble on gruyere cheese, eat barbecue sandwiches off soggy paper plates, watch basketball games, listen to string quartets, and make small talk, endless hours of small talk that wasn't small at all.

Joe's visiting position was dependent on a year-end review, his next job was dependent on letters of recommendation from colleagues, and there was talk of a tenure-track opening up, so he had to strategize his small talk carefully. He had to be mindful of hidden agendas, secret alliances, false friends who would pat you on the back only because they were looking for a good place to insert the knife, and moles who would make a few cryptic remarks, then report your reactions to an enemy. Being seen talking to the wrong person, even for a few seconds at the refreshment table, could cause trouble later.

At a party in September of Joe's first year in Wisconsin, Dr. Angstrom, a boisterous professor of Women's Studies, whom he thought was a lesbian until her "life partner" turned out to be a live-in boyfriend, pointed out four professors that he should "watch out for."

The first was homophobic.

The second resented him getting the job over the candidate he wanted.

The third didn't like him because *her* enemy voted to hire him.

And the fourth just didn't like him, period.

But how could Joe tell if Dr. Angstrom was really trying to help, or was a "false friend," trying to steer him away from professors who would be important allies?

Being gay put Joe at a serious advantage in the Machiavellian power struggles, since most of the alliances were based on shared heterosexual experiences. His year end review, letters of recommendation, and chance of being offered a tenure-track, should one open up, had little to do with his teaching or research and everything to do with exhibiting "collegiality" with heterosexuals: chuckles over the husband's refusal to ask for directions, the wife's credit-card mania, the temper tantrums of the five-year old, the incessant text-messaging of the teenager, the interference of the in-laws, the nosiness of the neighbors.

Scholars have noted that gay employees are not promoted as readily, do not rise to management as often as heterosexuals, due in part to the Family Man Syndrome (the men have no wives and kids and are therefore unreliable), and in part to homophobia, but mostly to a "lavender ceiling": promotion decisions are made based upon chummy, informal interactions among heterosexuals, and gay people simply have nothing to say.

Joe had no experiences to share, except for memories of his own childhood thirty years ago, and he did not feel qualified to speculate on this straight world that still, after three years, seemed artificial and oppressive, like a smug 1950s *Leave It to Beaver.* So he was forced to sit back quietly and be branded cool, aloof, not a team-player, or to change the subject and be branded self-centered, a grandstander.

Joe usually avoided parties where "husbands, wives, and kids" were invited; though he knew his absence would be strategically unwise, he thought the excuse of a "prior commitment" would make him seem more interested and engaged in Kansas than actually attending and sitting alone and embarrassed.

One party that he did attend consisted almost entirely of heterosexual professors and spouses and their rambunctious children – a baby kept spitting on him, while her anthropologist mother, oblivious, rattled on about 2:00 am feedings.

A few unmarried heterosexuals appeared with boyfriends and girlfriends in tow; they were considerably more effusive about their physical attraction, always holding hands, finishing each other's sentences, and feeding each other cake.

An elderly professor sat with his new, younger girlfriend on his lap; as he orated about his new research project, every now and then he would turn her face toward his, plant a kiss on her lips, and turn back to him with a triumphant grin, like a toddler who's just learned to tie his own shoes. Joe was expected to share in his triumph, to congratulate him with his eyes instead of turning away in embarrassment. He couldn't help it – he turned away, wondering if he had just jeopardized his year-end review.

When Joe saw seemingly unattached men at faculty parties, he approached them with his most winning smile and a repertoire of anecdotes that made him seem charmingly self-effacing yet an important voice in gay scholarship. But his gay references flew by unnoticed ("So you met Quentin Crisp? Who's that?"), and sooner or later, usually sooner, a girlfriend or wife was sure to arrive, kiss him intimately on the cheek, and say something incomprehensible about heterosexuality ("Katie and John said that they're coming too").

Perhaps most disconcerting of all, several of the women Joe spoke to threw in casual references to a "single" sister or female neighbor or female friend, waiting for the spark of interest so they could arrange an introduction. He was at the party alone, so obviously he was single and heterosexual.

When Joe brought a date to a party, female faculty or faculty wives still threw in casual references about the single women they knew. Granted, he did not hold his date in his lap, or kiss him loudly and graphically at random moments, wary of the enemies such gestures might create. But still, what two men would attend a faculty party together, unless they were dating?

Apparently no one made that logical deduction.

---

[1] *Church of the Nazarene Manual*. Kansas City: Beacon Publishing, 2001.
[2] "Pass It On," Fox Valley Christian Church,
http://www.fvcc.com/fvcc/SermonPassItOn2-25.html

3 "Response to the ECUSA General Convention," Reformed Church Website, http://rechurch.org/recus/recus /ecusastmt.html
4 United Church of Gainesville, http://www.uc gaines-ville.org/
5 "Welcoming Gay and Lesbian People," Social Policy Actions of the ELCA, http://www.elca.org/ socialpolicyresolutions
6 Trinity Lutheran Church, http://www.geocities.com/tlcloyaloak/061008.html
7 McFague, Sally. Models of God.
8 The others belong to smaller sects or are unaffiliated.
9Emanu-El B'ne Jeshurum http://www.ceebj.org/
10 Cabezon, Jose Ignacio. "Homosexuality and Buddhism." In Winston Leyland, ed., *Queer Dharma: Voices of Gay Buddhists*. Gay Sunshine Press, 2000: 29-44.
11 Dalai Lama
12 Thomas Cleary, *Practical Taoism*. Shamballa, 1996: 62. Alan Watts. Tao: The Water-Course Way. Pantheon Books, 1975: 21
13 Yao, Xinzhong. *Introduction to Confucianism*. Cambridge University Press, 2000.
14 Woolfolk, Joanna, and Martine. *Sexual Astrology: A Sign-by-Sign Guide to Your Sensual Stars*. Dell, 1979.
15 Goodman, Linda. Linda Goodman's Love Signs: A New Approach to the Human Heart. Collins, 1992: 23.
16 Astrology Online, www.astrology-online.com/daily.htm
17 Vega, Phyllis. *Romancing the Tarot*. Fireside Books, 2001.
18 Fiore, Edith. *The Unquiet Dead: A Psychologist Looks at Demon Possession*. Ballantine Books, 1995.
19 Jameison, Bryan. *In Search of Past Lives*. Driftwood Publications, 2002.

Chapter Eight
Prime Time, Straight Time

In 1985, Joe and his roommates used to watch *The Golden Girls* every Saturday night before heading out to the Rage.

In 1990, he and his partner never missed *Designing Women* or *Twin Peaks*.

In 1995, they used to host *Melrose Place* parties on Monday nights.

In 2000, Sunday night meant ordering orange chicken from the Empire Szechuan Village to eat in front of *The Simpsons*.

And that was all, perhaps two or three hours of television per week. No dramas, no cop shows, and certainly no network news (an hour of pundits arguing over who hates gay people the most?).

There was really no time; in any given week he might have a meeting of the Pride Committee, a book signing at the Different Light, dinner with friends, a night answering the phones at the Gay Community Center, Bear Night at the Eagle, a dinner-movie date, and a concert at the MCC.

Besides, television was an intrusion from Kansas, to be approached with caution, like the propaganda pamphlets dropped from airplanes during the Vietnam War. A program might seem welcoming, or at least tolerant, but at any moment, it could drop its pretense and reveal its true colors:

Blanche on *The Golden Girls* would be horrified to discover that her brother is gay, or Homer Simpson would call one of Bart's classmates a "pansy," and he would realize that they were friends after all.

But in Kansas, life was not at all crowded. Northland offered only "family friendly" activities, for straights and their young children: the County Fair, the Dairyland Surf Classic, the Kennel Club Show, the Civil War Reenactment, the Fall Family Fun Festival.

And after spending every daylight hour wandering alone amid the crowds of men and women holding hands or kissing on doorsteps, listening to their joyful proclamations that all desire is straight desire, all love is straight love, Joe preferred to stay home in the evening, among his gay books and movies and artwork, his little outpost in the wilderness. He found himself flipping on the television often, to watch almost-out gay characters on *Malcolm in the Middle,* teenage nerds in love on *Drake and Josh,* gay couples getting their master bedrooms redone on *Extreme Makeover,* and body-building explorers looking for yet another excuse to appear semi-naked on the Discovery Channel and Animal Planet.

Television in Wisconsin was much more amenable than either Hollywood movies or *New York Times* bestsellers, perhaps because there were so many choices, sixty at any moment. Joe could spend an hour or two almost every night with gay characters or same-sex romances, a welcome respite from the giggly proclamations of universal straight desire that deadened life elsewhere in Kansas

Caution was necessary, of course:

It was impossible to channel-surf for more than a few seconds without encountering straights kissing.

Fox News and MSNBC apparently featured twenty-four hours of homophobic rants every day.

And even the most seemingly gay-friendly program could at any moment proclaim that gay people did not exist at all.

On the Discovery Channel series *It Takes a Thief*, reformed crooks Matt Johnston and Jon Douglas Rainey test home security precautions by faking burglaries. When then they encounter two men living together, they speculate that the pair must be "roommates" or "business partners," refusing to know that gay people exist. Their clients are equally anxious to not know: a grateful homeowner jokes that Jon is welcome to take one of his credit cards and "Buy something nice for your lady," as if it is inconceivable that he could have a man.

Back-Stories Shrouded in Mystery

The television series Joe watched in Wisconsin displayed men desiring each other or falling in love with men extraordinarily often, but eventually those men would also desire or fall in love with women.

When he found a male character who both formed strong same-sex bonds *and* failed to express straight interest, Joe watched him, cautiously but hopefully, for an episode or a season, thinking, "Ok, this isn't a subtext. He is scripted as gay." But if the program endured, the character always, eventually, got around to a lustful gaze at a girl, "proving" once again that there are no gay characters on television

A film has two hours or less for character development, a novel about 300 pages, or about five hours of reading time, but a single season of a television series lasts between ten and twenty hours, and a popular series can easily last ten seasons. There are hundreds of hours, ample time for characters to change jobs, change romantic partners, face crises, experience emotional growth, and, unfortunately, display a hitherto-unacknowledged straight interest.

A male character may ignore women in a movie or novel not because he is scripted as gay, but because there is no time to give him any straight involvement; but in a television series, the writers can always wait until the third season to give him a girlfriend.

Or, if they become aware that audiences perceive the male character as gay, they can correct their "mistake", as happened with the character Zack of *Heroes*: he was so frequently identified as gay on internet fansites that the producers scripted a heterosexual crush for him. Audiences may even enjoy "questioning the masculinity" of a male character, as long as they are eventually reassured that he is not *really* gay.

Often Joe found that the "mistake" was corrected in just a few episodes. One night he channel-surfed onto *Hustle*, a British comedy-drama about a group of amiable con artists. Young-gun Danny Blue has just met Troy in a bar. They talk for hours. Then Danny says goodbye, starts to walk away, realizes that he doesn't want to part, and rushes back to Troy again, surely a "falling in love" moment. In the next scene, apparently the morning after a sexual intimacy, he is introducing Troy to his colleagues and petitioning to include him in their latest con. Throughout, Danny and Troy have a remarkably expressive physical bond, with full-body hugs, arms around shoulders, hands pressed against chests.

"Obviously a gay couple," Joe thought.

He tuned in the next week, and the next. Troy never appeared again, but Danny's job in the con always involved bonding with attractive men, and never flirting with women, not even a receptionist or secretary. When he had to pretend to have sex with a female colleague (so the mark could hear them through the wall and conclude that they are a couple), he could barely restrain his giggles.

Off duty, he was seen only with guys. He gazed with palpable desire at gang leader Mickey Bricks.

Obviously gay, Joe thought.

Then, in the fourth episode that Joe saw (not the fourth episode of the series), Danny was juggling girlfriends from all over the world, using different cell phones to keep track of the lies he used to woo them.

Hustle corrected the "mistake" in just four weeks.

But ABC's *Lost* took a whopping two seasons.

Joe calculated that of the 48 survivors of an airplane crash facing paranormal peril on a desert island, at least five must be gay. During an early episode, the main characters were strategizing about something or other when a pair of hunky extras, obviously lovers, ran joyfully with fishing poles toward the beach. "We will see their home life soon," Joe thought. But they never appeared again.

Early on, fans speculated that young surgeon Jack, the unofficial leader of the castaways, would turn out to be gay, but that seemed impossible. Villains are usually gay, transvestite, pedophile, or all three at once, but never stalwarts, action heroes, leaders of the good guys.

Joe was rooting for Charlie, a rock musician and recovering heroin addict. During lengthy flashbacks to their lives before the plane crash, each of the fourteen main characters revealed a straight romance, with a single exception: Charlie. His flashback was about his brother.

Nor did Charlie exhibit the slightest romantic interest in the female castaways – he bonded with the extremely pregnant Claire, but they never kissed or cuddled. They were obviously just friends. Instead, Charlie chased around

Locke, a bald, wiry wilderness expert who would not look out of place in a leather bar on Folsom Street.

Joe waited patiently for someone to mention Charlie's gayness through all of the twenty-two episodes of the first season. Nothing.

Early in the second season, executive producer Carlton Cuse responded to an inquiry on the internet fansite, The Fuselage: "When will a gay character appear?" He said: "To spill about whether a character currently on the island is gay would be at cross-purposes to our mission of keeping the characters' back stories shrouded in mystery."[1]

Joe thought he was merely expressing homophobia: straightness can be celebrated, but gayness must always be a secret. Instead, he was preparing for a monumental "correction."

Later that fall, in an interview for *TV Guide,* Cuse explained why laid-back con artist Sawyer was displayed semi-nude so often: "Women like it when he takes his shirt off."

Now Joe began to get nervous. If Cuse didn't believe that there were any men in the real world who would like to see Sawyer take his shirt off, why would he script any on his island?

In November of the second season, a newly introduced castaway, haunted cop Ana Lucia, asks Sawyer the standard straight ice-breaker, "Are you married?"

He is not.

She then asks, "Are you gay?"

He responds, "Very funny!"

It was a legitimate question. Why, Joe wondered, did Sawyer think she was joking? Why did he find it ridiculous? Maybe because in his world, gay people are mythical creatures, logical impossibilities? A man who is attracted to men -- Anna Lucia might as well have asked, "Are you a hobbit?"

Still hoping that Charlie would redeem *Lost*, Joe kept watching. Another new castaway arrived, Mr. Eko, a reformed drug runner with a bodybuilder's physique. His flashback was also about his brother rather than a straight romance. What could be a more perfect pair, he thought, than a reformed drug runner and a recovering drug addict? And sure enough, Charlie instantly dumped Locke to chase Mr. Eko around the island. The two were even shown sleeping together.

Then came the second season finale. Mr. Eko was apparently killed in an explosion, and Charlie returned to platonic pal Claire – except now they shared a brief, chaste kiss. Surely this was not merely correcting a "misinterpretation." It was a tease! he could hear Carlton Cuse chuckling, "Fooled you! Charlie is straight after all! Gay people and hobbits do not exist!"

Joe tuned in occasionally for the remaining seasons, to see if any new characters might be gay. Finally in the midst of Season Four, a character was "outed." He was a villain, one of the evil Others, and like Dumbledore in the Harry Potter books, no one suspected until long after his death. The real people, the people we deal with in everyday life, are always straight or passing.

Years of Straightness

Finding a network television program with a strong homoerotic subtext wasn't difficult, but "real" gay characters were scarce.

If you watch every feature-length movie released in the United States in any given year, you will spend about 450 hours in the theater, and see ten or so gay people, plus twenty or so gay male "girls" and half a dozen temporary lesbians.

If you watch four hours of television every day, not an excessive amount, at the end of the year you will have devoted 1,460 hours to television, and unless you search very carefully, no gay people, no gay male "girls," no temporary lesbians, who prefer men, nothing but men and women kissing, nothing but endless assurances that gay people do not exist.

During the daytime, game shows and talk shows have mostly given way to judge shows, televised arbitrations with real litigants suing each other over fender-benders, money lent to boyfriends or girlfriends, inept wedding photographers, and ebay purchases gone awry. Although a small percentage of the litigants are gay or lesbian, more often the judge assumes that no gay people exist.

Judge Marilyn Milian of the *People's Court* constantly asks litigants "Are you married?" or "Do you have a boyfriend/girlfriend?", without determining their sexual orientation first.

Judge Judy Scheindlin, *Judge Judy,* goes even farther, denouncing unmarried litigants: "Why don't you grow up and get married!", voraciously equating straight practice with maturity, condemning gay people to perpetual adolescence.

Judge David Young is gay himself (and flamboyantly "one of the girls"), yet even he constantly forgets that gay people exist. "Are you a woman who has been taken advantage of by a man?" he asks, unaware that a woman might be taken advantage of by a woman. He advises a male litigant who has just graduated from high school to continue his education, because: "There are a lot of cute girls in college

who would like you!" The young man has not once mentioned being straight.

Most soap operas involve nothing but the endlessly
protracted amours of horny straights for 260 or so episodes
per year, every year, decade after decade, but a few include
a gay character or two, usually conflicted and closeted.
There have been four conflicted, closeted gay characters
amid the 500 or so introduced to date on *All My Children*
(0.8%), three on *One Life to Live* (0.6%), two on *As the World
Turns* (0.4%), and one on *General Hospital* (0.2%). But they are
usually so "discrete," and their relationships drawn so skittishly, if they are allowed relationships at all, that one must
watch very closely to figure out that they are gay. No doubt
most soap opera fans never see one of the gay characters, or
never notice.

Network sitcoms tend to be about single straights
searching for "the one" (*How he Met Your Mother, The New
Adventures of Old Christine, Scrubs*), married straights negotiating their relationships (*According to Jim, The King of
Queens, George Lopez*), or teenagers negotiating straight
crushes (*That 70s Show, Everybody Hates Chris, Malcolm in the
Middle*). A gay character might appear as a walk-on once or
twice per season, or never at all.

However, straight characters are mistaken for gay
fairly often. On *Reba*, Reba's ex-husband and his friend are
mistaken for a gay couple; on *Everybody Loves Raymond*,
Raymond mistakenly believes that his brother is gay; on
Hope and Faith, the sisters mistakenly believes that their father is gay. The straight characters are merely embarrassed
by these "false accusations," never traumatized or enraged,
not homophobic; but the effect is to assert, as confidently as
Sawyer's "Very funny!" on *Lost*, that there is no such thing
as a real gay person. If you suspect that someone is gay, you

are mistaken. You are jumping to the wrong conclusion based on an "innocent" misunderstanding.

The Gilmore Girls, a comedy-drama about free-spirit Lorelai attempting to be best friends with her daughter Rory, was set in a small Connecticut town full of colorful, eccentric characters. Yet none of them was gay, nor even mistaken-for-gay. One gets the impression that the producers are not merely forgetting that gay people exist, they are literally unaware, so there is nothing to jump to the wrong conclusion *about*. In an episode he watched in April of his year in Wisconsin, Lorelai confesses, "I hoped Rory would be the one girl on earth who wouldn't [begin to] notice boys until she was 48." It would be impossible for episode writer Linda Loiselle Guzik to script the line with such certainty, or for Lauren Graham to deliver it with such conviction, if they realized that far more than one girl on earth doesn't begin to notice boys at all.

Including a gay character in a sitcom cast does not provide any protection against the assurance of universal straight desire or practice. *My Name is Earl*, about a reformed ne'er-do-well trying to assist those he's wronged in the past, included an occasional visit from the closeted nerd Kenny James. Yet in the episodes where Kenny is not featured, Earl assumes that everyone he encounters is straight.

He tries to boost the spirits of the suicidal Philo by fixing him up with a girl, without first asking whether he is interested in girls or not.

When Earl reunites with Albie, a boy he frightened while robbing a house several years ago, he judges that the fourteen-year old is ready for a heart-to-heart talk about girls, again without asking if Albie happens to like girls.

Contemporary dramatic series are overwhelmingly about solving murders (*Law and Order, Boston Legal, CSI,*

Criminal Minds), sometimes by paranormal means *(Supernatural, Veronica Mars)*, but the cops, detectives, and psychics, always straight, take ample time off to search for "the one," and they invariably assume that all victims, clients, and killers are straight.

A young woman is murdered, and the cops immediately ask her parents if she had a "boyfriend," oblivious to the possibility that she might be a lesbian.

A man is discovered bound, gagged, and stabbed in a hotel room, and the detectives immediately seek out all of the female prostitutes in the neighborhood who specialize in bondage, certain that the prostitute must be female.

A businessman vanishes, and the psychic immediately tries to conjure up a vision of the "women" in his life," unaware that men exist who have men in their lives.

On *Law and Order: Criminal Intent*, Detective Earnes actually finds a gay magazine in a suspect's apartment, but even so cannot bring herself to believe that he is gay. She merely rolls her eyes and exclaims "He's got issues!", oddly homophobic in a gay-free New York. (And, in fact, he isn't gay, he's an actor, using the magazine to research a role).

On *Homicide: Life on the Streets*, comedian Lily Tomlin plays Rose Halligan, a wealthy dowager accused of murder. As two detectives transport her to the police station, she decides that it would be pleasant to pass the time with the "let's all demonstrate how straight we are!" game. She asks, "Are either of you boys married?"

Detective Pembleton states, "I'm not the marrying kind." The phrase is usually code for "gay," but the detective appears to mean that he enjoys straight promiscuity too much to marry.

Rose finds that response insufficient; the game requires a specific assertion of heterosexuality. So she continues to push: "Maybe you haven't met the right young lady."

Lily Tomlin herself is gay, but she happily allows her character to erase all gay people everywhere from existence. Oddly, the other detective, Tim Bayless, who would be skittishly outed as bisexual several seasons hence, is spared the brunt of Rose's inquisition; she merely forces him to admit that he is divorced and "it's complicated."

Dexter, about a forensics scientist who moonlights as a serial killer, starred Michael C. Hall, fresh from playing the gay character David Fisher on *Six Feet Under*, and it was introduced through a full-page ad in *The Advocate*, openly inviting gay viewers. Naturally, one assumed that it would be gay-friendly. Yet the opening scenes scream loudly, over and over, that in this Miami, gay people ABSOLUTELY DO NOT EXIST.

First Dexter trots off to a crime scene, where one of the investigators exclaims that his sister is hot and the other announces that the dismembered woman had a "great ass."

Their heterosexuality established, Dexter goes to the station. He asks, "How are the families?" of two coworkers.

He then drops in on a third coworker, an older woman who advises, "You should find a pretty girl," utterly unaware that gay people exist.

Then – and only five minutes of air time have passed -- it's Friday night, "date night in Miami; everybody's having sex." Many shots of men and women dining al fresco in the heart of a gay world that is utterly gay free.

Dexter tells us that doesn't experience emotions, and although he "appreciates women" like every other man on the planet, he doesn't care for sex. But in order to maintain his façade of being like "everybody else" in the world, he is dating a woman.

Why go through the trouble of advertising a television program to an audience, and then telling them over and over that they do not exist?

I Thought You Were.. .Um. . . .

When presumably gay characters do appear on television, the word "gay" must never be spoken, in order to keep their identity as hidden as possible.

On *The Nanny*, Mary Ruth works at a hair salon with the effeminate Claude. She complains that it's hard for her to find a man to date: "They say they're all married, or they have relationship issues, or they're. . . ."

Claude stares at her, daring her to say it.

But she won't. Blanching, overcome by embarrassment, she stammers, "Um. . .I think that's all they say."

Why is she so afraid to admit that some men are gay in front of a stereotypic gay man? Surely he knows! But then the silence would be broken, and Mary Ruth could no longer pretend that she is unaware that gay people exist. Nor could the audience.

On *Seinfeld*, George is upset to discover that his new girlfriend has a male roommate. Jerry suggests, "Maybe he's. . . .," accompanied by a hand flutter. Why does Jerry feel the need to use a silence and hand flutter instead of the short, easy word "gay"? Perhaps because the word is not at all easy for him to say.

On *The Simpsons*, an episode set in the future finds a young adult Bart Simpson encountering office sycophant Waylon Smithers, apparently on a date with a woman. Shocked, Bart says, "I though you were. . . um. . . ."

Again, he refuses to use the word.

Why would Smithers object? Surely he knows that people think he is gay – he has been demonstrating that he is "one of the girls" in every way possible since the program began. He even buys estrogen at a garage sale "for a friend. . .who is trapped in the body of another friend."

Yet only in a few later episodes has he used the word "gay" to describe himself, and no one else ever uses the word "gay." If they must reference his sexual identity, they hesitate, gulp, prevaricate, struggle to find euphemisms, as if the word is too difficult to say or too difficult to hear.

Why must the word "gay' be forever unspoken? Perhaps because it would provide a positive identification that must be forever vague, forever open to interpretation. One must always say "I thought you were. . . ." and leave the audience pretending not to know.

Fagmalion

Real, open, overt gay characters on prime time are vanishingly rare. According to GLAAD, the Gay and Lesbian Alliance against Defamation, less than 2%, usually much less, of the regular and recurring characters on prime time in any given season are identified as gay, lesbian, bisexual, or transgendered. The few gay men are assistants, subordinates, outsiders, far removed from the main action of the series, and invariably "girls," like "male nurse" Yosh Takata on *ER*, or fashion editor Wilhemina Slater's "fairy" assistant Marc on *Ugly Betty*.

Will and Grace was a partial exception, with two gay men, lawyer Will and ne'er-do-well Jack, in starring roles. However, they went to great lengths to demonstrate that they, like Yosh and Marc, were really "girls," that whatever desire they experience is really straight, feminine drawn to masculine, woman drawn to man. Jack is slightly more feminine, frequently wearing women's clothing instead of restricting himself to shopping and show tunes, but both consider themselves "girls."

In one episode, Will's cousin states that he is planning his wedding, and he needs "a woman's opinion." "Sure, I'd be glad to help," Will responds with no camp, no irony, only the utter conviction that "woman" means him.

Will and Jack also accept being called "fags," "homos," "fairies," and "sissies" by straight characters, friends and strangers alike, meekly, with little or no protest. They examine every homophobic myth ever invented, and assert that each one is absolutely true.

When a gay man must feign interest in a woman, he complains that he doesn't know how. "Treat her like your mother," gal pal Grace suggests, referring to the long-discredited theory that "homosexuality" arises through unresolved Oedipal conflicts. Will starts to protest about Grace's staggering homophobia, but she gives him a withering look, and he is forced to admit that she is right: all gay men are indeed in love with their mothers

While both Will and Jack know a few Cher- and shopping obsessed "fags," they do not have much use for gay friends, nor do they have any idea that gay community institutions exist (except for a few drag bars). Instead, they enjoy permanent quasi-romantic relationships with straight women, Grace and Karen (who are identified merely as "women," since no lesbians exist), and they associate primarily with other male-female couples. Thus they demonstrate that every man needs a woman, if not a lover than a "lady friend," or he is doomed to spend his life alone.

In the series finale, Will marries his cop beau, and they adopt a baby girl. Flash forward twenty years, and Will's daughter is marrying Grace's son. Regardless of the momentary glitch Will's gayness made in the Order of Things, happy endings always involve a girl walking down the aisle into the arms of a boy. Meanwhile, Jack has been living with his own partner, Karen, for the last twenty years. Same-sex loves come and go, but the bond between a man and a woman lasts forever.

Even though it devotes ample time to denigrating "fags," asserting that all gay men are really "girls," and insisting that being gay is a meaningless trifle, destined to fade away in the face of straight "true love," *Will and Grace* still finds time to proclaim that gay people do not exist at all.

At the beginning of an episode offensively entitled "Fagmalion," Will is sitting in a restaurant, waiting for his blind date to arrive. Since Will is gay, obviously his date is a man. He starts a conversation with the man at the next table, Barry, who states that *he* is also waiting for a blind date.

Anyone with a minimum of intelligence would immediately conclude that they are each other's dates. But Will doesn't. He jokes, "You know how women are, they always like to make an entrance." Why is he so eager to believe an impossible coincidence, that two blind dates have been set up for the same restaurant at the same moment, one gay and one straight, rather than admit that gay people might exist?

When Joe showed this scene to the students in *Sociology of Sexuality* class at Wesley College, they were confused by his objection. Why on earth would Will think that the Barry could be gay? They were in a restaurant, a real place in the real world, not in a gay bar!

Joe explained that gay people exist in many places beyond bars, in grocery stores and book stores, in dentist offices and post offices. They even go to restaurants.

The students stared. They had never thought of such an obvious fact before.

Just as grade school children believe that their teachers exist only in the classroom, they believed that gay people exist only in small, circumscribes spaces, in gay bars.

Certainly they could reason it out and conclude that gay people must somehow manage to buy groceries, mail letters, and get their teeth cleaned, but still it seemed an outlandish, alien idea, and somewhat disquieting. The class homophobe joked that he now had to be careful *everywhere*.

But Joe's students were all straight, or passing. The scene was written by executive producer John Kinnally, who is "openly" gay, that is, not straight, not passing. Shouldn't he realize that gay people sometimes go to restaurants?

Evidently not. The DVD commentary to the episode reveals not a hint that he found anything amiss in the scene – he failed to give it a second thought. Like his character, Kinnally eagerly participates in his own erasure, triumphantly proclaiming that he himself does not exist.

War is Gay

Joe's students at Wesley College loved the animated tv series aimed at the *Jackass* generation. Fox offered a few on Sunday nights, when no game was scheduled, and Comedy Central one or two others, but most appeared on the Cartoon Network's late-night "Adult Swim" block. In November of his second year in Wisconsin, Joe taped and watched four episodes each of the five programs they recommended: *South Park, Family Guy, American Dad, King of the Hill, and The Venture Brothers.*

It was a horrifying spectacle, endless blatant, bitter homophobia. Characters constantly call each other "fag," "homo," "queer," "gay-wad," and anything bad, ineffective, uncool, or otherwise to be avoided is labeled "gay."

On *Family Guy,* dozens of jokes invited viewers to snicker at the possibility that pop culture figures might be gay: Bert and Ernie from *Sesame Street,* Richie and Potsie from *Happy Days,* Peppermint Patty and Marcie from the *Peanuts* comic strip, Luke Perry (outed in the school paper, he sues for "slander"), and Rob Lowe (Stewie is astonished to discover that he is actually straight: "He sure hides it well!").

When Patriarch Peter Griffith is paired with effeminate actor Tony Randall on *Match Game,* the word Tony must guess is "flaming." Peter's only clue is "you." Apparently "real" gay people exist only in the artificial world of mass culture, far removed from the universal heterosexuality of Quahog, Rhode Island.

The word "gay" did not appear often on *King of the Hill;* redneck Hank Hill generally used the expression "not right" instead. For instance, discussing his twelve year old son: "Bobby wants to join the drama club. I'm telling you, the boy ain't right." Thus he cannily manages to have his cake and eat it too, pretend that he is unaware that gay people exist while still characterizing them as abnormal, as freakish misfits.

Hank's wife Peggy Hill did use the word twice, always in connection with a secret life. While working as a substitute teacher, she states: "I have never had a problem keeping a secret. Ask any of the gay teachers I've worked with. But you couldn't, because I would not tell you who they were." It is inconceivable to her that a gay person might exist who is not trying to pass.

When Peggy becomes a magician's assistant, she refuses to explain how the tricks work to her family, stating that "nothing is more important to magicians than keeping secrets, probably because so many of them are gay." People who are gay, or "not right," must always pretend to be straight; straights must spend their lives certain that there are none. And, of course, there are none in Arlen, Texas.

Bobby has a girlfriend. Apparently he is "right" after all.

In *The Venture Brothers,* a parody of the 1960's children's adventure show *Jonny Quest,* every central character and most minor characters, good or evil, made homophobic comments. Bodyguard Brock Sampson rejects a fancy spy gadget as "gay." Dr. Venture is working on a cure for "homosexuality." Teenagers Hank and Dean, accused of being juvenile delinquents, are sent to jail to be "scared straight" by veiled descriptions of "what happens there."

None of the programs introduced any gay characters during the programs analyzed, except for the psychotic teacher Ms. Garrison of *South Park,* who had gone from being a straight male to a gay male to a male-to-female transsexual, making jaw-droppingly vicious homophobic statements in every incarnation. Some programs did feature mincing stereotypes, but their obsession with their nails and jokes about anal sex were always "redeemed" by an expression of interest in women.

On *American Dad,* Roger, a flamboyantly feminine space alien, visits the Middle East disguised as a woman, whereupon he is sold into a harem of an offensively stereotyped Arab sheik, and consents to sex (but only after noticing that his "husband" has an abnormally small penis). Yet in another episode he joins the teenage Steve in a quest after girls ("Do he even like girls? Sure, he must like girls").

On *Family Guy,* the homicidal infant Stewie, who talks like an effeminate James Bond villain, has erotic dreams of well-muscled men, but he also falls in love with a series of girls and women.

On *The Venture Brothers*, a villain named The Monarch is stereotypically flamboyant and theatrical, gay-coded; but he also has a sexual relationship with Dr. Girlfriend (whose deep voice causes her to be often mistaken for a "dude").

What is the function of this homophobia in the absence of actual gay characters? Perhaps the producers of these programs are demonizing gay people as folk devils, like the Jews of Renaissance England – though no Jews had lived in England since 1290, Shakespeare, Christopher Marlowe, and other playwrights frequently trotted Jewish characters onto the stage for audiences to boo, hiss at, and hate.[2]

But teenage animated sitcoms offer no actual gay characters, not even to hate. Instead, the joke is usually about "accusing" someone of being gay who actually is not, like the "mistaken for gay" plotlines of adult sitcoms. Bert and Ernie on *Sesame Street* are not *really* gay; nor are Brock and Dr. Venture; nor is Stewie, or Roger, or Bobby Hill. The fear is in the possibility that gay people might exist, but audiences are assured that it is groundless, that all people are really straight. Thus, most episodes contain at least one proclamation of universal straight desire. On *Family Guy*, Peter tells his son, "As men, it's only natural for us to look at naked girls. *Every man* does it."

It's Just a Cartoon!

In television programs aimed at audiences of preteens, the proclamation that all desire is straight desire is intensified by the homophobic insistence that children must not know that gay people exist, less they develop "homosexual tendencies" that result in "confusion," and could eventually cause them to "decide" to become gay. Gay media figures who are completely "out" elsewhere get all stilted and anxious around children, and homophobic censors keep their eyes firmly attached to every frame of every kid's tv show. Children must grow up thinking that everyone on Earth is avidly, obsessively, irreparably straight.

Joe could stomach analyzing children's television for only three nights, one night per network. He saw preteens of every age and description are expressing straight desire, swooning over hotties, asking each other out, having boyfriends and girlfriends, going steady, breaking up, but not a word suggests that gay people exist. Even androgyny was promoted in an utterly gay-free world. The Disney channel produced several tv-movies about teenage boys with gender-bending interests, like cooking (*Eddie's Million Dollar Cookoff*), dramatics (*High School Musical*), and jumping rope (*Jump In*), but they all invariably featured straight romance.

Timmy Turner, a ten-year old beset-up by inept fairy godparents on Nickelodeon's *Fairly Oddparents*, becomes so frustrated by the complexities of preteen hetero-romance he wishes men and women to opposite sides of the planet. But now Cupid, an effeminate young man in a diaper, has nothing to do. Not: less to do. Not: a significantly smaller case load. Nothing. Without men and women, no one could possibly fall in love!

When hints of same-sex desire did occur, viewers were determined to not notice, to not believe it. In the Cartoon Network's *Grim Adventures of Billy and Mandy*, a parody of the Harry Potter books is set at Toadblatt's School of Wizardry. A misdirected love potion makes Dean Toadblatt, a human-sized toad (voiced by John Vernon of *Animal House* fame), fall in love one of the male teachers, the human-sized Squid Hat (voiced by Weird Al Yankovic). In the next scene, they kiss rather graphically, then ride away on a broom decorated with tin cans and a "Just Married" banner, while the students cheer. The sequence lasts for only a few seconds, and is not relevant to the plot of the episode; but still, it drops a broad hint that same-sex relationships are possible.

Fans who wrote in to the *Billy and Mandy* message board seemed perplexed by the scene. Several asked "What was up with Dean Toadblatt and the Squid Hat? Are they supposed to be gay, or what?"

The responses suggested a deliberate attempt to not know, to not be aware that gay people exist:

"Dean Toadblatt drank a love potion, so he isn't responsible for his actions."

"The Squid Hat must be female."

"They can't be gay, they're not even human."

"Lighten up, it's just a cartoon!"

My Gym Partner is a Monkey, on the Cartoon Network, is about a human boy, Adam Lyon, accidentally enrolled in a middle school for animals. In one episode, Jake Spidermonkey asks Adam to the school dance. Adam refuses, declaring that he wants to take a girl. Seething with jealousy, Jake tries to sabotage the date, and the two boys end up fighting. Evidently same-sex dates are commonplace at this particular middle school: the principal sees the fight, assumes that they are dancing, and cautions that touching one's partner is forbidden. As the episode ends, the two boys are photographed as a couple, and Adam looks dismayed as Jake's long tail curves into the form of a heart.

But viewers did not notice the romantic interest, or tried not to notice. When a thread on the *Gym Partner* message board asked "Is Jake into Adam?", fans invariably rejected the idea:

"Jake is only twelve years old, too young to be gay."

"Jake acts gay to make the cartoon funnier, but everybody knows he's not."

"Can't two guys be best friends without everybody thinking there's something wrong with them?"

And the ubiquitous "Lighten up! It's just a cartoon!"

The last comment is particularly suggestive: the fan believes that cartoons are lightweight entertainment, not designed to depict sad or threatening aspects of life. We will never see a drive-by shooting or a terrorist attack on *My Gym Partner*, nor will any student be a victim of cancer, or child abuse. So why would we see a gay character? Surely that's just as disturbing.

Gay-Free New Worlds

The science fiction series *Babylon Five* made front page news in when two of its male characters, Franklin and Garibaldi, went undercover as newlyweds on their honeymoon. They did not balk at the assignment, and no one at the posh resort raised an eyebrow in surprise. Therefore, in the far-future society of *Babylon Five*, same-sex marriage must be perfectly ordinary. Gay fans were ecstatic.

When faced with constant erasure, the slightest hint that you exist is a cause for celebration. However, there were no real gay characters in the episode, or in any other of the 110 episodes of *Babylon 5*. Joe checked, and found no real gay characters in 97 episodes of *Quantum Leap*, 87 episodes of *Sliders*, 61 episodes of *Roswell*, 110 episodes of *Andromeda*, or 701 episodes of the five *Star Trek* series (*Star Trek: The Original Series*, *The Next Generation*, *Voyager*, *Deep Space Nine*, and *Enterprise*). He didn't count the occasional effeminate men, of course, or the male aliens who temporary occupy the bodies of females.

During his second year in Wisconsin, Joe began going to the gym in the afternoons rather than the mornings, and all he could find to watch on tv while jogging on the treadmill was *Star Trek: The Next Generation*. One episode had the middle-aged Captain Jean-Luc Picard returning to a Parisian cafe that he frequented in his youth. He tells the waiter that twenty years ago he had a rendezvous in this very spot with "someone very special." The waiter instantly interprets "someone" as a "young lady." Why is he so absolutely certain that Picard did not have a rendezvous with a young man? Because Picard is a man, and therefore by definition finds only ladies "very special."

On another day on the treadmill, ship's doctor Beverly Crusher fell in love with Odan, an alien parasite whose non-sentient host happened to be a hot guy. When its male host dies, Odan moves on to another, this time a woman. Odan wants to continue the romance, but Dr. Crusher explains that humans are incapable of purely spiritual love. They need sex, too, and obviously that can't happen with two female bodies.

"Perhaps someday," she muses, "Our ability to love won't be so limited." She is unaware that women who love women exist.

The constant reminders that gay people do not exist may stem from the producers' belief that viewers are children and adolescents, who must never, never find out. Or it may recall fan objections similar to those rendered against the same-sex kiss in *The Grim Adventures of Billy and Mandy*, that cartoons are supposed to be lighthearted and funny, far removed from the "trouble" of everyday life. In the same way, science fiction series are usually set in a future utopia, where every conceivable social problem has been solved, and there's nothing left to do but explore strange new worlds and make peace with the Klingons.

The producers envision gay people as one of the social problems, a "trouble" that is certainly absent in the brave new world.

Or else there are no gay people in the twenty-fifth century because there are none in the twentieth. *Star Trek: The Next Generation* was filmed at Paramount Studios, less than a mile from the border of Oz, yet no doubt the writers, directors, and actors still conducted their daily lives as if everyone, everywhere was straight. So when it came time to create their fictional worlds, of course the space ship lounge would contain only male-female couples, Captain Picard could only have a female "someone very special," and Dr. Crusher must carefully explain that two women cannot be a couple because her species requires physical love.

When Whoopi Goldberg's character, font-of-wisdom bartender Guinan, was scripted as saying "when a man and a woman are in love. . . .", she adamantly refused. The director allowed her to substitute "two people" for "a man and a woman," but he was utterly mystified. What difference could it possibly make? Weren't the two statements identical?

Enjoy It with the Mrs.

Television series last so long that "misinterpretations" can be corrected and the myth of a gay-free world retained, but television commercials have twenty seconds or less to establish the setting, create characters, and tell a story. With so little time, "misinterpretations" would seem quite common. In fact, they are not. In movies, novels, and television series, the main plot always involves straight romance; the primary characters are always a man and a woman who fall into each other's arms at fade out. It is the secondary characters, like the bickering crocodile expert and small-town sheriff in *Lake Placid* or the surfer-dudes in *Orange County*, who can be read or misread as falling in love. It is the subplot that can be queered. But commercials feature only primary characters, either a man and a woman in love or a single person looking for "the one," and only a single plot, about how product for sale facilitates straight romance. There is no room left for same-sex bonds of any sort.

Every cleaning product was advertised as if it was used exclusively by straight women, housewives who must eliminate their children's grubby fingerprints from the kitchen counter before their husbands come breezing through the door. Every food item was advertised as if it was prepared exclusively by straight women, housewives who serve it to their husbands and children and are rewarded with a cry of "Great meal, honey!"

A man is eating alone in a suburban kitchen. A wall fades away to an old-fashioned country store in "a simpler time." A wizened old grocer hands him a box of some cereal "full of natural ingredients" and encourages him to "Enjoy it with the missus." How did the grocer know that the man was straight, and married? Because every man who eats cereal, or who buys cereal, is straight, and married.

Snacks were sold not as snacks, but as a means to the end of straight coupling. A man reclines in a deck chair by the pool, messily eating an ice cream cone. A bikini-clad woman approaches, finds him disgusting, and moves on. The next man is eating Dibs, a compact, neat ice cream novelty. The woman judges him worthy of sex, so she smiles and reclines next to him.

Beer was consumed entirely by unmarried straight men consorting with bikini models, or by married straight men glued to the game while their wives fume.

Wine was consumed entirely by elegantly attired straight couples out for a romantic dinner.

Soda was sold through a straight morality play: A guy tries to kiss a girl at the end of their date. She refuses, and he walks off, despondent. But a swig of Diet Coke suddenly makes him sexy, and he rushes back to sweep the girl off her feet. In a year of commercial-watching, Joe found only one beverage not being sold only to straights: Mountain Dew, which displayed muscular young men engaging in extreme sports, not trying to pick up girls.

Commercials for restaurants displayed either nuclear families or young, attractive straight couples who offered to feed each other, but then backed off at the last minute and laughed playfully. When there were mixed male-female groups, they were clearly divided into romantic couples. Two men were never shown dining together, unless they were obsessively discussing their hetero-mania: "Do you like blondes, brunettes, or redheads?" "Yes!"

Lesbians were at least able to buy clothing; commercials for ladies' garments rarely showed men overcome by hetero-longing. But gay men must make do with homespun: whenever a man bought a shirt or a suit, a slim red-nailed hand inevitably pressed on his shoulder to indicate feminine approval.

Commercials for women's deodorant were all about being confident in sales meetings, but men rolled on their deodorant and immediately got caressed by red-nailed hands.

Every commercial for shaving cream, without exception, ended with the guy being manhandled by a supermodel, or more commonly an army of supermodels, driven into a frenzy of lust by a clean-shaven face. Perhaps that is why the Castro clones used to wear moustaches, Jeff thought, to ward off the sexual assaults.

Even getting sick was no escape. Allergies ruin the picnics of boy-girl couples. If you get diarrhea, your wife can suggest "soothing relief." If you catch a cold while on the road, you can buy a product that's almost as good as being home "with your wife."

The advertisers probably had no intention of alienating potential gay customers. They simply had no idea that some viewers might be gay, because they had no idea that gay people exist.

We Never Intended....

Some commercials do not involve husbands or wives, men do not gaze longingly at ladies, and ladies do not gaze longingly at men, so theoretically the characters could be gay. Sometimes there are two of them, so why not assume that they are a gay couple? It may be a remedy to the incessant erasure of the other 400 commercials one sits through every day. But when the producers hear that someone has "misinterpreted" their commercial, they shrink away in horror and protest "They're straight! Gay people do not exist!" Just to be on the safe side, they immediately remove the commercial from circulation, lest anyone get the "wrong" idea.

Several years ago, Volkswagen aired a dialogue free commercial in which two young men are driving aimlessly about, when they see a discarded easy chair on the side of the road. They load it into their car (it fits perfectly because of the hatchback), and drive away, only to be overwhelmed by the smell and discard it again. What else could they be but a gay couple? The producers shrieked that "We had no intention of implying such a thing!", and pulled it from circulation.

Later Volkswagen aired another commercial, again dialogue-free, with two young men stopping at a service station. While one buys snacks, the other pumps gas (they don't need much because Volkswagens are so fuel-efficient). They switch seats, exchange a romantic smile, and continue on their journey. Again, obviously a gay couple. The producers again shrieked "We never meant to suggest. . . .", and pulled it from circulation.

When long-time cartoon antagonists Popeye and Bluto drink Minute Maid Orange Juice, they reconcile – and perhaps realize that their bickering has been a cover for romance. They pick flowers, hug, and ride off on a bicycle built for two, while Olive Oyl, their usual object of competition, stares suspiciously (she should have suspected before, when she dated Popeye for seventy years without even a kiss). When speculation about the Popeye-Bluto pairing hit the internet, the producers protested much more than usual: "We would never think that! Nobody would think that! Anybody who knows anything about the characters knows that it is utterly ridiculous!" The commercial was instantly dropped.

A more recent series of commercials for t-mobile direct, an internet company, stars two mature men. Both apparently live alone. They visit each other, watch tv, go out to coffee shops. The white one complains about his slow internet service, and the Asian one recommends t-mobile direct. No women appear in their lives. There are no references to women except once the white man, watching tv, comments on the intrigue of a soap opera. Nor are there any other markers of heterosexuality, such as sports, mentioned, or in their apartment décor (he froze the frame and did a thorough analysis). What else could they be but two middle-aged gay men, long term friends hanging out?

But neither wears a sign stating "I am gay," so it is very unlikely that straights will notice.

Gay magazines often run ads for these same products, so advertisers know that gay people exist, and want their money. But television commercials are intended for "a mass audience," and while producers are quite certain that may residents are homophobic, they do not believe that a single one is gay. So they populate their commercials with straight people. If you think a character is gay, you are mistaken. If you think gay people exist, you are mistaken.

---

[1] "Gay Characters on *Lost*" thread, The Fuselage, http://www.thefuselage.com/Threaded/archive/index.php/t-44046.html

[2] Glassman, Bernard. *Anti-Semitic Stereotypes without Jews: Images of Jews in England, 1290-1700.* Wayne State University Press, 1975.

Chapter Nine
Daily Chores in Ohio

Joe's second year at Wesley College was ending, and there was no sign of his visiting position being upgraded to a tenure-track, so he went on the job market again. Again he limited his search to colleges within sixty miles of Oz, close enough for weekend visits.

Except when the towns were monstrosities. A Lutheran college in Minnesota, fifty miles from Oz, sat amid a gun store, a strip club, and a run-down Family Video store.

Or when the colleges themselves were monstrosities. A state university in Georgia, thirty miles from Oz, had a parking lot was crowded with red pick-up trucks with confederate flags in the window and a course catalog that hadn't been revised since the Truman administration: *Sociology of Women, Marriage and the Family.*

Near the end of June, Joe finally received two job offers, both visiting rather than tenure-track, both with depressingly low salaries:

A tenure-track at a liberal arts college in rural eastern Ohio, fifty miles from Oz, but on narrow, winding country roads that would be treacherous in the winter.

A two-year visiting position at Chester State University in Ohio, seventy miles from Oz, but about an hour's drive on a modern interstate highway.

He chose Ohio.

It was more rustic than he expected, all forests and farmland, with a rich and somewhat disquieting assortment of cultural oddities, including a pre-Columbian Serpent Mound and an extremely active UFO-chasing club.

The town of Chester seemed time-warped to the Eisenhower Era. Main Street began at an air force base and extended for six blocks, past three cheap hotels, a tattoo parlor, a comic book store, a Christian bookstore, a boarded-up movie palace where they sometimes held swap meets, and Luigi's Italian Restaurant, with a neon sign of a stereotypic Italian chef holding up a "pizza pie."

Broad Street offered a used car dealership, a boarded-up Thrift Town department store, and a row of fast-food restaurants, including a Dogs N Suds (elsewhere the 1950s chain had long since fallen a victim to the proliferation of McDonalds). High Street (high because at one point it soared over a deserted railroad track) offered Pentecostal, Southern Baptist, Nazarene, and generic fundamentalist churches, but nothing progressive. The residential streets were quiet and shady, with garage sales and kiddie pools.

There was a small gay presence: a bar, two welcoming churches, a gift shop with gay-themed cards, and two organizations, one with the oddly closeted name "Friends of the Italian Opera" ("we do not go to the opera or discuss the opera"). There was even a tiny, three-block long Gay Pride Parade, unannounced in the media, so straight people on the sidewalks kept staring and pointing, and rushing into buildings and dragging out their friends to gawk at the spectacle. Joe usually drove to Columbus, where Germantown was as bright and vibrant and open as Dupont Circle or the Rue Ste. Catherine. But still, he could spend only about ten hours per week in Oz; 95% of his life, 158 hours out of 168 every week, took place in Chester.

One perk of the proximity to the air force base was the endless parade of muscular soldiers sunning themselves by the pool in his apartment building or jogging shirtless on the fitness path at Chester City Park. He discovered the drawback later: a surprisingly large number were studying at Chester State with the goal of becoming FBI agents and catching pedophiles or terrorists, so they all enrolled in his fall courses in *Criminology, Juvenile Delinquency,* and for some reason even the seemingly irrelevant *Sociology of Gender.* Classrooms full of muscular soldiers may be visually appealing, especially while it was still warm enough for chest-hugging t-shirts, but the opinions they expressed were uniformly 1950s conservative: crime is caused by a namby-pamby penal system, and delinquency by broken homes and violent video games; and "homosexuals" are very sick, too sick to enlist in the military, most likely conspiring with the pedophiles and terrorists to take away our freedom.

Just Put Down "Single"

Joe's first stop at Chester State was the Human Resources department, where he met Teresa, a bubbly, rather plump woman glittering with bracelets and rings and reeking of perfume. Her cubicle was decorated with pictures of an attractive middle-aged man, probably her husband, and a lot of kids of various ages in "family-fun" poses: at a water-slide, at a picnic, face-painted for Halloween, unwrapping Christmas presents. The screen saver on her computer consisted of cats in funny predicaments, and a cat calendar hung over her desk. Every Human Resources Officer appears to be cast from the same mold: they are always bubbly and plump, they always wear too much perfume, and they always decorate their cubicles with pictures of husbands, kids, and cats.

Teresa omitted the usual "Are you married?" question, but her gushing about the upcoming "family fun" activities that he might want to try – the County Fair, the Caramel Festival, the Fall Fun Festival, Civil War Days -- just as effectively conveyed the message that she believed he had a wife and kids at home, waiting breathlessly for an answer to the question "What shall we do this weekend?"

The erasure began in earnest with the new employee paperwork: W-2, Retirement Account, Citizenship Verification, Life Insurance, Long-Term Disability Insurance, Medical and Dental Insurance. Every form, without exception, required him to mark whether he was a married heterosexual or a single heterosexual. Joe tried to leave the spaces blank, but Teresa helpfully pointed out his "omission." he tried to "refuse to answer," but, smiling, oblivious, perhaps thinking that he was Brad Pitt (who refused to marry until gay people could), Teresa said that the forms with blank spaces would just be returned for "correction."

"I'm gay, so I don't fit in either category."

Smiling, composed, she chirped "Then you're not married, right? Just put down *single*. That's what you *are*."

The insurance forms also wanted to know the names of his wife and kids. Many businesses allow same-sex partners to be included as dependents in an employee's insurance program, but Chester State did not, so he put down "none." The "beneficiary" should not have been a problem; theoretically he could name anyone at all, his parents, his high school gym teacher, the Dalai Lama if he had his address. He didn't want Teresa to think that gay people never form permanent relationships, so he named Jan, even though they had broken up a long time ago. "Relationship: Partner," she read, wrinkling her nose. "Business partner?"

"No," Joe said. "Life partner. You know, long-term companion. . ."

"Sounds too much like a business partner. Better say *friend*. That's what you *are*."

"I have a lot of friends. How about *lover*? I only have one of those. Of course, I'm new in town. Give him a few weeks."

Reddening, unaware that he was joking, she agreed to let "Partner" stand.

Dating Female Students

Joe needed to jump one last human resources hurdle before starting his new job: Sexual Harassment Training. Nearly every company requires it of new employees. In Wisconsin, it was two hours long, with a filmstrip, a discussion, and a booklet to take home. But at Chester State, it was a strenuous six-hour affair, with a different filmstrip, a lecture, a catered lunch, another lecture, a role-playing game, a discussion section, and a test.

He heard a rumor that a few years before, a professor became obsessed with one of his students and began calling her cell phone twenty times a day, staking out her apartment, accosting her in public. He was fired, and the President pressured Human Resources to increase sexual harassment training, as if that could have prevented the situation.

Sexual harassment means using a power differential to pressure a subordinate (in his case, a student) into dating or sex, or making risqué comments to anyone in the workplace. Obviously Joe could pressure only *male* students into dating or sex, and any risqué comment he might make would involve their butts or bulges.

But every moment of the six hours presumed that sexual harassment was exclusively heterosexual, that men only ever pressure women, or women men, into dating or sex, that the only risqué comments that exist involve women's breasts.

The film showed twelve "wrong way – right way" scenarios: nine men ogling their female employees, complementing them on their outfits, touching their shoulders, and offering promotions in exchange for sex; a man tacking a *Playboy* centerfold to his cubicle wall; a man telling a joke about breasts to his horrified coworkers; a woman asking a male subordinate out for coffee. And nothing else.

After lunch, the Vice President of Academic Affairs, a portly middle-aged man wearing a gleaming wedding ring, talked about the need to maintain professional distance when working in close proximity with older students, especially graduate students "of the opposite sex."

Joe raised his hand and asked, "Would he be allowed to date a graduate student if he was not taking any of his classes?"

Without even a blink of surprise, he responded, "No. You shouldn't ask for or accept a date with any student. She might enroll in your classes in the future, or feel uncomfortable about enrolling in a class that was required for her major." The pronoun-shift was so quick and easy that it must have been unconscious.

During the role playing game, they paired off and learned how to initiate a pleasant, non-harassing social contact with a coworker of the "opposite sex." Joe asked for a same-sex partner, but was told, "Oh, no, this training has to be for everybody."

Obviously, "everybody" meant heterosexuals only, since gay people did not and could not exist in the workplace.

Family Medical Group

In Ohio, Joe's research took him beyond school and work, friends and romantic partners, books and movies and television, to everyday chores: trips to the doctor and the therapist, workouts at the gym, oil changes at the garage, taxi rides, airplane trips, jaunts to the mall in search of a birthday present. Some are easily overlooked because they take so little time, an hour or two per month, much less than the time we spend working, pursuing relationships, or even watching television. Some are easily forgotten because they recur with little variation, so in the end they feel like a single event. Some are easily dismissed as trivial because they come and go with little emotional impact, little significance. Yet they provide a backdrop for our lives, daily rhythms that give us order and show us where we belong.

Most of these events take place among strangers, people who will probably never see us again, or will see us only after checking a chart. Friends, neighbors, and coworkers at least try to remember that you are gay, if only to preserve the peace, but professionals can safely forget.

They can be infinitely surprised every time they encounter someone who is gay, or refuse to believe it, whispering "There is no such thing as a gay person" in a stilted, frantic voice, as someone might walk through a haunted house whispering "There are no such things as ghosts." Thus, the backdrop for our lives tells us, over and over, day after day, year after year, that we do not and cannot exist.

Whenever Joe moved to a new town, he selected "family physicians" over specialists because they were cheaper, even though the term "family" specifically excluded gay people.

In Chester, at the Family Medical Group, the intake form asked him to check off the diseases that he (or anyone in his biological family) suffered from. "Heart disease. . .hemophilia. . . ." he read. "Hernia. . . . homosexuality. . . incontinence. . . ."

Homosexuality?

None of the major suppliers of medical forms include "homosexuality" among the diseases covered. A report from the University of Michigan Medical School suggests that medical practitioners who want to provide a welcoming environment for LGBT patients need only change the "Married/Single" question on the intake form. To include "homosexuality" was evidently an in-house decision.[1]

Joe circled "homosexuality," put a lot of checks next to it, and waited to yell and scream at the doctor. He came into the little examination room, scanned through the list, and said "Hmmm. . .I see there's a history of heart disease in your family. . ."

Why did he ignore the "homosexuality"? If he didn't believe it was a disease, why did he include it on the intake form?

As Joe walked out into the parking lot, he reflected that this was a good way to express homophobia and erasure at the same time. The doctor could express his opinion that "homosexuality" is a disease, but back off when someone called him on it.

There was no "homosexuality" on the intake form at the next family physician Joe tried, nor at his new optometrist, dentist, dermatologist, or urologist, but every medical examination seemed to find its own way to proclaim "There are no gay people here," if not to Joe than to someone within in earshot.

Later in the year, he got the flu, and his new doctor wrote out a prescription for an antibiotic. "You're still contagious," he said, "So tell your wife to sleep on the couch for a few days."

Though he had a fever of 102, he still managed to reply "You mean my boyfriend?" The doctor just smiled.

Joe had a question for the dentist: "I know you're not supposed to brush your teeth or floss right before or after sex, but how long do you have to wait?"

He looked puzzled and said, "I can't see any problem with brushing and flossing after sex."

Joe told him that HIV can be transmitted through tiny tears in the gums.

Still puzzled, he said "But that's in your mouth. . .you don't use. . .what do you mean?"

After all the work of getting him to understand, he didn't know the answer. He had heard of oral sex, but it never occurred to him that any man actually practiced it *with another man*.

Sometimes Joe simply overheard the erasure:

While he was sitting in the waiting room at his doctor's office, a pharmaceutical sales representative came in and told the receptionist about a party to celebrate the introduction of a new drug: "Everyone is welcome. The doctor and his wife, or you and your husband." How did he know that the doctor and the receptionist were both straight?

Diversity

The moment he arrived on the campus, Joe petitioned to join the campus-wide Diversity Committee, assuming that its charge of increasing the awareness of "diversity" in the campus community would include gay people. But the sixty-page long *Diversity Report,* about how Chester State responded to the "rich cultural diversity of the region," mentioned only ethnic minorities, Appalachians, and women.

At the first meeting, they divided the academic year into months and assigned each to a different minority group, which would receive a month-worth of big-name guest speakers, ethnic food festivals, craft shows, films, workshops, concerts, and parties. Different committee members suggested Hispanics, Arab-Americans, African-Americans, Asian-Americans, Women, and Jews.

"What about Gay Pride?" Joe asked, finally getting his chance.

"When is it?" the Dean asked.

"Well. . .usually it's in June, but National Coming Out Day is October 11th, so we could schedule it for October."

"September is too short notice for Hispanic Heritage," someone said. "Let's move *that* to October."

"What about Gay Pride?" he asked again.

"We just have the budget for real minorities," someone sniped.

The Dean stared him down. "Now, now, let's be collegial. Some of our colleagues come from super-liberal colleges, so they don't understand how controversial Gay Pride Month would be around here. This is Ohio. Many of our students are in the military. They don't want anybody's life in danger."

"It's a good idea," a female faculty member said, "But not for Chester State."

The Rainbow Coalition put up a booth on the quad on October 11th, but one booth was not the same as official recognition, with posters on a hundred campus bulletin boards and a flurry of guest speakers, workshops, concerts, and parties. Yet gay people, deemed not a "real minority" or "too controversial," were erased from the place where they should have been most obviously present, a celebration of difference in contemporary society.

For many years, African-Americans were erased in the mass media. There weren't any at all in the movies, not even a face in the crowd, except for a few stereotypic servants. Today every Pizza Hut commercial comes in two versions, one with white actors, the other with black, often saying exactly the same lines. Every commercial for Chocolate Sugar Bombs Cereal depicts exactly three children, always with the same racial and gender configuration: a white male, a white female, and a black male. Thus, diversity, albeit of a labored, self-conscious sort, is promoted.

However, diversity means only ethnic and sometimes religious minorities. Another job of the Diversity Committee was to promote a course called *Majority-Minority Relations*. Joe saw the sample syllabus: White, Black, Asian, Hispanic, Native American. Midterm. Catholic, Protestant, Jewish, Muslim, Buddhist, Hindu. Final Exam. Sexual orientation was absent.

Asexuality
After nearly six years in Kansas, Joe thought he had heard every type of erasure, but a visit to the urologist in March of his first year in Ohio revealed a new one. Dr. Myers was tall, thin, and white-haired, in the business forty years, with a grandson at Chester State – never a favorable sign, since the elderly are less likely than the young to be aware that gay people exist, and more likely to recoil in horror when they meet a "homosexual" face to face.

He looked at Joe's intake form and asked the usual questions: When was his last prostate exam? Was he having

difficulty in urination? And so on. Then, suddenly, a nonse-
quiter in the midst of a diagnosis, he asked the usual ice-
breaker: "Are you married?"

Just a few days before, Joe had to do everything but
draw a diagram to get the dentist to understand his flossing
and HIV question, so he was in a bad mood, and he didn't
feel like playing the "I can't get married in this state" game.
"I don't care to answer," he said.

Dr. Myers looked up in complete surprise. "Huh?"

"I said, I don't care to answer. Next question?"

Annoyed, the doctor persisted. "I just need to know if
you have been having problems in your sex life."

Joe laughed. "You've been to medical school, Doctor.
Surely one of your lectures mentioned that people can have
sex even when they aren't married."

"Ok. Then tell me this: has there been a decline in the
frequency of your sexual intercourse recently, or a general
decrease in your desire to be with a woman sexually?"

"Well, let's see," Joe said. "I have never had 'sexual
intercourse' at all, and my desire to be with a woman sexually is as strong as it ever was: non-existent. You'd have to put
a gun to my head to get me to fondle a lady's breast."

Dr. Myers seemed somewhat taken aback by this revelation, but did he conclude that Joe was therefore gay?

Not for an instant. He said: "Well, you know, a small
percentage of men have no interest in sex. It's called asexuality. It's perfectly normal, nothing to be concerned about."

"I am interested in sex," Joe protested. "I'm just not
interested in sex with women."

Dr. Myers stared, completely baffled, and wordlessly
looked down at his chart. He could imagine the wheels turning in his head. Sex, but not with women? Who else is there?
Surely he doesn't mean with children! Or farm animals!

Worried that he would scribble something about pedophilia or bestiality, Joe told him "I'm gay. I only have sex with men."

He looked up instantly. "Oh. Why didn't you say so in the first place?"

He would never have come up with the word "gay" on his own. He must have seen thousands of patients over the years. Surely some of them were gay. Maybe the gay patients were passing, even at the doctor's office. Or maybe they were open, but Dr. Myers was so eager to believe that everyone on Earth is straight that he instantly forgot.

The Androgyny Scale

During his first year in Chester, Joe became depressed, so he drove to Chester Psychiatric Services, a standalone brick building surrounded by cornfields, and made an appointment with one of the three licensed clinical psychologists. He didn't bother to check their background for potential homophobia: the American Psychiatric Association removed "homosexuality" from its list of mental disorders in 1973, before any psychologist currently practicing had enrolled in freshman psychology.

In his naiveté, Joe didn't realize that being "not a sickness" does not translate to gay-friendly. Many psychologists believe that the gay person is disabled, an incomplete, immature version of a straight, a "negative outcome" of a traumatic childhood or adolescence. Others believe that while being gay is theoretically neutral, growing up in a homophobic society causes tremendous feelings of guilt and shame, with the same "negative outcome": an adult who is traumatized, victimized, incomplete, missing. But his psychologist, Dr. Nagel, simply refused to believe that gay people exist.

He was a smiling, rather rotund man in his mid-forties, with a tanned, balding head, thick hands like sausages, and the brash, chummy demeanor of a Sunday school teacher. He received his Ph.D. in Counseling Psychology from Ohio State University only five years ago, but before that he had spent many years as a school counselor at Chester High. On his desk Joe saw photographs of two teenage boys but no woman, so naturally he assumed that Dr. Nagel was gay.

He changed his mind when Dr. Nagel gazed out of the window at the grassy lawn and the foot-high corn beyond and said, "My oldest boy is seventeen, and you know what that means: girls, girls, girls, morning, noon, and night!" Surely a gay man would not be so eager to buy into the myth that all teenage boys, without exception, are wild about girls.

When Joe described his symptoms and his worries, Dr. Nagel prescribed the *Minnesota Multiphasic Personality Inventory* (MMPI-2), a battery of 567 true-false questions used for everything from evaluating drug addicts to screening applicants to seminaries. It was first developed in 1942, but there have been several revisions, most recently in 1982, long after "homosexuality" ceased being a disease. Therefore, Joe did not expect questions that demonize gay people.

He was wrong. There were several:

"I am sometimes attracted to people of the same sex."

"I sometimes fantasize about members of the same sex."

"If it were socially acceptable, he would like to have sex with someone of the same sex."

Obviously psychologists still believed that same-sex desire was a symptom of emotional dysfunction, like contemplating suicide, or even of psychosis, like believing that an outside force is controlling your thoughts.

Doing some research, Joe discovered that the questions about same-sex desire, along with some about gender transgressions, like "I would enjoy being a florist" or "I would enjoy singing in a musical," belonged to Scale #5, *Masculinity-Femininity*. It was originally developed to identify and boot out gay recruits during World War II, but now most therapists use it to determine if your "gender roles" are adequately developed. Men should score highly on the masculine pole, and low on the feminine.

A few gender-transgressions don't hurt, but men who consistently fail to score low on the masculine pole (little interest in sports, mechanical gadgets, and women) or high on the feminine (significant interest in Broadway shows, flower shops, and men) are in trouble. They have "sexual problems," "conflicts in sexual identity," and "effeminate behaviors." The old stereotype of gay men as really women trapped in male bodies stands. The old stereotype of gay men as "confused," as "problems," stands.[2]

When the results of the test came in, Dr. Nagel noticed that he was exceptionally low on the masculine pole, and high on the feminine (he may have helped a bit by declaring an avid interest in the show tunes, flower shops, dress-making, and interior design). He suggested that the cause was role confusion: "You grew up in the Midwest, but you haven't lived here as an adult. Then suddenly, in middle age, you're back again. You're regressing to a childlike state, and that's bound to include some androgyny."

"What about the questions about being attracted to men?" Joe asked, impatient.

Dr. Nagel looked down to check his chart, or to avoid his stare. "Oh. . .yes, I see that you marked them all 'yes.'

That may suggest a possibility that you have homosexual tendencies."

May suggest a possibility?

"But," he assured Joe, "It may also be due to your regression to a childlike state. It certainly doesn't mean that you are gay."

Again, the gay person as a child, as trapped in a perpetual adolescence, unwilling or unable to "settle down" into adult straight practice!

To combat his depression, Dr. Nagel suggested that he make a list of the positive things about his life. In order to jump-start his realization that gay people exist, Joe included as #3 the gym, the massive chests straining beneath 280-lb barbells, the unabashed frontal nudity in the showers.

"Lots of guys are sensitive to the physical attractiveness of other guys," Dr. Nagel said in a soothing tone. "It doesn't mean that you are gay."

Would anything, ever, under any circumstances, mean that he was gay?

"Let's talk about your love life," he continued. "Having a caring wife or girlfriend to talk to. . . ."

This was the last straw. "I've never had a wife or a girlfriend. Would a boyfriend do?" And then, before Dr. Nagel could assure him, "Having a boyfriend doesn't mean that you are gay," Joe told him that he was gay.

Dr. Nagel smiled. "I'm pleased that you feel comfortable enough with him to reveal your secret."

My secret?

Is She Cute?

One major benefit of living in Oz is the minimal driving required. In West Hollywood, in the heart of car-obsessed Los Angeles, Joe drove perhaps once a week. In the West Village, he didn't even own a car.

But in Kansas, residences and amenities are miles apart, and public transportation severely limited – God forbid that you be forced to interact with anyone other than your husband or wife – so Joe had to drive to the drug store, the supermarket, the gym, and the bank, plus to Oz, which meant an extra 120 miles per week. He drove more miles in a week in Chester than he had in two months in West Hollywood, and consequently spent much more time in gas stations, auto garages, and the Jiffy Lube.

When Joe kept hearing a pinging sound when he was driving, Dr. Allen, an economics professor from across the hall, gave him the business card of a mechanic: "I go to him all the time. He's a family man, so he does a good job."

Joe was expecting the Family Man Syndrome, the belief that men who have married and reproduced are especially competent, so he countered, "How does having sex with a woman make you a good mechanic? I didn't think the two skills were connected."

Dr. Allen stared for a second as if he was speaking gibberish, then returned to the Family Man litany. "No, no. . .I just meant that he's a family man, so you can trust him. He won't cheat you."

"Isn't that like telling a Jewish person, 'He's not Jewish, so you can trust him?'" Joe said, letting the sarcasm ooze into his voice. "Gay men are notoriously dishonest."

Dr. Allen's comment sounds like heterosexism rather than erasure: straights are better, more competent, more honorable than gay people. However, the point of the Family Man Syndrome is not to be straight per se, but to marry and reproduce. Not even every heterosexual does this: it is a point of honor, a sign that you are better, more competent, more honorable than *other heterosexuals*. So if you are not a Family Man, customers will avoid your products and services, and supervisors will pass you over for promotions, but not because they assume you to be gay: gay people do not exist. You are a failed heterosexual.

Joe did not choose the Family Man for his repair. But still, almost every time he entered an auto shop in Kansas, a mechanic made a joyous comment that revealed his certainty that he was straight:

At the Oil Plus, he was told: "Why don't you have a seat in the waiting room? There's some *Esquires* and *Maxims* in there. That will keep you busy, right?"

At Action Lube, he said he needed the car by 5:00 pm. The mechanic grinned. "Hot date, huh? Is she cute?"

At Midas, he pulled out his checkbook to pay the bill, and glanced up to check the date to a calendar of semi-nude ladies. The mechanic, noticing his glance, chirped "She's pretty hot, huh? Almost makes [the amount you spent] worth it."

To add insult to insult, as he walked off to retrieve his car, he called "Be good to the girls, now." Whatever that meant, it surely meant he perceived him as straight.

Joe refrained from "coming out" to any mechanic, judging it not worthwhile to spend the next hour fielding questions about "what causes it" and whether he tried sex with a woman before deciding to "switch teams."

He just clammed up, read his book, and tried to ignore the ambient assurances of universal heterosexuality: discussions among the staff of the girl they dated last night, the girl they would like to date, and the breasts of female celebrities. He reflected that most blue-collar workplaces must be like this, full of men or women judging each other's straight interests and proclaiming that no gay people exist.

How do the gay employees manage? Do they grin and bear it, or do they fight back?

He suspect that most grin and bear it.

Gifts for Him

The best cure for depression is to pull out your credit card and yell "Charge!" Shopping is not only a means of acquiring necessities and luxuries, it is a means of expressing an identity, stating who we are and who we would like to be. However, in the purchase of most items, we have no choice: the identity we are required to express is straight. Even in Oz, where the *Gay Yellow Pages* has the heft of a telephone directory, everyday purchases require entering "straight" stores, gay only by virtue of their location.

But still, two men could shop at the "gay" Safeway and ask each other "Are we out of toothpaste?" without weird looks, or drop into Laurel Hardware for without any quips about "getting away from the wives." Not so at the Kroger or True Value in Chester.

Joe could shop for a bouquet at West Hollywood Florist without being asked about "Her favorites." Not so at the Flowerland in Chester.

For burning off the last shreds of our disposable income, Oz offered shops like Dorothy's Surrender and Don't Panic, with rainbow key chains, penis-shaped candles, birthday cards emblazoned with muscle men, and t-shirts that read "I'm can't even think straight." But Chester offered Cozy Country Gifts, with a patchwork quilt of a boy and a girl grinning at each other in the ecstasies of a prepubescent hetero-crush, or a figurine of a boy plucking petals off a flower, with the caption "She loves me...she loves me not."

Online shopping offered erasure of its own.

Allposters.com suggested that teenage boys might like posters of sports stars, and teenage girls posters of cute animals, no hot babes of either gender. But men got posters of female breasts (labeled "Goals"), and women lowering their panties and asking us to "Lend a hand."

A total of 25% of the 274 posters for men and 36% of the 131 posters for women asserted that they were straight, and not one admitted that any of them are gay or lesbian.

Oddly, there was also a Gay and Lesbian category, with some rainbow flags, Gay Games posters, and precisely the same beefcake and cheesecake that straights receive. So the management of allposters.com knew that gay people exist, they were just not "men" and "women."[3]

Calendars.com offered *The Boyfriend of the Month*, featuring "that perfect guy that anyone would consider a great catch," and *The Uniforms Calendar*: "What could be better than a man in uniform? A man out of uniform!" So far, so good.

But there was also a *Chippendales Calendar*, "a must have for every female!"

The *Sports Illustrated Swimsuit Calendar* was "a favorite with men around the world!"

The category of Men's Satire Calendars consisted mostly of ladies in bikinis making jokes, and Women's Satire Calendars, mostly of dour-looking ladies explaining why "men are like new shoes" (they're hard to break in, and when they're worn out, it's time to replace them). Almost all of the calendars sold to men presumed that they all wanted to spend the year looking at ladies, and women, that they wanted to spend the year complaining about men.[4]

At *Gifts.com*, the category For Him offered lots of gifts for straight weddings and anniversaries, personalized His N Her Pillow Cases, a "Weekend of Love Kit" with an image of a man and woman from the *Kama Sutra*, and "Life Lesson Figurines," about men getting into humorous scrapes that assume hetero-coupling: "Just because you like it, doesn't mean *she* will"; "When she asks for a backrub, sometimes she just means a backrub."

The "Metro Guy" (a closeted curtailment of "Metrosexual") might enjoy *King Magazine*: "sexy women, fast cars, sports, real money, and mad music."

Teenage Boys might enjoy a book, *Essential Manners for Men,* which seems to be inclusive in its advice on "How to Live with a Significant Other or Spouse," but actually isn't (the significant other is assumed female). There's also a gay-free chapter on "Things Men Do Wrong that Make Women Wince."[5]

Amazon.com, the mega book and everything else site, won the award for the most egregious insistence that gay people do not exist

The introduction to the Boyfriends/Husbands Gift category amply referenced the "white knight" who has "swept her off her feet."

The introduction to the Girlfriends/Wives category rhapsodized about the "woman in his life," with never a same-sex partner acknowledged or implied.

The introduction to the Teenage Boys category suggested: "Give the young fresh fellows something loud and crashy, action packed, or inappropriately funny," followed by a smug, simpering: " Just don't be offended if their interest in what's in the box falls below their interest in girls." Amazingly, when Joe emailed amazon.com to complain, they changed the "interest in girls" line to an inclusive "Rock on!"[6]

Ebay, the online auction giant, displayed the least erasure of any of the websites he observed, perhaps because the item descriptions were not written by homophobic advertising agencies, but by private individuals selling off their discards or running small businesses, and trying to reach the widest possible customer base.[7]

Orlando Bloom, star of *The Lord of the Rings* and *The Pirates of the Caribbean* series, appeared on 728 items up for auction, but less than ten of the item descriptions expressed the belief that no gay men exist: a photo "for the ladies"; a *Pirates of the Caribbean* t-shirt that is "perfect for guys -- no picture of Orlando Bloom on the front!"; a poster of a shirtless Bloom reclining on a large white pillow ("Great poster, ladies!). Oddly, another seller advertised the same white-pillow poster with a telegraphic yet inclusive "new girls n guys Orlando Bloom dreamy."

192 auctions offered items emblazoned with the likeness of Zac Efron the star of *Hairspray* and the popular *High School Musical* franchise. There were posters, photos, articles of clothing, school supplies, pillowcases, and even light switch covers. But only four of item descriptions specified that all potential bidders, and all potential recipients, must be girls. The others exclaimed: "*Everybody's* favorite teen hunk!", not "*Every girl's* favorite teen hunk," or "A great addition to *any fan's* collection!", not "*any girl's* collection." The t-shirt emblazoned with "It's a Zac Efron thing!" was specified as unisex.

Still, it wasn't hard to find erasure:

A dart board emblazoned with a picture of a male model, advertised as "Ladies, here is your dart board! Get'em while supplies last!"

A mug showing ladies in a state of undress "for the men!"

Euphoria Cologne, to "attract the opposite sex!"

A photo of Joaquin Phoenix "for the ladies."

A T-shirt emblazoned with "Got boys?" in a parody of the popular "Got milk?" ads, "tailored for the ladies!"

A fishing lure in the form of a mermaid, "Guaranteed to catch all fishermen!"

A Hawaiian hula boy bobbler for a car's dashboard, "looking for a hula girl."

The Lady of the House

When he arrived in Ohio, Joe immediately registered for the state's Do Not Call list, to keep the telephone from ringing a dozen times a day. Through most of the year, he received news of "amazing offers" only from his credit card companies (your own creditors are exempt) and from the Policeman's Fund.

But in May of his first year in Chester, he suddenly began receiving two or three calls per week asking for "the lady of the house." First he hung up. Then, as the calls continued, with different voices each time, he devised a long, withering response: "How dare you limit your calls to straight married couples? This isn't the 1950's, you know. How do you come off alienating half of your potential customers?"

The callers usually hung up before he got far, but one stayed on the line long enough for him to find out the source of the "lady of the house" calls. A fundamentalist watchdog group had solicited volunteers from local churches to call everyone in the telephone book. After the Lady of the House answered three questions (about whether there is too little or too much pornography, violence, and witchcraft on television), she would be asked to join.

Why "The Lady of the House"? Even if the watchdog group believed that every single household in the United States consists of straight married couples, surely the husband was as qualified as the wife to offer an opinion about the flood of pornography, violence, and witchcraft on television. The caller was not sure about this, and it is not explained on the watchdog group's official website

Telling them that he was gay did not get Joe removed from the "to-call" list. Eventually he discovered that there was no provision made in the volunteers' instructions for households without a lady. It had never occurred to anyone in the watchdog group that either gay people or unmarried adult straights exist.

So instead of "do not call," the volunteers were marking his number with "lady of the house unavailable," as if his wife were merely out shopping. The next evening a new volunteer arrived, retrieved his number, and tried to reach "Her" again. It took several angry emails to the watchdog group itself to finally end the calls.

Lots of Fine Ladies Here

In Oz, a gym membership is a must, especially when warm climates do not allow excess pounds to be hidden beneath bulky sweaters. In West Hollywood, Joe spent at least twelve hours per week at the Hollywood Spa; in Wilton Manors, at least ten hours per week at Gold's Gym; but in Ohio, he squeaked by with a few hours a week in the campus gym, and Chester had many fast-food restaurants but not a lot of organic produce. So Joe started to develop a standard Midwestern belly-bulge.

During his second year in Chester, he went to the Better Bodies Fitness Center and signed up for a session with a personal trainer.

Thomas was bronze, buffed, and cheery, with a severe military buzz-cut and the granite-chiseled jaw of a sports announcer. He graduated from Chester State with a degree in biology, washed out of medical school, and now was a semi-pro bodybuilder, with a few minor awards but not enough money or endorsements to quit his day job.

Gay or straight? Not enough evidence to determine, until he read from his chart, "So you want to lose weight, increase your muscle mass, get popular with the ladies."

Joe protested that he didn't want to get popular with the ladies, but Thomas was already heading toward an incline press machine.

Three sets of twelve reps later, he returned to the ladies: "You have pretty broad shoulders already, so you should concentrate on your pecs. Women go crazy over a nice chest."

Joe decided to go for a shock reveal: "So do I. But I go even crazier over six-pack abs. And biceps! He could be the poster boy for ugly and eat cats for breakfast, and I'm still asking him out to dinner and a movie.'"

But Thomas continued without comment or expression of surprise. "For the lateral raise, we'll start you at thirty pounds." He demonstrated, brick-wall chest against his back. Then he said: "If you like the toned, athletic type, you should come in on Tuesday nights. You can take your pick of the muscle babes."

Surely Thomas meant male "muscle babes"? At least, Joe pretended that was what he meant. "Great!" he exclaimed. "Are any of them gay?"

"No, no. I don't think so, anyway.." Thomas relieved him of the thirty-pound dumbbells. "Too light. Try forty. He never saw anybody hooking up, if that's what you mean. But if you run into a lesbian, just move on to the next. There's plenty of girls to go around."

He *still* thought Joe was straight! It was time to get blatant. "I only like men. Gay men, preferably."

Surprisingly, he laughed. "Like I said, plenty of girls to go around! Now let's work on your triceps."

Joe couldn't tell if he was being homophobic or not.

Even when he worked out on his own, the men on either side of him were murmuring "bzz bzz bzz girls bzz bzz bzz girls bzz bzz bzz girls" like background music. If he got closer, he heard snippets of:

"Lots of fine ladies here tonight!"

"Man, she was hot!"

"I wish he was single, he'd bag her in a minute!"

When the gym closed for Memorial Day, a big sign explained the straight motive: "We are closing to spend time with our families."

One day as Joe was plodding along on the treadmill at his middle-aged speed, the tall, lanky hunk on the treadmill to his left kept glancing over at him. Was he interested, Joe wondered, or just waiting to administer CPR when his heart gave out? They jogged in silence for awhile, and his glances became more bold, more openly appreciative. So Joe smiled and said hello.

He smiled in return. "She's pretty hot, huh?

She?

It seems that the whole time he had been glancing past Joe, at a lady jogging to his right.

The mistake was rather commonplace – how often has one returned a startlingly enthusiastic greeting from an acquaintance or stranger, only to discover that someone else is being addressed? Today, however, it reinforced his awareness that he was an interloper in Kansas, a stranger in the land – it had never occurred to Joe that he might be looking at the lady to his right, and it had never occurred to him that Joe might be looking at anyone else.

[1] Ambrose, Matthew, and Lisa Ladewski. *Caring for Gay, Lesbian, Bisexual, and Transgendered Patients: A Resource Guide.* Ann Arbor: University of Michigan Medical School, 2005.

[2] Graham, John R. *MMPI: Assessing Personality and Psychopathology.* Oxford: Oxford University Press, 2005.

[3] Allposters.com, http://www.allposters.com

[4] Calendars.com, http://www.calendars.com

[5] Gifts.com, http://www.gifts.com

[6] Amazon.com, http://www.amazon.com

[7] Ebay.com, http://www.ebay.com

Chapter Ten
Oscar Wilde's Wife

One bright, warm Wednesday in April of his junior year in college, shortly after he discovered that gay people exist, Joe was sitting in a classroom in East Hall, a rambling Victorian house on the edge of the campus. While a fat, balding, querulous hobbit named Dr. Lindstrom was leading a desultory discussion of *The Sun Also Rises*, he was gazing out the window onto the quad, at three boys tossing a Frisbee, and a fourth dozing on the grass with a paperback open on his lap.

A generation later he remember every detail of the day, perhaps because it started so idyllic, the stuff of catalog photographs, and so suddenly turned grim and threatening. Sometime near the end of the hour, thinking of the scene where Bill Gorton asks Jake Barnes to run away to South America with him, he raised his hand and asked if Ernest Hemingway might have had "homosexual tendencies."

One of the back-of-the-room jocks stifled a snicker. Otherwise the room became absolutely silent. Dr. Lindstrom stared at him, quite visibly frightened. Joe realized that he had made a mistake, speaking a word that must never be spoken, like the Deplorable Word in the Narnia books that can destroy the world. Far away, in the hall, he heard shuffling footsteps. He wished that he was in the hall, or out on the quad, tossing a Frisbee, safe.

Finally Dr. Lindstrom turned away, toward the window, as if he, too, wished to be out on the quad. "No, of course not," he said in a curiously detached tone. "No evidence of that whatsoever, whatsoever."

He turned back to the podium, closed his sheaf of notes, and began an impromptu lecture on William Faulkner. No questions about Hemingway appeared on our final exam. The Deplorable Word was never spoken in any of the other 1,600 class sessions Joe would sit through between freshman orientation and graduation.

Ten years later, after a few years away from academe, Joe was in graduate school in History, and the Deplorable Word was still never spoken. In over 500 class sessions in the bright California sun, he heard many lectures on gay people of the past – Michelangelo and Leonardo Da Vinci, – but never a word hinting that they were gay.

He did hear the word "homosexual" twice, in *Victorian Poetry*, by a tall, simpering, sneering woman with a Ph.D. from Brown. Ernest Dowson wrote *Vitae Summa Brevis* ("they are not long, the days of wine and roses") to illustrate "the emptiness of his homosexual lifestyle." And Gerard Manley Hopkins, author of *The Hound of Heaven*, "wasn't manly at all; he was a homosexual!" he dropped the class before we got to Oscar Wilde.

Ten years later, after still more years away from academe, Joe was in graduate school again, in Sociology, and the Deplorable Word was *still* never spoken. No gay people were mentioned in his classes in *Social Theory, Research Methods, Criminology, Sociology of the Family, Urban Sociology,* or *Social Movements,* unless he brought them up himself. *The Sociology of Deviance* did devote one of its weekly three-hour sessions to "homosexuality," but he skipped class that day, not interested in hearing how deviant he was.

When he began teaching his own classes, Joe tried to break the silence by speaking the Deplorable Word whenever possible.

There were gay Christians in *Sociology of Religion*.

There were gay parents in *Sociology of the Family*.

When the textbook said "husbands and wives," he said "husbands, wives, and same-sex partners."

When the textbook asked what we find attractive in "the opposite sex," he said "potential romantic partners."

In *Research Methods*, for a quick illustration of some statistical concept, he would begin with "John and his boyfriend" instead of the textbook's "John and his girlfriend."[1]

Joe's students sat through his presentation on gay Christians with only occasional gasps of surprise.

They asked respectful questions about gay parents.

But when Joe mentioned gay people casually, in anecdotes or illustrations, he was suddenly back in East Hall a generation ago, asking if Hemingway might have had "homosexual tendencies." A few back-of-the-room jocks snickered, and the rest of the class became deadly silent. The students stared, embarrassed, uncomfortable, not sure how to respond.

Thirty years after Stonewall, gay people were permissible in the classroom, as long as they appeared only in their own special, carefully contained units. They did not belong in everyday life, in discussions of linear regressions or secondary socialization; there, only husbands and wives should exist, and people named John must never have boyfriends. To suggest otherwise was hilarious to some and distressing the rest. Students complained on their course evaluations that "every lecture was about sex" and "He kept hitting you on the head with his sex life."

On a cold afternoon in November of his second year in Chester, Joe sat in his office at Chester State University, looking out at a quad covered with new snow, while group after group of dripping, boot-stamping students bustled in to talk about their projects in *Research Methods*. Four groups planned to study physical attraction or romantic relationships, and every one presumed that only straight attraction or romance exists.

A group of sorority sisters, one in a "Hello-kitty" vest, planned a survey of fifty high school girls, half from an exclusive private school, half from a public high school in a poor neighborhood. They hypothesized that girls from the upper class would "start to notice boys" at an earlier age than those from the working or lower class. "How will you make sure that your respondents are all straight?" he asked.

They stared, not comprehending.

"Only straight girls notice boys," he explained. "Gay girls notice girls."

They stared, still not comprehending.

"Ask them when they first experienced romantic desire," he said with a sigh.

A group led by a senior criminal justice major, who spent most class sessions grinning at him as if sharing a secret, yet expressed so many homophobic opinions that he was sure he couldn't be gay, planned to conduct an experiment about the influence of physical attraction on helping behavior. An attractive girl would walk across the campus, and whenever she saw a guy standing alone, she would "accidentally" drop her books. The next day, an unattractive girl would repeat the experiment. The group hypothesized that guys would be more likely to help someone they were attracted to.

"What if the guys are gay?" Joe asked.

The leader stared. Even though he was homophobic, it had never occurred to him, or to his classmates, that anyone might be gay here, in Chester, Ohio, in real life.

"Maybe we tell the girls to just pick, you know, masculine guys?" he suggested.

"Have both men and women drop the books," Joe said with a sigh.

A group led by a smart-alecky education major, who always seemed to expect an A just for showing up, hypothesized that we are culturally conditioned to find members of our own race more attractive than members of other races. They would ask fifty respondents to rate photographs of "members of the opposite sex," white, black, Asian, and mixed.

"What if some of your respondents are gay?" he asked.

The smart-alecky education major rolled her eyes, obviously thinking that he was an idiot. There wouldn't be any gay respondents! This wasn't San Francisco!

"Well. . . if any of them tell us they're gay, we'll just show them the other set of pictures."

"Show everyone both sets of pictures," he said with a sigh.

The fourth group, consisting of a girl in a wheelchair and a girl who often missed class because of her radiation therapy, hypothesized that athletic men have "stricter dating requirements" than non-athletic men. They were perfectly inclusive: none of their survey questions assumed that all men date women: "would you date someone who was significantly taller or shorter than you? Was too masculine or too feminine? Wore too much perfume or cologne?"

But when it came time for the oral presentation to the entire class, they forgot and talked constantly about whether the guys would date "a girl who was too tall" or a girl who "wore too much perfume."

Somehow, in between the proposal and the presentation, they had forgotten that gay people exist.

My Husband Can't Drive

Why was it so difficult to overcome student insistence that all the world was straight?

Their textbooks erased gay people, of course, but what about the lectures and discussions? Surely at least a few of the 1,600 class sessions between freshman orientation and graduation presented gay people as ordinary, expected, everyday, as present in the world. Or did they hear only silence, as pristine and unbroken as the silence at East Hall on that bright spring day a thousand years ago?

As part of his duties at Chester State University, Joe had to observe eight sociology classes taught by four different professors. Three were straight (they kept photographs of husbands or wives on their desks, brought them to office parties, and used the term "we" in casual conversation). One did none of those things, so he assumes she was gay.

He was astonished by how often the straight professors freely, easily, casually evoked their romantic partners in class: "My husband never asks for directions"; "My wife lived in Baltimore when she was growing up"; "Last summer his wife and he went to Ireland." "This weekend his husband and he. . . .."

Sometimes the evocations were related to the class materials, but usually they were thrown in at random, evidently as attempts to bond with the thirty young adults who all, they believed, would someday be straight husbands or wives.

But in the classes taught by the lesbian professor, he heard nothing. She evoked a rock-climbing vacation and a visit to the movies with no companions, just the pronoun "I," and gave the distinct impression that she shared her Victorian house in Yellow Springs with no one at all. No doubt the students never realized that she was gay.

More surprising was the shuddering refusal to speak the Deplorable Word. In every class session, regardless of whether the professors were gay or straight, they invariably discussed "husbands and wives," excluding same-sex partners, and invariably gave John a "girlfriend." Again and again they presented straight experience as universal human experience. Again and again they behaved as if there were no gay people in that classroom, on the Chester State campus, or anywhere in the world.

Guys, Ask Your Girlfriends

Was sociology uniquely homophobic as a discipline, or was the Deplorable Word left unspoken in all of the thousands of classes that met at Chester State, in the Engineering Building and the Creative Arts Center and the Business School and the Honors College?

To find out, Joe explained the concept of erasure to his *Sociology of Sexuality* students and sent them out in the field to gather examples from their other classes. Many returned with blank notebooks, unable to see erasure even when they were specifically looking for it. Some confused erasure with homophobia, and returned with big, blatant, scabrous examples that he hoped were fictional. But many returned with their notebooks full.

An Education professor tells the class, "Children's toys are very gender-specific: boys get cars, girls get dolls. Why shouldn't boys get dolls, too? After all, those boys are going to be daddies someday, and they need to practice changing diapers just as much as their future wives do." Is every boy on Earth really going to someday engage in straight intercourse and become a father? Of course – every boy on Earth is straight.

One would expect little discussion of gay or straight people in *Introduction to Chemistry*; ions and isotopes have no sexual orientation. But still, the professor manages to evoke universal straight desire: "Are you prepared for a little pop quiz today? I realize the *Sports Illustrated* swimsuit issue just came out, so the guys have other things on their minds."

A Freshman Composition professor assigns a brief essay: "Imagine your life ten years from today. Describe your future job and where you want to live. Describe your future husband or wife." The professor is unaware that some students imagine futures with same-sex partners.

In a History class, the students are watching a movie about the counterculture of the 1960s, when a muscular, shirtless man appears on the screen. Eager for any opportunity to erase gay people, even the most tenuous, the professor smirks: "There's a little something for you ladies to look at."

When a female student arrives in her Biology class with her arm in a sling, the professor is sympathetic: "Can you get your boyfriend to take notes for you? In another class, the professor jokes, "Next time your boyfriend wants the tv remote, just give it to him."

A Criminal Justice professor lectures on a serial killer: "He couldn't manage to get it together. He dropped out of two colleges, got fired from a succession of jobs, and never had a sexual relationship with a woman. You know that's just violence waiting to happen."

This sounds like homophobia, but the professor probably would not suggest that all gay men are serial killers. It is a lack of sexual relations in general, not a lack of straight relations, that drives men to hockey masks and chainsaws. He specifies "with a woman" only because he is unaware that gay men exist.

Ironically, it was in the units about gay people that professors were most insistent that everyone here, now, is straight.

In *College Survival Skills*, the professor introduces the unit by insisting that there are no gay students here: "We usually stereotype gays as effeminate queens, but in fact, you can't tell by the way they look or act. There might even be a gay person in this classroom, and we would never know." He twice assumes that everyone on earth is straight, and then concedes that there might be a gay person in this classroom, but it would be an outlandish, extraordinary event rather than part of everyday experience, and it would be secret – the rest of "us" would never know.

In *Cultural Diversity* for Education majors, the professor introduces a panel from the Gay-Straight Alliance: "I realize that the subject of homosexuality makes you uncomfortable, but it's an important part of your education to be exposed to different opinions and lifestyles." Even while attempting to be inclusive, the professor is absolutely certain that everyone in the class is both straight and homophobic.

Everyday life at most high schools and many colleges is infused by heterosexist contempt or homophobic hatred, where a culture of adolescence determines prestige solely through straight practice, where athletes motivate each other with taunts of "fag," where "gay" is an all-purpose term for anything bad, silly, or inept.[2] But most research, written by professional academics, exonerates the academics them-

selves, framing the students, or sometimes the campus police, librarians, teaching assistants, or resident hall monitors,
as homophobes who need to be enlightened.

Two important collections of essays, *School Experiences
of Gay and Lesbian Youth: The Invisible Minority* and *Addressing Heterosexism and Homophobia on College Campuses*, never
mention the possibility that teachers or professors might
themselves be homophobic.[3] Many, perhaps most, are not.
But as they sit in their offices planning lectures, or in the daily give-and-take of a classroom discussion, they usually forget that gay people exist. And many of their students never
find out.

Strategies of Mate Selection

Nearly every college student takes a course in psychology; nearly a third of the students in liberal arts colleges
major in it. Since the American Psychiatric Association removed "homosexuality" from its list of mental disorders in
1973, before most professors teaching psychology today had
even graduated from high school, one finds little homophobia in psychology class. Instead, one finds that gay people
do not exist.

David G. Meyers makes his erasure plain in the first
sentence of his introductory textbook, *Psychology*, when he
goes into detail about his "wife."

Later in the book, he devotes five pages to what causes the disease of "homosexuality."

Outside of those five pages, everyone in the textbook
is straight. In the chapter on "Childhood and Adolescence,"
Meyers repeats the old chestnut about puberty initiating a
sudden, luxurious, hormone-drenched hetero-mania. In the
chapter on "Mate Selection," he discusses why we (all
people who have ever lived) are attracted to certain traits "in

the opposite sex." He covers romantic relationships, falling in love and breaking up, without mentioning even once that it is possible to fall in love or break up with someone of the same sex. When he doesn't have to think of gay people as victims of a mental illness, he pretends they do not exist.[4]

Psychology professors and advanced students spend most of their time designing experiments, and soliciting research subjects for them. Several online websites allow them to reach a wide range of potential subjects for studies of perception, attitudes, memory, and every other imaginable topic.[5] Sexual orientation is irrelevant to some studies, such as *Optimism in College Students* (Miami University) or *Creativity and Thinking Styles* (California State University, San Bernardino), but many involve physical attraction, romance, and interpersonal relationships, and would make little sense if the answers of gay people were counted as straight, or vice versa.

Still, when Joe became a "subject" of twenty such experiments, only about 50% asked his sexual orientation, and less than 25% included same-sex partners among the examples ("Jen and Karen have been dating for two years"). The rest assumed explicitly that physical attraction only occurs between male and female, that every date, every romance, every sexual encounter necessarily involves "the man" and "the woman."

Personality and Relationships (Towson University) asked, "Have you ever been concerned about your ability to attract members of the opposite sex?" he answered: "No." Towson University is near Oz, yet still the graduate students there have no idea that gay people exist.

Relationship Attitudes (Rutgers University) asked Joe to agree or disagree with the statement, "I am attractive to the opposite sex." He tried to answer "Why, precisely, should he care?", but the only two choices available were "agree" or "disagree."

Human Mate Choice Experiment (University of Edinburgh) wanted to see if "vocabulary influences mate selection in humans." First it asked his gender. He stated "male." Then he read various scenarios in which he met women, and asked how likely he would be to ask her out on a date.

Signs of Love or Lust (California State University, San Bernardino) asked if he was likely to date people based on photographs rather than written scenarios. But still, after he stated that he was male, he was shown photographs only of women. This was a student experiment, but wouldn't the supervising professor ask "What if some of the respondents are gay?" Evidently not.

Women's Perceptions of Romantic Partners (University of Southern California) sounded inclusive, so Joe pretended that he was a lesbian and signed up. However, his sexual orientation was not asked, and the possible choices of his "romantic partner" were all male: was he interested in "a guy with broad shoulders," "a guy with big muscles," "a tough guy," or a "bad boy"? The graduate students who developed the experiment are studying at USC, about six miles from Oz, yet still they refused to believe that lesbians exist.

The German Word for "Kiss"

In junior high, Joe was given the choice of two foreign languages, Spanish and French. But there was really no choice: 90% of the students in French class were girls, since any boy who dared to attempt a conjugation of "aimer. . .to love" was likely to be beat up for talking like a "fag." Joe chose Spanish. But in college, he became a foreign language nut: he took enough French and Spanish to make myself understood in Paris or Madrid, plus German, Latin, and a bit of

Greek and Russian. As an adult he tried (successfully or not) to learn Italian, Norwegian, Portuguese, Icelandic, Mandarin Chinese, and Japanese. That means sweating through twelve or so introductory language textbooks.

Most are organized like a story, with ongoing characters and a simple plot to add interest to the dry grammatical rules, and "like all stories," it is about straight romance:

> Antonio e un ragazzo italiano. Christina e una ragazza americana. Antonio e Christina sono amici. . .

> Marc est francais. Julie est américaine. Ils sont amis.[6]

Typically, an American college boy visits Madrid, Paris, Munich, or Moscow, goes to a café, and tries to pick up a local girl. In the first dialogue, he asks "What is your name?"

In the second, he states, "Your country is beautiful."

Soon we learn where each is studying, and how many brothers and sisters each has. They begin to date.

The American boy learns to tell the time so he won't be late for the cinema, learns the names of food so he can order in the restaurant, gets an overview of national history as they tour the museums, and eventually, when the girl gives him a book of her favorite poems, reads the national literature in the original language.

If you stick with your language studies through Chapter 20, you will learn the Spanish, French, German, or Russian word for "kiss." The semester always ended before we got to Chapter 30, but no doubt it featured the words for "green card" and "wedding," as the college boy plans a new life with the girl of his dreams.

Why does language study so often require a celebration of straight romance? Why couldn't the American boy tour Paris or Moscow with a local boy, or an American girl tour with a local girl? They wouldn't even need to date; just showing same-sex bonds of any sort exist would be a welcome change from endless boy-girl romance.

Maybe the authors feel that straight romance is of universal interest, even to gay people. Or maybe they believe that the target audience consists entirely of heterosexual youth, who are obsessed with dating and mate selection.

For this reason, they invariably exclude the word for "gay" from vocabulary lists, and the reading selections of national literature may include García Lorca, Thomas Mann, and Paul Verlaine, but refuse to admit that they were gay.

Tuttle, the Asian book publisher, has gone even farther, with a series of books entitled *Making Out*: *Making out in Chinese, Making out in Japanese,* and so on through Korean, Thai, Vietnamese, Indonesian, and Arabic.

Most volumes have a male symbol in blue facing a female symbol in pink, so you know that the intended audience is straight.

The instructions tell you what to say "When you see someone you would like to meet, who is not accompanied by a member of the opposite sex." Theoretically the object of interest could be of the same sex, but the line drawings of men and women together leave little uncertainty that only male-female pairings are intended.

The chapter on "The Language of Love" never suggests that anyone ever speaks the language of love to someone of the same sex. And, of course, none of the books teach the local word for "gay." They expect that anyone who wants to "make out" in a foreign language must necessarily wish opposite-sex making out.

Gather the Faces of Women

Many, perhaps most of the readings assigned to Joe as an undergraduate literature major jubilantly proclaimed the absence of gay people from the world. He remembered three in particular with anger and fear.

Carl Sandburg tells him to "gather the faces of women," but later "Loosen your hands, let go and say goodbye." Women's faces but not men's faces must be collected like songs.

In a John Updike story, a teenage boy working at a small-town A&P reminisces: "In walks these three girls in nothing but bathing suits." He goes on to describe their legs in exacting detail, as if girls in bathing suits but not boys in bathing suits require description.

Alan Dugan is at a party, when the secret police come to take him away. "I take one last drink," he writes, "A last puff on a cigarette, a last kiss at a girl. . . ."[7] The last kiss must always be with a girl.

Why did the professor select these three authors? Because there is only the briefest of glimpses, or no glimpse at all, of the possibility of same-sex love anywhere in their works.

Carl Sandburg, who wrote copied Whitman's free-form style but not his "manly love of comrades"; his is a world of "slender supple girls with shapely legs," of "luck and love, women worth dying for."

When he writes of men, he writes of the Shovel-Man, dreamed of by "a dark-eyed woman in the old country," or Jack, who "married a tough woman and they had eight children," or a Polish boy, "out with his best girl" on a Saturday night. Men only and always long for women.[8]

John Updike, the darling of the angst-ridden suburban 1960s, writes endlessly about men noticing women, kissing women, and marrying women. Men exist only as conduits of straight desire: "We are all Solomons lusting for Sheba's salvation," says the narrator of "Lifeguard," characterizing every man who ever lived as searching for women.

"In a Bar in Charlotte Amalie" does feature a drag queen, but he is a pathetic, lonely outcast, with no desire for women and therefore no reason for living.[9]

Alan Dugan was "the poet of masturbation," endlessly describing his straight desires and exploits, with no mention of men except for barroom cronies. His "Night Song for a Boy" is not about a boy, but about his depression over his failure to get enough women.

In old age, Dugan has a homoerotic dream about a deceased friend, but in perhaps the most homophobic line in any poem since Catullus, he is horrified at the thought that his dream self might be "an impotent homosexual necrophiliac," and longs for the "right" sort of dreams, dreams about women, again.[10]

Every selection on the syllabus of that long-ago class came from an author who obsessed over a mystifying, alien sort of passion and erased nearly every trace of same-sex love from the world. When they are forced to describe men, their descriptions are bare and lifeless, as if too trivial to mention amid the endless paragraphs devoted to girls' legs. There were many famous gay writers in mid-20th century America to choose from: Truman Capote, John Cheever, Robert Duncan, Thom Gunn, Allen Ginsburg, Carson McCullers, Tennessee Williams, Gore Vidal. But one of them might have been forced to speak the Deplorable Word.

Joe found courses in Gay Literature taught at dozens of colleges, from Stanford to Frostburg State University in Maryland to Foothill Community College in Los Altos Hills, California, and gay people occasionally mentioned in other literature courses.

Contemporary Literary Theory at Lawrence University devotes a week to "gay, lesbian, and queer theory."

The Literature of the American 1950s at the University of Pennsylvania refers to Tennessee Williams as gay.

But in most courses, especially those for non-majors, gay authors were presented as straight or omitted altogether, and even stories of same-sex friendship were censored, lest anyone suggest that the author might have "homosexual tendencies."

Introduction to Modern Fiction at California State University, Pomona, assigns "A&P," the same John Updike story that he read as an undergraduate, but no stories with gay characters or same-sex friendships.

Introduction to American Literature at George Washington University includes two authors who were gay, Herman Melville and Emily Dickensen, but assigns none of their works that allude even vaguely to same-sex desire.

Introduction to American Literature at the University of Akron aggressively "breaks the canon," assigning the Iroquois Creation Story and a book about Sojourner Truth. But again, the only gay authors are Herman Melville and Emily Dickensen, and again the assigned readings omit any references to same-sex love.

Most survey courses depend on the venerable *Norton Anthology of English Literature*. There have been many changes since Joe bought his copy, with many women and people of color added, and a few dead white men dropped. The latest edition comes in three volumes instead of two.

However, the number of gay or bisexual authors included has remained constant for thirty years. There are seven: William Shakespeare, Lord Byron, Algernon Swinburne, Oscar Wilde, A. E. Housman, Virginia Woolf, and W. H. Auden. They are not identified as gay or bisexual in their author biographies, though marriages and sundry affairs form the basis for the straight authors' biographies. Even English majors may graduate with an unwavering certainty that Walt Whitman was straight, that all men gather the faces of women, that same-sex desire does not exist.

Ritualized Homosexuality

For nearly two centuries, anthropologists have scoured the globe, investigating the tiniest of backwoods tribes, observing, interviewing, taking notes, and then returning to their university departments to publish papers. They write about every aspect of a culture, from food production to religious practices, from tribal government to games and recreation, but when it comes to teaching their classes, they can't teach what they don't believe exists.

Sometimes anthropologists observe two men or two women of the culture who seem quite taken with each other, so they have no choice but to record the affection. But they are quick to insist that such behavior does not signify "homosexuality."

Men among the nomads of Mali walk around holding hands? A sign of friendship, not gay.

Men in Fiji lie on hammocks casually fondle each other's testicles? A sign of friendship, not gay.

Men in the highlands of New Guinea flirt and preen for each other, discuss potential partners with their friends, and finally take "the one" home to meet the folks? They're like brothers, not gay.

Men in ancient Mesopotamia spent their lives together, lived in the same hut, referred to each other as "his beloved," and never sought out female partners? Adult adoption, not gay.

Women in Zimbabwe give each other flowers, write each other love poems, and become enraged when their partner flirts with someone else? Practice for heterosexual romance, not gay.

Women in northern Nigeria marry each other? Economic transaction, not gay.

Well, what counts as gay? There has to be *sex*, say the anthropologists. Intimate contact (other than that testicle fondling), arousal, penetration, and orgasm.

Since most people do not engage in such activities in full view of anthropologists taking notes, there is rarely any proof of intimate contact between same-sex partners. An anthropologist who used the same criteria in West Hollywood would have to conclude that "Homosexuality does not exist in this culture," simply because men wait until they get home rather than penetrating each other on the sidewalk outside the Café Etoile.

Sometimes anthropologists go as far as to ask a native informant, "Does it ever happen that two men have sex with each other, or two women have sex with each other?"

"No, that never happens," the informant says.

"No homosexuality in this culture," the anthropologist dutifully records.

Try asking that question of any blue-haired Baptist lady in Tupelo, Mississippi, and see what answer you get.

Sometimes the men of the culture (rarely the women) do have same-sex arousals and orgasms right out in public for everybody to see, or else informants mention them. Then anthropologists have no choice but to record the existence of same-sex erotic behavior in the culture. Still, they find all sorts of ingenious ways to explain that the behavior is about something other than "homosexuality." The men are not really into each other at all.

In aboriginal Australia, older men seek out younger men for sex? It's a civic ritual, an introduction to the rights and responsibilities of citizenship, not gay.

In Mexico, masculine men seek out feminine men for sex? It's a heterosexual bond, sex irrelevant as long as the gender roles are complementary, not gay.

In Oman on the Arabian Peninsula, men pay for sex with male prostitutes? It's an economic transaction, not gay.

So if same-sex romance doesn't count as gay, and same-sex orgasm doesn't count as gay, what does?

Nothing. Anthropologists cannot believe that gay people exist, so like his straight friends, they are incapable of seeing anyone gay. They see people of the same sex seeking each other out, falling in love, having sex, and spending their lives together, yet they still manage to conclude that "There is no homosexuality in this culture." Students will therefore graduate with degrees in anthropology, or with a single anthropology course, and believe that gay people exist, if at all, only in the decadent West.

Pretty Girls in Physics Class

Molecules and subatomic particles have no gender, no sexual orientation, so the Physics Building should be free from heteronormativity. But it is not. Here is how Albert Einstein explains the theory of relativity:

> When a man sits with a pretty girl for an hour,
> it seems like a minute. But let him sit on a hot stove
> for a minute and it's longer than any hour.[11]

Einstein, who died fourteen years before Stonewall, probably had no idea that every man does not care to sit with pretty girls, or with girls of any sort. But physics teachers in Kansas have been repeating his quip to classrooms full of gay and straight students ever since.

Animals Shy Away

Not only are there no gay people – there are no gay animals.

Same-sex behavior has been documented in hundreds of animal species. Everyone can see non-neutered male dogs trying to mount anything, without regard to its gender or species; if even pants legs are not safe, why would they "shy away" from other male dogs? When non-spayed female cats are in heat, they will present themselves to any other cat, dog, or human, not "shying away" from anything. Some animals have distinctive preferences for same-sex behavior, and some select life-long same-sex mates. Some species have never been observed engaging in straight copulation.[12]

However, you will never hear this information in Kansas, no matter if you take *Introduction to Biology, Zoology, Ecology,* or *Animal Behavior:* there the professor, textbook, and other students will depict only male and female animals incessantly seeking each other out.

Straights eagerly search for evidence that straight desire is instinctive, universal across all species, and while same-sex desire, if it exists at all, is limited to a handful of humans.

The popular textbook *Zoology,* by Stephen A Miller and John P. Harley,[13] is loaded down with male and female snails, minnows, elephants, and opossums trying to attract each other, having sex with each other, settling down, and raising families, with not a word to suggest that any animal has ever engaged in same-sex behavior.

At Lewis and Clark College in Oregon, the professor teaching *Animal Behavior* helpfully put all of his lecture notes online. Two class sessions are devoted to "Mating Systems," or "collective behavioral and morphological traits associated with interactions between the sexes for the purposes of sexual reproduction." He mentions several types of mating systems, including monogamy, polygyny (one male with several females), polyandry (one female with several males), and promiscuity (both sexes have multiple opposite-sex partners), but no same-sex partners.

The lecture on "Human Mating Systems" pretends that even among humans, sex only ever occurs between males and females.[14]

But the absence of references to same-sex practice in biology class cannot explain the hysterical fervor with which residents of Kansas proclaim that every animal on Earth is straight.

In Joe's own *Sociology of Sexuality* class at Chester State, a dozen students wrote on their midterm exams that same-sex activity occurs only among humans. Five used the precise phrase "animals shy away from that sort of thing," though they were sitting in different parts of the room and could not have been copying from each other. He had devoted an entire lecture talking about the hundreds of animal species where same-sex activity is common.

No student will deliberately contradict a lecture on a written exam. In *Popular Culture* class, a student once listened to Joe state that after World War II, the studio system went into decline, and actors were no longer hired for long-term contracts. But he heard only "no longer hired," and wrote on his exam, "There have been no movies with actors in them since World War II."

When Joe questioned him, the student agreed that the statement was completely ludicrous; he agreed that he had seen many movies with actors in them, and that no fictional movie could be made without actors. But he wrote it anyway, because he thought Joe had said it. He had no interest in logic or common sense, or in his real life experiences; he wanted a good grade.

If Joe told the class "There were no men in the world before 1958, when they first were cloned in a lab in Fresno, California," most students would record the statement in their notebooks with no protest or question. They might laugh at the absurdity, in private, but on the test they would certainly write about the first men who ever existed being cloned in a lab in Fresno, California.

So why was his lecture on same-sex practice among animals different? Even if the students thought the information ridiculous, even if they knew, with absolute certainty, that all animals were straight, why didn't their interest in getting a good grade discourage them from writing "animals shy away."

Perhaps they never heard about same-sex practice among animals at all; they zoned out, like the fundamentalist students during the presentation on gay Christians. Or perhaps believing that "animals shy away" was much more important, more important than anything. They might be ok with the existence of gay Christians, or gay parents, or gay people existing in places other than bars, but there *must not* be gay animals. To state otherwise, even on a test, would be giving up something vital about their straight identity, something immeasurably precious. Something they were willing to fight for.

[1] Not "Barbara and her girlfriend" because the term "girlfriend" could mean a non-romantic friend as well as a romantic partner.

[2] Elia, J. P. "Homophobia in the High School: A Problem in Need of a Resolution." *The High School Journal* 77 (1994): 177-185; Kielwasser, A. P., & Wolf, M.A. "Silence, Difference, and Annihilation: Understanding the Impact of Mediated Heterosexism on High School Students." *The High School Journal* 77 (1994): 58-79; Martino, Wayne. "Policing Masculinity: Investigating the Role of Homophobia and Heteronormativity in the Lives of Adolescent School Boys." *Journal of Men's Studies* 8.2 (2000): 213-236; Lance, Larry M. "Heterosexism and Homophobia among College Students." *College Student Journal* 36.3 (2002): 410-414.

[3] Cramer, Elizabeth P., ed. *Addressing Homophobia and Heterosexism on College Campuses.* Binghamton, New York: Harrington Park Press, 2003. Harris, Mary B. *School Experiences of Gay and Lesbian Youth: The Invisible Minority.* Binghamton, New York: Harrington Park Press, 1998.

[4] Meyers, David G. *Psychology.* 7th edition. Houston: Worth Publishers, 2004.

[5] Social Psychology Experiments in the Web, http://www.socialpsychology.org/expts.htm#pinterpersonal; Online Psychology Experiments, http://psych. hanover.edu/research/exponnet.html

[6] Sagesse, Riccardo. *Easy Italian Reader.* McGraw-Hill, 2005. De Sales, R. de Roussy. *Easy French Reader.* McGraw-Hill, 2004.

[7] Sandburg, Carl. "Chicago," "Songs, Stars, Faces." *The Complete Poems of Carl Sandburg.* New York: 11, 207 Harcourt, 2003; Dugan, Alan. "Tribute to Kafka for Someone Taken." *Poems Seven: New and Complete Poems.* New York: Seven Sto-

ries Press, 2001: 45. Updike, John. "A&P." *The Early Stories, 1953-1975*. New York: Ballantine Books, 2004: 596-601.

[8] Sandburg, Carl. "Poems Done on a Late Night Car," "The Red Son," "Dream Girl," "The Shovel-Man," "Jack," "Back Yard." Ibid: 61, 74, 68, 9, 22, 53.

[9] Updike, John. "Lifeguard," "In a Bar at Charlotte Amalie." Ibid: 602-607, 269-283.

[10] Dugan, Alan. "Night Song for a Boy," "In Memoriam: Donald Mark Fall." Ibid: 172, 393.

[11] Calaprice, Alice, ed. *The New Quotable Einstein.* Princeton: Princeton University Press, 2005.

[12] Bagemihl, Bruce. *Biological Exuberance: Animal Homosexuality and Natural Diversity*. New York St. Martin's Press, 2000.

[13] Miller, Stephen A., & John P. Harley, *Zoology*. New York: McGraw Hill, 2004.

[14]Animal Behavior Syllabus, http://www.lclark.edu/%7Eclifton/behav/home.htm

Chapter Eleven
She Hates a Gut!

During the summer of his first year in Ohio, Joe was rendered speechless by a passage in *TV Guide* about summer television for teenagers:

> The guys of Fridays may be the best time teens and tweens can have without breaking curfew. For laughs, there's a 12-episode marathon of *Hannah Montana*, with Jason Earle. . . Sporty sorts can crush on Ross Thomas's surf hunk Bailey on *Beyond the Break*. . . and for anyone into enigmatic oddballs with killer eyes and zero bellybuttons, you can't do much better than Matt Dallas of ABC Family's impressive *Kyle XY*. [1]

He read the passage two, three, four times, but no, there was not a hint of erasure. Every other magazine article that he read in Kansas went to great lengths to pretend that all men were interested in female actors, and all women in male actors, that all teen boys "crush" only on girls and all teen girls only on boys, that there was no such thing as same-sex desire.

But here, for perhaps the first time in the history of journalism, a writer was admitting that "sporty sorts," not just girls, could crush on a surf hunk, and "anyone," not just girls, could be into enigmatic oddballs with killer eyes.

Joe had already investigated the erasure of gay people from books, movies, music, and television, but he planned to skip magazines and newspapers, even though a half dozen appeared in his mailbox every month. They were supremely trivial, to be glanced over briefly, used to pass the time on the subway or at the doctor's office, and then discarded. Movies that premiered seventy years ago still appear on television, novels written two centuries ago could still make World's Greatest lists, but magazines and newspapers from just a few months old were of interest only to historians looking for glimpses into the past.

However, novels, movies, television programs, and popular songs are *stories*.. They can be resisted. However loudly they proclaim that every journey ends with a man and a woman falling into each other's arms, there are always subtexts that producers didn't notice or forgot to suppress.

Magazines and newspapers, on the other hand, supposedly contain journalism, cold, hard, objective fact, not an artist's interpretation of experience but experience itself, not story but "information." Therefore, a half-hour spent glancing through a magazine or a newspaper can have a more profound impact on how we perceive the world than six hours spent watching television or reading a novel. When *Time, Newsweek, Entertainment Weekly,* or *TV Guide* tells us that all desire is heterosexual desire, all romance heterosexual romance, that no gay people exist, we find it harder to resist, harder to realize that they are lying.

Every Man's Fantasy

Joe's first stop was a pile of old *TV Guides* that had been accumulating for a year as they awaited the recycling bin. *TV Guide* had one of the highest circulations of any magazine in United States, with 3.2 million copies sold every week. Aside from the television listings, there were interviews with stars, articles about specific programs, reviews, and fan letters, and, in nearly every issue, Every Man's Fantasy.

Erica Durence plays a young Lois Lane in *Smallville*, about the adventures of a teenage Clark Kent (soon to be Superman). She is so hot that she "can make any guy a Man of Steel." Do all men, gay and straight, really become steel-like upon viewing Ms. Durence?

Venerable Sophia Loren, whose bosoms made her a sex symbol in the 1960s, is told that "You affect guys like an aphrodisiac." She still has it, but only guys notice. Every guy, gay or straight, becomes steel-like in her presence, while girls feel nothing but jealousy.

Olivia Munn, host of *Attack of the Show!*, has "model good looks." Therefore she is "mobbed by her male fans." Why does reporter Joseph Hudak take the time to specify "male fans"? It would be easier, and take fewer words to just say "fans." But that would imply that some, or a few of the individuals attracted to Ms. Munn's good looks are female. And of course, none of them are. Not one.

Even more common is Every Woman's Fantasy.

Patrick Dempsey of *Grey's Anatomy* is so cute that "young female fans can't get enough of him" – no young male fans.

Eric Mabius may be winning accolades as the metrosexual editor of a fashion magazine on *Ugly Betty*, but "discerning women have been swooning over him since he made his feature-film debut" – no discerning men.

David James Elliott, hunky star of *Close to Home*, doesn't disrobe often, to the dismay of his "largely female audience" – obviously the male portion is perfectly satisfied![2]

Curtis Stone, star of *Take Home Chef*, "has attracted plenty of female viewers. . .it's no wonder women seem to get flustered around him" – no flustered men.[3]

When statements failed to limit the celebrity's appeal to a specific gender, they seemed accidental, as if the writer left the "female" off "female fans" or the "male" off "male fans" because it was too obvious to include.

Damien Holbrook wrote the crack about Erica Durence arousing "any guy," but also said that ever since Connor Trinneer of *Star Trek: Enterprise* started taking his shirt off, "oodles of Trekkers have been dreaming of boarding more than just the Enterprise."

When John Stamos, former *Full House* heartthrob, joins the cast of the medical series *ER*, he is displayed naked in every episode, thus "soaking up new viewers for the show," not "new *female* viewers." But the apparent inclusivity is buried amid endless speculation about what ladies on the show the hunky doctor might be hooking up with, not to mention four photos of male-female characters being in love.[4]

Entertainment Weekly, devoted to trends in every type of popular culture, from movies and television to books and Broadway, was less consistent. Some issues were perfectly inclusive, but others evoked Every Man's Fantasy or Every Woman's Fantasy a dozen times.

When Tom Hanks sported a new, longer hairstyle in *The Da Vinci Code*, "Women really, really dug it" – no men, of course, even though Tom Hanks himself played a gay man in *Philadelphia*.

A new medical series stars Stanley Tucci, a balding bear who makes "women swoon" and "men glower" – no man ever swoons, and no woman ever glowers!

There were many other assertions of the universality of straight desire. The movie *Blood Diamond* gives Jennifer Connelly the line "Not every American girl wants a storybook wedding." Reviewer Owen Gleiberman responds, "Really, how many American girls *don't* want a storybook wedding?" Obviously he is not aware that some American girls are lesbians, and do not dream about walking down the aisle into the arms of Prince Charming.

At the Country Music Awards, most men dress in casual shirts and jeans, "because a gentleman never overshadows his lady." Fashionista Adam Markovitz concurs: "In fashion, no girl wants to be upstaged by her guy." Every girl has a guy, every gentleman has a lady, no gay men or lesbians exist.

People was the worst offender, screaming again and again, in every issue, that celebrities could only possibly draw fans of the "opposite sex." When the editors decided on their annual list of the "Sexiest Men Alive," [5] they asked every candidate "Are you married?" and if he was not, "What do you look for in a woman?" They "knew," somehow, that every candidate's fans were exclusively female; readers were informed of what "women" like best about sexy speed demon Helio Castroneves, why "women" are drawn to sexy adventurer Josh Bernstein, and how "women" dig funny guys like sexy nerd Rainn Wilson.

The editors did realize that men might be reading the article, but obviously not to look at the sexy men; they wanted to learn how to become sexier themselves. Therefore, sexy CEO Tom Ford offers them such advice as "Be polite. Stand up when a woman comes to the table."

Bachelors are men who are available for romantic interaction, so surely some of "Summer's Hottest Bachelors" were gay. Yet *People* asked each candidate "What kind of women do you like?", "Where do you meet women?", and "What's your ideal date with a woman?" with the hetero-normative urgency of *Tiger Beat*.

The #1 Hottest Bachelor, Mario Lopez, was asked if he "minds" being a heartthrob to gay men (he's fine with it), so whoever interviewed him was aware that gay men exist. The other interviewers were absolutely unaware. Brett Michaels "rocks the hearts of ladies young and cougar," but rocks no man's heart. Gerard Butler "first made the ladies swoon in *300*," but has never made a man swoon. "The ladies," but not the men, "are crazy for David Cook!"

She Hates a Gut!

Some so-called men's magazines are devoted to photographs of naked women (*Playboy, Penthouse*), and obviously appeal only to straight men (and perhaps lesbians, but they tend to reject the sexist portrayal of women as playthings). But others are devoted to fitness (*Men's Fitness, Men's Health*) or fashion (*GQ, Esquire*), topics of interest to men of any sexual orientation.

Still, every cover, every article that Joe analyzed assumed that all men are straight, and read magazines to either look at women or learn how to attract women.

Men's Fitness offers some ab-crunch exercises, because "She Hates a Gut!" and "She Wants You Ripped!" – no man seeks fitness for his health, or to attract men.

Maxim advertises a "Monster NFL Blowout!" with profiles of "The hardest hitters! And the cheerleaders!"

Esquire abandons all pretense that it is about anything but straight display, and advertises "The Sexiest Woman Alive!"

In case you have any doubt that to be a man is to be obsessed with straight desire or practice, the editors carefully omit any mention of gay people. In a full year of *Men's Fitness,* the word "gay" appeared exactly twice, both times when celebrities happened to mention gay people during interviews, and the reporters couldn't shush them fast enough.

It appeared amid the endless straight ruminations of *Esquire* only once, when the "Answer Fella" fielded the question "Is there a gay accent?" (Yes, there is, he answered, mimicry of female intonation).[6]

It appeared in *Maxim* three times, in the form of homophobic jibes, as in an article about movies with pairs of male friends whose intimacy "makes you squirm" because it almost makes them seem gay.

Magazines marketed to "women" were just as likely to be convinced that only straight women exist. Since women were not particularly interested in looking at men, they obviously bought magazines for only one reason: to learn how to attract men.

Cosmopolitan offers "40 Girlie Moves that Make Guys Melt!", certain that every girl *wants* to make guys melt, and every guy *will* melt if approached with the proper girlie movie.

Seventeen offers tips on how to "Make Him Want to be Your Boyfriend!", as if no girl ever wanted a girl, and no boy ever declined to be wanted by a girl.

Redbook, for more mature women, tells readers about "What Men Really Want at 25, 35, 45." What they want occurs in the bedroom, and it is entirely straight -- there are no gay 25, 35, or 45 year olds.

In a year of issues, the words "gay" or "lesbian" did not appear at all in *Seventeen* (perhaps the audience of high schoolers was deemed too innocent to hear about such "sordid" matters).

The word "gay" appeared twice in *Cosmopolitan*, not in articles but in letters sent in by anxious readers to Amy Levine, the "Carnal Counselor" advice columnist. When a woman wonders if her boyfriend is gay, Levine responds that he can't be, he's just sensitive (no such thing as a gay man). When a woman wonders, "Am he gay if he have erotic thoughts about women?", Levine answers with an unequivocal "no!" Lots of women fantasize about other women; it doesn't mean that you are gay. Apparently *nothing* means that you are gay.

In *Redbook,* a woman wrote into the reader-response column, "Sex and the Single Mom," that she met a man on the internet, but when they got together for dinner, he turned out to be "gay, gay, gay!"

Readers advised that he probably wasn't gay, just clumsy and socially inept, though one suggested that he might be a pedophile in search of children to molest.

Later in the year, real gay people appeared, in a serious article that asked if gay youth are at higher risk for suicide than straight youth. It answered that we don't know: "sexual orientation is a personal characteristic that people can, and often do choose to hide, so. . .it is difficult to know for certain."

Joe did know for certain – gay youth are much more likely to attempt and commit suicide – but the author was careful to minimize the impact of external homophobia, and to trivialize sexual orientation, making it a "personal characteristic" like hair color. At least she was aware that gay people exist.[7]

The most interesting erasure occurred in the erotic magazine *Playgirl*, which announced that it provides "frank photography of the opposite sex" for women (meaning, of course, straight women). Many gay and bisexual men also enjoy the romantic softcore focus of *Playgirl*. In fact, about half of the subscribers are men. Yet a thorough search of the official website and a year's worth of issues reveal a concerted effort to pretend that there are no male subscribers or readers at all – same-sex desire does not exist, so no man could possibly be interested in the "frank photography" of men. Products are advertised "for her"; fiction contains straight coupling only. Even the models are presumed absolutely straight, invariably asked the sorts of "women" they find attractive.

How to Snag a Guy

News magazines like *Time, Newsweek,* and *U.S. News and World Report* do not specialize in entertainment, so they should not be subject to Every Man's Fantasy or Every Woman's Fantasy. Since they are aimed at an audience of both men and women, they should not fall prey to the rigid association of gender and sexual orientation that compels men's and women's magazines to erase the possibility of same-sex desire or practice. After all, news should consist of hard truth only, with no attempt to ignore a phenomenon just because the reporter or editor would just as soon not know about it.

Nevertheless, a sample issue of *Time Magazine* erased gay people five times.

First Giuliano De Pandi advises women on "how to snag a guy." No woman wants to snag a woman, nor would any man decline being snagged by a woman. When the interviewer complains that De Pandi makes all men sound alike, she says simply, "They are." They are all straight, period.

Next, a reporter interviews sociologist Peggy Giordano, who studied teenage boys, and dismantled the myth of their indefatigable horniness. They aren't just about sex; they want romance, too. But only with girls: throughout the article, only straight desires, behaviors, and relationships are mentioned. Obviously there is no such thing as a gay teenage boy.

An article in the "Health" section tells about a new microbicide "that women can use vaginally prior to intercourse to stop the transmission of HIV." There is a problem, however: the women's male partners don't like it. So 100% of AIDS cases can now be prevented, as long as "the woman" uses the microbicide. The authors are either unaware that HIV can be transmitted through same-sex contact, or they are unaware that same-sex contact occurs at all. Sex by definition involves "the man" and "the woman."[8]

A review of *Little Miss Sunshine* refuses to let on that the character of Proust scholar Uncle Frank is gay. Fortunately, a related article about Marcel Proust does manage to out Uncle Frank, in scorchingly homophobic language, as a "depressed, suicidal homosexual" (aren't they all?). But then it refuses to let on that *Proust himself* was gay.

When a Girl Starts Noticing Boys

Joe grew up with the daily newspaper. One of his earliest memories was of his mother sitting in a rocking chair, doing the *Daily Journal* crossword puzzle while his brother and he watch cartoons. When he was ten years old, he got up 4:00 am, summer and winter, to wrap and deliver copies. When he was fifteen, he won a judo competition and got his picture in the Local News section, and his parents bought thirty copies to mail to all of their relatives.

He even learned about the existence of gay men from *The Journal:* sometime in his early teens, a local critic savaged a movie (he didn't remember which one): "Two men lie in bed. They embrace. Hairy body against hairy body. Porno-graphy." he was fantasizing about hairy body against hairy body for weeks.

When Joe moved to Oz, he abandoned straight-world newspapers. If it wasn't in *Frontiers, The Advocate,* or *The Edge,* then it was irrelevant at best, and more likely biased, homophobic, vicious, "Hairy body against hairy body: por-nography."

But in Kansas, millions of people still subscribed to daily newspapers, or read them online, as a significant source of information about the world, even more "fact" than magazines. So, during his second year in Chester, Joe subscribed to the Sunday edition of the *Chester Daily News.*

And suddenly he was back in small-town Indiana. Nothing had changed in thirty years, not even the heady smell of the pulp paper or the black ink that smudged your fingers. Ads showed smiling, happy people drawn from some straight suburban fantasy of the 1960s, husbands rid-ing lawn mowers and barbecuing outdoors, wives in aprons removing pot roasts from ovens, a little boy carving a pumpkin, two little girls having a pretend tea party, a tee-nage boy and girl grinning at each other on a porch swing.

The Real Estate section discussed neighborhoods that were great "for raising a family."

The *Parade Magazine* insert was part flag-waving, part parenting tips, with no mention of gay people in 52 issues, except for one question in the celebrity-gossip column about Clyde Tolliver, J. Edgar Hoover's live-in "roommate"; the columnist insisted that there was no evidence that the two were "homosexuals." Gay people do not exist.

The Life and Arts section was the worst offender. A parenting specialist fields a question about when a girl should start "noticing boys" (some as early as six or seven, some as late as fourteen or fifteen, but don't worry, it's normal, natural, and inevitable).

A homespun wisdom columnist describes the sweettender agony of waiting for her son to come home from his first date with a girl.

The Nightlife page once reviewed the gay-themed play *La Cage aux Folles,* being performed at the local community college, but none of Dayton's gay clubs appeared in the "live music" listings.

"Life's Memorable Moments" displayed endless photographs of beaming men and women celebrating engagements, weddings, and anniversaries. The official form used for posting your event requires the name of "the husband/groom" and "the wife/bride," omitting the possibility of same-sex commitments.

The Obituary section did mention two gay national figures: AIDS activist Jeff Getty (survived by his partner of 26 years, Ken Klueh), and former Congressman Gerry Studds (survived by his husband, Dean Hara). But in 52 issues he found only one local obituary that mentioned a same-sex partner: David P. Gillis, age 46, an assembly line worker from Troy, Ohio, preceded in death by his partner, Bruce. Surely other gay people in Dayton died sometime during the year, but *Daily News* editors changed partners to roommates or companions, or didn't mention them at all, presuming that "survivors" mean only straight survivors.

In the Entertainment section, none of the word jumbles, crossword puzzles, and cryptograms offered any hint that gay people exist, though straight husbands and wives were ubiquitous.

There was an outcry in 2001 concerning an edition of the *New York Times Crossword Puzzle* (which appears in the *Daily News* and hundreds of other local newspapers) called

"Homonames." Readers complained that the clues were "sexually suggestive," and the answers were all "people who were known to be gay." Crossword Editor Will Shortz called the controversy "asinine," explained that "homonames" was a play on "homonyms," and went on to proclaim, like the advertising VIPs who handle "rumors" of gay characters in television commercials, that he had no intention whatever of mentioning gay people, that he would never approve a puzzle that had the slightest hint of inclusion.[9] *The New York Times* officially framed the problem as about homophobia: "Slurs involving sexual orientation would be a violation of *The Time's* standards"; therefore, no "allusions to gay life" were intended. Evidently they believe that every mention of a gay person is by definition homophobic, so the only way to be non-bigoted is through erasure.[10]

Looking at the offending puzzle, Joe saw no sexually suggestive references. The people "known to be gay" in the answers include Bette Midler, Phil Specter, Kurt Russell, Doc Holiday, Niels Bohr, Jim Nabors, Jules Feiffer, Claude Rains. No one on the list is (or was) openly gay, and only two are subject to rumors. Some of them are gay-friendly; perhaps that is sufficient to make crossword aficionados recoil.

Straights lazying around with the crossword puzzle on Sunday morning, are trying to enter a different world, a new bright world with no worries or concerns. They think of gay people as one of the troubles, distressing, distasteful, tawdry, ugly, something that they shouldn't have to be reminded of, even if the reminder is all in their imagination.

Have You Ever Kissed a Girl?

The comics page of the daily newspaper is the most trivial segment of a trivial medium: three panels of minimalist line drawings, a few recurring characters and situations, a dialogue of fifty words or less, a sight gag or (hopefully) wry observation. The constraints of the structure make ongoing stories difficult, and change is rare: few characters grow older, find new jobs, learn from their mistakes, or even change their clothes. But the repetition itself, day after day, year after year, makes the characters and situations iconic, especially in popular strips can last forever: Garfield has been eating lasagna since 1978; Charlie Brown has been getting the football pulled away since 1950; Dagwood Bumstead has been rushing out of the house and knocking over the postman since 1930.

They are a tiny, inconsequential part of our daily routine, returned to again and again because they are mildly amusing or simply a habit, but they since they are always there, day after day, year after year, from childhood to the grave, they have a profound impact on our sense of what is real and true. And, as in forms of mass media, what is real is panoply of straight desire and romance.

The world of the comic strip is overwhelmingly the world of the television commercial. Most strips (*Hi and Lois, Family Circus, Blondie, Baby Blues, For Better and For Worse, Foxtrot, Zits*) evoke the same suburban nuclear families as the ads: husbands continuously nap on couches, wives worry over the dishes, teenage sons strum guitars, teenage daughters spend hours on the telephone, kids sell lemonade by the side of the road, and babies make friends with Mr. Sun.

Strips about young men (*Dilbert, Frazz, Herb and Jamal*) are usually set at work, and mostly concern insane bosses and backstabbing coworkers, but occasionally the workday is done, and the young men strike out on hapless quests after women.

Strips about young women (*Cathy, The Meaning of Lila*) devote some time to work, but most time is spent during endless, dismal dates with wolves and losers.

Children (*Cow & Boy, Dennis the Menace, Peanuts*) spend an inordinate number of strips pursuing straight romances of their own, and even when they are not themselves interested, they judge others on their successful straight practice. In *Soup to Nuts,* when a zookeeper exhibits unwelcome intellectual ability, six-year old Andrew humiliates him by asking "Have you ever kissed a girl?"

Straight desire is not only depicted as the universal human condition, it is the universal animal condition. The venerable cat *Garfield* is mainly concerned with sleeping and food, but he has a girlfriend, a pink cat named Arlene. Bucky Katt of *Get Fuzzy* is more active, frequently dating female cats with "bad reputations," while his fellow pet Satchel Pooch frequently gets crushes on the female dogs in his play group, as well as human women on tv.

Do You Know What You've Done?

For the first 100 years of comic strip history, the "openly" gay character was law student Andy Lippincott, who appeared in *Doonesbury* in 1976 just long enough to reject the romantic advances of classmate Joanie Caucus and come out ("Are they sure?" Joanie asks), and returned for a few strips in 1984 in order to die of AIDS.

A second "openly" gay character appeared in 1993, when the nuclear family strip *For Better or for Worse* featured a story arc about teenage Michael's friend Lawrence Poirier revealing "his secret." Cartoonist Lynn Johnston reflects: "Although he have focused on the lighter side, it has been important to him to explore those things in life which are not necessarily laughable, but things which pose a challenge, things that must be dealt with seriously and worked through." Other characters are horrified at first, but eventually they learn to accept Michael's "lifestyle."

Not so the readers: forty newspapers refused to run the story arc, and fourteen cancelled the strip outright. The phone at the Johnston residence rang day and night. 30% of the 2,500 letters that poured in were negative, not so much angry as agonized, expressing an amazing amount of pain: "do you know what you've done?" and "you have no right to do this to people!"[11]

How could a mere comic strip cause such trauma in readers? Gay characters had been appearing regularly on tv and in the movies for over twenty years, with spurts of homophobic outrage, but little psychic suffering. Johnston herself did not understand why over 800 people felt victimized by a simple coming out story, and she donated the letters, or "boxes of emotion," to a local university for detailed analysis. Perhaps it was because Lawrence was seventeen years old, a high school boy, and teenagers must never be portrayed as gay, not under any circumstances; some of the letter writers were certain that "homosexuals" reading the strip would thereby be encouraged to descend upon the nearest playground with child molestation and murder on their minds.

Or perhaps it was, as Lee Salem of the Universal Press Syndicate states, people "look on the [comics] section as kind of sacrosanct."[12] The comics, like the crossword puzzle, speak to the safest, most comfortable, most childlike part of the straight soul, to an hour in pajamas on Sunday morning, where the bad things of life, like crime and war and gay people, can be momentarily forgotten.

In 1998, Greg Evans considered having Aaron Hill, long-time friend and "crush" of the teenage *Luann,* realize that he was gay. He went as far as to have Luann and her friends discuss the possibility; someone even asked, "What if Aaron is gay?" Soon he was receiving up to 25 emails per day (five times more than usual), over half supporting the idea of Aaron coming out, the other half vociferously opposed. But Aaron was not a minor character like Lawrence Poirier; he could not be dropped without radically changing the strip, so if he came out, *Luann* would have an ongoing gay presence, and with only 300 newspapers subscribing, even a dozen cancellations would put Evans out of business. At the last moment, he decided to drop the storyline and "keep Aaron straight" (though over the years he has hinted, more than once, that gay people are commonplace in Luann's world).[13]

Often the author's intention is insufficient. Stephan Pastis, who draws the acerbic *Pearls Before Swine*, is extremely homophobic, littering his strip with "pansies" and "fairies" and effeminate stereotypes. When he wrote a gag about Rat (his mouthpiece character) talking the impossibility of platonic male-female friendships, he specified "straight men" to keep hundreds of pansies and fairies from mincing over to their lavender computes and lisping they were perfectly happy with platonic friendships (according to Pastis, every strip evokes outraged email; even a strip that omitted the gag to encourage remembering the soldiers fighting in Iraq received outraged emails about his "slap in the face" to veterans of other wars; however, he always tries to minimize the fallout if he can do it without detracting from the humor).

The syndicate told him that "straight" had to go, because children might ask what "straight" means, and the answer implies that men who are "not straight" exist. (Oddly, in another strip the syndicate allowed "bisexual," as long it was made very clear that bisexuals "choose" to be attracted to both sexes). So he wrote "No man," bowing to the pressure to erase gay people from the world.[14]

Most cartoonists either drop the idea of mentioning gay characters before they ever appear, or succumb to the bullying of their gay characters before they ever appear, or never think of it in the first place. Today King Features Syndicate offers local newspapers a choice of 65 strips, Universal Press Syndicate 49, United Media Comics 49, and Creators Syndicate 34. There are doddering relics of the past (*Barney Google, Prince Valiant*) and postmodern hipsters (*My Cage, Secret Agent Man*), wildly popular mega-hits (*Dilbert, Garfield*) and struggling obscurities (*Adam @ Home, Pooch Café*). Most of the strips have recurring characters, usually at least ten, sometimes more than fifty. Precisely four of them, less than 0.2%, are explicitly gay, and even those four rarely take center stage.[15]

In Gary Trudeau's *Doonesbury*, longtime character Mark Slackmeyer came out in 1993, and married Chase Talbott, the conservative nemesis on his talk radio program, in 2003 (the couple has since divorced); but neither Mark nor Chase appear more than a few times a year.

In Brooke McEldowney's *9 Chickweed Lane*, the daughter of the central character has moved to New York to pursue a career in ballet, where she rooms with fellow dancer Seth, an "unabashed wearer of the Green Carnation," as his United Features Syndicate biography closets him; the roommate of a supporting character, his appearances are rare.

The fourth, the only gay person in a starring role is Boyd, the stereotypic "gal pal" who makes wise-cracks at the titular character in *The Meaning of Lila*; but even he took two years to actually use the word.

Another gay character appeared in 2006 in Jim Borgman and Jerry Scott's *Zits*. Fifteen-year old Jeremy Duncan mocks newly-introduced classmate Billy, claiming that his shoes "look so gay." Billy responds that he *is* gay. Jeremy says he knows that, but he meant "gay" as in "lame." Then the self-involved teenager then muses: "Why do people always misinterpret what I say?" There is no record of howls of outrage or newspapers cancelling the strip, probably because *Zits* is far edgier to begin with than the stuffy *For Better or for Worse*, and because there was no angst-ridden "coming out" story arc; Jeremy, and no doubt everyone else at school, already knew.

Billy appeared later that year in a continuity involving Jeremy's poker game. This time, however, no one mentions his gayness; in fact, to up the ante, he bets "One conspicuous nose pick in front of a hot girl." Perhaps the artists disagreed about making him gay: Jim Borgman is an infamously liberal editorial cartoonist for *The Cincinnati Enquirer*, who would prefer to see *Zits* deal with "serious issues" like AIDS, while Jerry Scott, creator of the conservative *Baby Blues* strip, "doesn't want to see the six o'clock news on the funny pages." Being gay is apparently a "serious issue," fit for the six o'clock news. Billy has not returned.[16]

Comics can be queered, of course, like other mass media. Though Greg Evans shied away from outing Aaron Hill in *Luann*, he has given Luann's older brother Tony an extremely tepid relationship with his girlfriend and a "roommate," a fastidious fashion bug named TJ, who never gives girls a second glance. Who can doubt that they are a romantic couple? E

Eight-year old Andrew in *Soup to Nutz* often behaves like a gay boy growing up in the 1970s, playing with Barbie dolls, lip-synching to the Village People, getting crushes on the Brawny paper towel man. Many fans believe that he is gay, but cartoonist Rick Stromolski refuses to "out" him, claiming "I don't know for sure myself."[17]

Sometimes the cartoonists themselves facilitate the queering with gags based upon the artifacts of gay culture (or the stereotypes of gay culture), though the word "gay" rarely appears. In *Get Fuzzy*, Satchel Pooch has been hiding in a closet and announces that he's "coming out."

Fellow pet Bucky Katt exclaims, "I've been waiting three years for him to say that!"

In another strip, Bucky complains to their owner, Rob, "Why are you guys hiding it from him? There's nothing wrong with it."

Rob begins to protest that Satchel is not. . .you know, whereupon the dog bursts into the room and exclaims that his new Barbra Streisand album is "Fabulous!" Bucky stares and points.

The joke depends on the reader deciphering clues, understanding what Streisand and "fabulous" signify, while leaving same-sex desire and identity unspoken. Whenever Bucky seems about to use the actual word "gay," Rob quickly cuts him off.

Drag Boy

Bill Amend's nuclear family strip *Foxtrot* is quick to establish the straight excesses of nearly every major character. Mom Andy and Dad Roger are devoted to each other, but occasionally experience glimmers of attraction to outside men or women. Teenage son Peter faints in orgiastic ecstasy over every girl he sees, and has dreams about swimsuit models divesting themselves of their bikini tops. Teenage daughter Paige keeps trying unsuccessfully to attract the attention of "dreamy boys," and has intricate romantic fantasies about a handsome Frenchman named Pierre. While both Peter and Paige have same-sex "best friends," the relationships are singularly lacking in passion. And, in 5,000 strips written over a period of sixteen years, not a single gay character, major or minor, has ever appeared.

Only one strip uses the word "gay." When unattractive nerd Morton Goldthwait asks Paige for a date, she considers three excuses to use in turning him down: she has a contagious disease (probably a euphemism for a venereal disease); she is gay; she is already married. But of course, Paige is grasping at straws: all three excuses are ridiculous, impossibilities in her world.

One strip plays with the possibility of same-sex desire. Peter is embarrassed to find that he is wearing the same shirt as Morton Goldthwait, and begs him to take it off. Morton will do so only for $5.00. The next panel shows Peter holding out the money and crying "Take it off! Take it off!" while Morton gyrates, shirtless, like a male stripper. Then Peter glances about in horror and cries "Put it on! This doesn't look good!" It is unclear whether he is worried about students thinking that he is paying for Morton to strip, or merely that he is gay.

Two strips play with the possibility of same-sex romance. At a school party, a shy boy named Tommy tries to work up the courage to ask Paige to dance. He closes his eyes and thinks encouraging thoughts. Then, unaware that she has walked away, he turns suddenly and says "Care to dance?" to another boy, who stares and stammers, "Huh?" Lest anyone think that Tommy "means" it, the other boy is drawn as an unattractive slob.

Later, Paige becomes upset because her best friend has accepted a date with the boy she has a crush on. She asks her mother, "How would *you* feel if *you* had to sit at home while your best friend dated a cute boy?" Andy replies: "Considering that his best friend is 45, male, and married. . ." Her best friend is her husband Roger, of course, but lest anyone think that she objects only because Roger is married or too old for high school boys, she carefully specifies that he is *male*: she disapproves of males dating males under any circumstances.[18]

However, there is a bright spot in the incessant erasure: ten-year old Jason, a math and science whiz. Jason shuns "boy interests" in cars, sports, and rock music in favor of Dungeons and Dragons, online gaming, and science fiction movies and television programs, for which he creates his own costumes. Sometimes he wears a costume that covers his entire body and uses his pet iguana, Quincy, as the head. He must have a gender-transgressive expertise in sewing and makeup to design costumes so well, and though many of them are science fiction characters or monsters, others are outright drag, such as Quincy's mother and Agent Scully from the *X Files*. He also appears in a girl's bikini.

Perhaps more suggestive than the gender transgression is Jason's relationship with friend Marcus. In sharp opposition to Peter and Paige's friends, Jason and Marcus are passionately devoted to each other, and literally inseparable. They are together so often, at school and at home, that one wonders if Marcus has a home of his own. When they build a tree house hideout, Marcus exclaims, eyes gleaming, that finally they have a place where they can be "alone. . .no one to bother us"; technically, one cannot be "alone" with another person, unless that person is more "other half" than buddy. Elsewhere they interact so intimately and joyously that one wonders if any love could ever separate them, and if they are indeed destined to part at a pubescent "discovery of girls," it will surely be a tragedy.

The other characters ignore Jason's relationship with Marcus as supremely trivial, but celebrate the tiniest, most circumstantial sign of an attachment to girls the way his parents once evoked his "girlfriend next door." When Jason writes a love letter (to the school snake), Mom thinks it is for a human girl, and gushes: "Our baby's growing up!" When he buys a pile of old *National Geographics* at a garage sale, Dad assumes that he wants to ogle the breasts of naked natives: "That ol' Y chromosome is doing its thing," he exclaims with a leer. But Jason is actually interested in photos of the 1969 moon landing. When he accepts an ice-skating date with a girl, his parents and siblings are so excessive with their praise, congratulations, and gushes of "growing up" that Jason must protest that he had a miserable time.[19]

The enthusiasm, or desperation, with which Jason's parents and siblings search for signs of his "growing up" into heterosexuality suggests an awareness of gay potential, a nagging suspicion that everyone in the world is not necessarily straight, that Jason may turn fifteen, twenty, and thirty and still pursue same-sex loves. But most readers no doubt fail to notice; like Jason's parents, they believe that it is just "a matter of time." And if Bill Amend were asked directly, he would probably say "Of course Jason is straight! Anybody who knows anything about the strip would know. . .he would never. . .he had no intention. . . ."

---

[1] Holbrook, Damian J. "The Boys of Summer." *TV Guide*, July 17-23, 2006: 65.

[2] Keeps, David A. "McDreamy Life." *TV Guide*, September 18-26, 2006: 32; Keeps, David A. "Who's the boss: when he's not *Ugly Betty*'s bad-boy editor, Eric Mabius proudly plays first-time daddy." TV Guide 54.47 (November 20-26, 2006): 32; Holbrook, Damian J. "Crushes." *TV Guide,* December 4-

10, 2006: 62; Sellers, John. "David's New Home: *JAG* veteran David James Elliott commands *Close* attention." *TV Guide* December 11-17, 2006: 35; "Sophia's Choice," G. J. Donnelly, *TV Guide* June 16-22, 2008: 43; Joseph Hudak, "She's Got Game." *TV Guide* August 11-24, 2008: 64.

3 Andrzejewicz, Karen, "Crushes." TV Guide 55.4 (January 22-28, 2007): 67.

4 Small. Jonathan. "Medical Miracle: Love, Happiness, and John Stamos Breathe New Life into *ER*." *TV Guide* 54:45 (November 6-12, 2006): 18-21.

5 Vol 68, No. 22 (November 28, 2007)

6 Pete Hammond, review of *Brokeback Mountain*. *Maxim*, January 2006; "The Answer Fella," *Esquire*, 146.4 (October 2006).

7 http://magazines.ivillage.com/cosmopolitan/experts/carnal/qas/0,,638356_680503,00.html; http://redbook.ivillage.com/health/0,,996b342x,00.htmlhttp://hotandbothered.redbook.ivillage.com/sex/2006/10/sex_and_the_single_mom_13.html

8 Time Magazine, August 11, 2006. Lilleyman, Sarah. "The Ubiquitous Proust."; Christine Gorman, Simon Robinson, & Bryan Walsh, "Giving AIDS Drug to Prevent AIDS Infection"; Giordano, Peggy. "The Secret Love Lives of Teenage Boys."

9 Dave Fisher, "Cross Words for A Crossword." About.com Puzzle Section, http://puzzles.about.com/library/weekly/aa010813.htm

10 Editor's Note, New York Times, August 5, 2001.

11 Lynn Johnston, "Lawrence's Story." *For Better or For Worse Official Website*, http://www.fborfw.com/features/lawrence/

[12] Jurkowitz, Mark. "Controversial Comics Raise Serious Dilemmas." *Boston Globe,* October 22nd, 2003.

[13] David Astor, "Teen Character in Luanne isn't Gay." *Editor and Publisher,* April 11, 1998: 28.

[14] Pastis, Stephan. *Da Brudderhood of Zeeba Zeeba Eata.* Kansas City: Andrews McMell, 2007.

[15] Not including comic books, web comics, and comic strips that appear exclusively in gay publications.

[16] Comic Alert Zits Archive, http://www.comicalert.com/comics/7439-zits/

[17] "Queer on the Funny Pages." *The Advocate,* June 21, 2005, Adam B. Vary.

[18] Amend, Bill. *Foxtrot: the Works.* Kansas City: Andrews McMeel, 1990: 115; Amend, Bill. *Wildly Foxtrot.* Kansas City: Andrews McMeel, 1995: 215; Amend, Bill. *Assorted Foxtrot.* Kansas City: Andrews McMell, 2000: 102.

[19] Amend, Bill. *Wildly Foxtrot.* Kansas City: Andrews McMeel, 1995: 176; Amend, Bill. *Assorted Foxtrot.* Kansas City: Andrews McMell, 2000: 28.

Chapter Twelve
A Family Company

Regardless of how many times you move as an adult, home is always the place where you spent the most significant years of your childhood, when the end of the block was an undiscovered country, every new experience was startling and strange, and you knew none of the rules, procedures, and protocols that the adults took for granted. In order to make sense of it all, to survive in this world you had been born into, you observed everyone – parents, teachers, older siblings, world-wise friends, strangers on the street – and consciously or unconsciously made their acts your acts, their rules of conduct your rules of conduct, their feelings your feelings.

True, some of their acts seemed bizarre, some of their rules were maddeningly unfair, and you didn't always feel what you were supposed to feel, but you embraced it all as absolute truth, absorbed it even when you tried not to. It remains part of you to this day, an unconscious sense of what is right, normal, natural, of how things are "supposed to be."

Most straights stay very close to home their entire lives, so there is a seamless transition between childhood and adolescence and young adulthood and middle age, no opportunity to learn which childhood "truths" were oppressive and which were a lie. But gay people tend to seek out gay worlds far away. Joe spent his adult life in California, New York, Maine, Florida, and Wisconsin, seeing home for about ten days a year, at Christmastime. His parents changed from middle aged to elderly overnight; his brother got grey overnight; he had to consult with his sister, or else he would accidentally give his twelve-year old nephew a gift appropriate for a six-year old.

But in Ohio, home was only two hours away, so suddenly Joe was able to visit several times a year. He was going to birthday parties, Thanksgiving dinners, kids' recitals, graduations. He talked to brothers and sisters, uncles and aunts, nieces and nephews, cousins and second cousins. He was part of a straight nuclear family, for the first time since he threw two suitcases and a box of books into his car and headed west. And he could see, for the first time since he was a child, how children are told, joyously and repeatedly, that they are, will be, must be straight.

The Girlfriend Next Door

Children grow up amid a brooding background noise of straight desire. Bedtime stories end with prince and princess declaring their love. Three-year olds are drafted into becoming ring-bearers at straight weddings. An advertising blurb extols the happy, carefree life of a boy and culminates with "the first time he brings a girl home for dinner," as if boyhood invariably ends, and manhood invariably begins, with girls.[1]

A full-page ad on the back cover of *TV Guide* tells us of Chris, a man who has recently been diagnosed with diabetes. He checks his blood sugar frequently. His reason: "Maya, my 4 ½ year old daughter. I will dance at her wedding."[2] It is highly unlikely that Chris envisions his daughter marrying a woman, but how can he be so certain that she is straight?

She is not even in kindergarten, so surely she has not expressed any romantic interests in anyone yet.

Yet Chris can be certain because he knows there are no gay children, period. He will therefore raise Maya to believe that she is straight, and more, to accept straight desire as ordinary, as everyday. The minutiae of its expression will be as familiar to her as her native language. She will learn about same-sex desire much later, if at all, as something bizarre and unknowable, something that intrudes upon her from outside. If she happens to be gay herself, she will feel herself bizarre and unknowable, an intrusion into the real world, the only true world, where all fathers dance at their daughters' weddings.

When straights are forced to acknowledge that gay people exist, they envision only adults. Adolescents and college students are at best "confused about their sexuality," and infants, toddlers, and children are always straight. They may not be interested in heterosexual practice at this moment, but sometime soon the boys will mature sufficiently to bring girls home for dinner, and the girls will mature sufficiently to be the recipients of the dinner invitations.

Straights insist on this point with surprising fervor. Throughout childhood, they obsessively evoke the far-off milestones of straight destiny: "When you start dating"; "When you get a steady girlfriend"; "When you get married"; "When you have a wife and kids."

Joe barely recalled the girl who lived in the little brown house next door to us when he was in kindergarten. She was a "grownup," in third grade, half babysitter and half friend. He used to visit after school, and we would play with her many dolls and marvelously intricate dollhouse.

His parents remembered very well, but did they see that long-ago gender transgression as evidence that their little boy was gay at the age of five?

Not for an instant. He was obviously using the dolls and dollhouse as an excuse to spend time with the girl of his dreams. Whatever he "chose" to become later, at the age of five he was straight.

A dozen times between kindergarten and high school, at Thanksgiving dinners, Christmas Eve parties, and Fourth of July barbecues, Joe's grandfather or an uncle or a neighbor would sidle up to him, comment on how much he had grown, and then ask, with an eager grin, "Do you like girls *yet*?"

They always included the *yet* to emphasize the inevitability of liking girls. They could not conceive of any possibility he would still be answering "no, he don't like girls" at age thirteen, or at age fifteen, or at age thirty. Sooner or later, he was bound to "grow up" into straight desire. A curt "No" sufficed when he was very young, but around junior high, the adults began pushing, prodding, cajoling, and wheedling: "Come on. . .you can tell me. . . . .don't be bashful. . . .is there a girl in your class that you like? What's her name? Is she cute?" By the time he was in high school, Joe could escape the interrogation only by inventing longing glances at a girl in chemistry class or evoking the girl next door walking in slow motion across the yard.

Only once have he ever heard a straight suggest that a child might be gay: more than twenty years ago, before he moved to West Hollywood, one of his college friends held a birthday party-barbecue. A neighborhood kid, perhaps eight years old, was hungry for male attention. He kept crawling onto the laps of the men present and taking their hands to wrap around himself in a sort of hug. After he left, the host turned to him and said in a low voice, as if sharing a juicy bit of gossip, "If he didn't know better, he'd think the boy had homosexual tendencies."

Perhaps the speculation was possible only because the boy was not his own, but even so, it was phrased with exacting caution: "homosexual tendencies," a psychic move in the direction of gayness, but certainly not gayness yet, and preluded with "If he didn't know better," to assure himself that he *did* know better. No child could really be gay.

The insistence that no child is gay may sometimes be based on homophobia, the belief that everyone starts out straight, but in adulthood some of us, due to debauchery, unhappy straight romance, or pure evil, decide to turn our backs on God and country and embrace gayness. Yet even parents who are completely nonchalant about the gayness of their adult sons and daughters still cannot bring themselves to believe that, twenty or thirty years ago, their little boys and girls were gay, so it may be a matter of exclusion, not homophobia, the assertion that "this person in front of him right now is straight." When parents insist that their preteen son's friendship with a girl is a romance, and his friendship with a boy is a meaningless trifle, they are not expressing homophobic disdain for gay people, they are simply unaware, at that moment, that gay people exist.

Girl-Crazy

If childhood is a period of eager anticipation of straight destiny, adolescence is a period of calm assurance that destiny is now. Everyone Joe asked asserted, with utter confidence, that all teenage boys, with no exceptions, are girl-crazy and all teenage girls, with no exceptions, are boy-crazy. It doesn't matter if they are young or old, male or female, gay or straight, parent of a gay teenager; even gay teenagers themselves, more often than not, are convinced that puberty invariably leads to a decade-long, hormone-drenched rush of straight mania, that no gay teenagers could possibly exist.

Shortly after talk show host Rosie O'Donnell revealed that she was a lesbian, she mentioned an adolescent crush on actor Tom Cruise. Confused straights asked, "If you experienced even a fleeting moment of straight desire twenty years ago, how can you then be gay?" She stated that it was simply part of being a teenage girl, irrelevant to her adult life. All teenagers everywhere are straight.

Ellen DeGeneres' character Ellen maked a similar statement on her sitcom: apprised that a girlfriend's daughter is crazy about boys, she says "I know how you feel. He was a teenager once." She may be gay now, but as a teenager, she was straight.

When Joe was sixteen years old and still preferred to spend his evenings with boys rather than girls, his parents began to get nervous. They bribed him with an increase in allowance, a later curfew, and use of the car, all if he planned an evening out with a girl instead of a boy. When he discovered that he could get the privileges just by *trying* to get dates, he began to ask the most popular girls in school, cheerleaders and beauty queens; then, "rejected," he was free to go out with a boy. But did they think he might be gay? Not for a moment. He may be shy, sensitive, a late bloomer, "socially awkward," but he was certainly straight, as wild about girls as every other teenage boy on the planet.

When his parents went away for the weekend, they had a single rule: no girls. Joe was free to invite a dozen boys over. They could all get naked and roll around on the floor in an orgy of Graeco-Roman wrestling, if they took a notion to. But no girl could so much as cross the threshold to work on a civics project. Joe's parents reasoned that if he was ever alone with a girl, they would be unable to keep our raging hormones under control, and sex might result; but nothing could possibly result from boys rolling on the floor in an orgy of Graeco-Roman wrestling.

Other adults in Joe's hometown likewise behaved as if no teenager in the history of the world had ever been gay. During high school, he never saw the inside of a girl's bedroom, not even for an instant; when he visited a girl for any reason, they were required to stay in the living room or the kitchen.

If she wanted to show off her new Shaun Cassidy poster, she would have to pull it down from her bedroom wall and carry it out to him, lest our hormones overcome us. But when he visited a boy, his mother might say, "He's still in bed. Why don't you go wake him up?" or "He's taking a shower. Go in and talk to him." No sex could ever result from being alone with a boy in his bedroom, or seeing him naked in the shower. There were no raging gay hormones. There were no gay teenagers.

His parents still believed that Joe was straight as a teenager, and only "decided" to become gay sometime in college. When he told his mother that he was writing a book about teenagers, she exclaimed: "You sure were wild about girls then!"

"What girls?" he asked in surprise. He had exactly five dates with girls during high school: twice a cheerleader unexpectedly said "yes" when he asked her out in the hope of being rejected, and three times a hunky football player asked him to double.

She named some of his female friends. "You were wild about Beth. . .you had a big crush on Anne. . .you were mooning over Terry for months. . . ."

He didn't recall any crushes, any mooning. At least not over girls. What about Nico, the exchange student from Italy? He broke his heart when he was a senior. What about Tom, the football player?"

She didn't remember them.

What about David? He was Joe's first boyfriend, in junior high: a chemistry club nerd with sandy brown hair and blue eyes that smiled behind his glasses, with warm hands and a pretentious, endearing way of calling him by his full name. They read comic books, played chess, and looked through his telescope at the stars; in the summertime we went swimming. He still remembered the night they heard Donny Osmond sing "The Twelfth of Never" on the radio.

"David? Sure, he was one of your friends when you were in junior high."

Joe's mother did remember him, but as a "one of his friends," no one special. Though they spent every day together for nearly three years, until his father was transferred and he moved away, she had no reason to remember him: a boy's friendships with boys were trivial, meaningless.

Only his friendships with girls deserved recognition, since any girl he mentioned, or telephoned, or brought into the house might be "the one," the girl of his dreams, the girl he would one day marry. Thus her name was memorized, photographs were taken, theater programs were carefully pressed into scrapbooks. It was inconceivable that any boy might be "the one."

It Doesn't Mean You're Gay

More than twenty years had passed since Joe was tee-nager, but little had changed: teenagers were still presumed universally straight. Of three bestselling advice books for teenagers:

The Complete Idiot's Guide to Dating for Teens does not mention gay people at all.

The How Rude! Handbook of Friendship and Dating Manners for Teens advises teens on how to respond if a friend reveals that he or she gay (in the chapter on "Problems and Secrets," as if being gay is always a problem or a secret), but never waivers from its assurance that everyone here, everyone reading the book, is straight.

The Teenage Guy's Survival Guide does tackle the "problem" of a guy who is "crushing" on another guy. Author Jeremy Daldry insists that it does not mean that you are gay, not even if things get sexual. If crushing on guys does not mean you are gay, and having sex with guys does not mean you are gay, what *does* mean you are gay?

Absolutely nothing – everything any teenage guy says, does, thinks, or feels is precisely what a straight guy says, does, thinks, or feels, because all teenage guys are straight. Daldry goes on to attack the pedophilia libel, and condemns "making mean jokes about girls or gays," but always with the assumption that the gay man is an adult, far removed from the teenage experience. The chapter on dating and romance discusses boys longing for girls only. Though Daldry advises tolerance of gay men, it is obvious that everyone "here" is straight.[3]

Look at the Pretty Girls

Joe never believed that any and all people should be assumed straight until they reveal their "secret," so he never sat down with his parents and had a momentous Coming Out Speech. However, he informed them of the details of every date he have been on since college: if he was handsome, muscular, or quirky-cute, what he wore, the movie we saw, what he ordered at the restaurant, whether he touched his hand awkwardly and sweetly, whether he thought he was "the one." He called called elated over infatuations, and devastated over breakups.

When Joe brought his first real boyfriend home for Christmas, he found the two twin beds in his old room thoughtfully pushed together to make a double; we received a joint gift, just like his brother and his wife; and we participated in the "couples only" photograph in front of the Christmas tree. That was more than twenty years ago, so obviously his parents "know."

But knowledge of gayness is never automatic, never reflexive; they have to make a mental adjustment. They have to *think* about it.

The Christmas after he moved to West Hollywood, his father took it upon himself to have a heart-to-heart. "I know they're crazy out in California," he said, "But you have to be careful. There are a lot of diseases you can get nowadays." Joe thought he meant AIDS, so he nodded his agreement.

Then Dad said: "Or you could get a girl pregnant."

His jaw dropped. How was it possible for his father to worry about him getting a girl pregnant? Did he still not "know"? Or did he believe that every man, gay or straight, had sex with women?

If his father had stopped to think about it, he would probably have figured out that gay men not only have sex with men, they fail to have sex with women. But the concern came quickly, as an afterthought, without conscious reasoning. He saw "male," and he knew, from years of listening to the proclamations of universal straight desire, that "male" meant "sex with females." In the heat of a conversation that must have been somewhat difficult for the reserved Midwesterner, he simply forgot to make the mental adjustment: "All males have sex with females, except in this one case in front of me right now."

The moments of forgetting, of failing to make the necessary mental adjustment when addressing the only gay person who exists, diminished during Joe's years of annual Christmas visits to the Midwest.

Perhaps meeting several boyfriends and long-term partners, hearing about his participation in gay organizations, and seeing his string of gay-themed publications made it sink in. Yet still once in a while the erasure came, in spite of everything, so ingrained, so instinctive was the association of humanness and heterosexuality.

On a bright, sunny day, his father suggests that he go to the park and "look at all the pretty girls."

His parents announce that they have purchased two cemetery plots, right next to theirs, for him and his "wife."

When he runs into an old friend at the mall, and make plans to get together with her later, his mother says, "Joe's wild about a girl he met today."

Extended Family

Come out to your parents, your brothers and sisters, your grandmother, your favorite aunt, keep coming out until you have checked off every name in your address book. Then wait for Thanksgiving, Christmas, Passover, any of those holidays where "extended family" gather – uncles and great-uncles, nieces and nephews, cousins and second cousins, people who you never call or email, whose homes you have never seen, whose addresses you probably have scribbled down somewhere.

Living in Ohio, Joe was able to go to his first Thanksgiving dinner with the family in over twenty years, and he realized with some trepidation that he would be seeing some of this extended family for the first time since college. Some of them scared him: an uncle, fat with a hairy belly jutting out from beneath his t-shirt, reclining on a Lazy Boy and laughing uproariously at a joke that he didn't understand; another uncle who stared at the tv in a dark room, silent, smoking endless cigarettes; an aunt, a petite blonde in Bermuda shorts, with a can of Coors beer in one hand and a *Soap Opera* digest in another, a cousin who had showed him his secret stash of *Playboy* magazines when we were both twelve; a great-uncle in bib overalls who called his judo *rasslin'*; a great-aunt who cautioned him, twenty years after the hippie movement had died, to never grow his hair long like the hippies, because short hair was the glory of man.

At Thanksgiving, Joe expected jingoistic warmongering ("Why don't we just drop a nice big bomb on Iraq, and wipe out terrorism once and for all?). He expected incomprehensible references to carburetors and batting averages. He expected beaming approval of the cousin who sat on the couch, warm and flustered, with his arm around his new girlfriend. But he didn't expect to be mistaken for straight.

By everyone.

The fat uncle with the hairy belly complemented him on his looks: "You must have to fight off the ladies with a stick!"

The cousin who once showed Joe his stash of *Playboys* asked him to evaluate the breasts of a female celebrity on tv.

His other cousin's new girlfriend got right to the point: "Do you have a girlfriend?"

Why did every one of them think that he was straight? Even though JOe hadn't seen or heard from them for many years, he heard *about* them: every visit and telephone conversation with his mother, brother, sister, and favorite aunt consisted primarily of discussions of these more distant relatives, their job prospects, medical problems, and straight romances. Surely the next day, when his mother, brother, sister, and favorite aunt got on the phone with those other relatives, they mentioned his job prospects, honors, medical problems, and same-sex romances.

Of course they did. Extended family members said things like "I hear you're a schoolteacher"; "I hear you're a writer"; and "How do you like it in Ohio?" One even knew that he threw his back out, an injury that happened five months ago, and was incapacitating for only a few days.

But that last thing, the people he was dating, in love with, sharing his apartment with, sharing his life with: no information. His mother, brother, sister, and favorite aunt failed to tell those other relatives anything about it. In conversation after conversation, year after year, they had forced him to pass. No one should know that Joe is gay.

It would take too long to come out to fifteen people, and besides, he didn't believe in pronouncements, as if he was revealing a secret, so he simply answered the questions as they arose.

To his uncle: "If a lady tried anything with me, I would run into the nearest gay bar and hide until she went away, or until I got lucky."

To the cousin with the stash of *Playboys*: "I wouldn't know about women's breasts, I'm too busy looking at guys' baskets."

To his other cousin's girlfriend: "No, I don't have a girlfriend. My boyfriend would get jealous."

They just stared, thinking that he was a wise guy making a silly joke, or not comprehending at all. But even if they concluded that Joe must be gay, would word get around, as his uncle called his sister, his cousin called his brother, his other cousin called his favorite aunt?

Never.

Six months later, at a Fourth of July barbecue, Joe went through the same thing all over again, with them or with other members of the extended family.

His niece's boyfriend asked "Are the girls in Ohio hot?"

His great-aunt said "You must be a real devil with the ladies!"

His cousin's new girlfriend asked, "Do you have a girlfriend?"

Why do family members keep so aggressively silent? Perhaps they are used to not thinking about it themselves, except when absolutely necessary. If he does not have his arm around a lover at that moment, if he is not discussing a Gay Pride parade at that moment, then they can forget. He returns, in their mind, to the default: male, therefore interested in women.

Family Research Centers

Everyone, gay or straight, has a genetic origin in two chromosomes, an X donated by a woman, and an X or a Y donated by a man, typically during an act of straight intercourse. In most cases the identity of the donors is a matter of public record, available at county courthouses and in churches, or through hundreds of Mormon-run Family Research Centers, so it is possible to trace your genetic material back in time, from your two donors to their four donors, then *their* eight donors, and so on. Assuming no duplicates, just 500 years ago, you had a million "ancestors," people whose donations of X or Y chromosomes combined to produce you.

Joe had a book-length list of over 2,000 such ancestors, donors of X or Y chromosomes from England, Ireland, France, Prussia, Switzerland, and the Chippewa and Mohawk nations, extending back well over 500 years, in some cases to before the Norman Conquest. Most entries consisted of little more than birth and death dates, with an occasional cryptic comment (what does "married by Squir Mil" mean? Is it the name of a person? A mill?). But sometimes there were hints of interesting lives:

His great-great-great-great grandfather William Allen (1783-1854), a cousin of famous patriot Ethan Allen, grew up in Patrick County, Virginia, but settled on the "frontier," the Lickin River of eastern Kentucky. He married another settler, Caty Gearheart, and had fifteen children. He was found dead in the woods after leaving a party that had lasted for four days.

Another great-great-great-great grandfather, Robert Hicks (1680-1718), was born on Long Island, New York, a few years after it was ceded to the English from the Dutch. He moved to the Chowan River, North Carolina, settled among the Cherokees, married, and had a son, all before his nineteenth birthday.

Joe's great-great-great-great-etc. grandmother Margaret de Umfreville (1397-1444), a descendant of Charlemagne, was born in Castle Harbottle, Northumberland, England. While still a teenager, she married William Lodington, an elderly judge. He died a few years later, and she immediately married a younger man, Sir John Constable.

But were his ancestors necessarily straight, simply because they engaged in a few acts of straight intercourse?

Perhaps William Allen's many children signify prudence rather than passion: children were an economic necessity in an agrarian society.

Perhaps Robert Hicks' early marriage was meant to ensure the goodwill of his adopted tribe, not a sign that he was in love, or attracted to the other sex at all.

Perhaps Margaret de Umfreville married her second husband so quickly because women in Medieval England could not inherit property, and she needed the financial security.

Did these ancestors seek out same-sex lovers? Or forge intense, passionate bonds with life-long friends? The record does not tell us. Like his mother's failure to remember his junior-high boyfriend, such relationships were assumed too trivial to record.

Only once in the book is a potential same-sex love named. Joe's great-grandfather William Henry Jackson (1839-1910) moved from New York to Columbus, Indiana at the age of 21, accompanied by a young man named Alvin Mooney. William, called "Small Bill" because he stood only 5'3", served in the Union Army during the Civil War, then married Hannah Matilda Moyer. They bought a farm in Lagrange County, Indiana, on the northern edge of the state, and had seven children.

Alvin Mooney appears only once in the record. What happened to him? Did he and Small Bill share a friendship, a romance, or something in between, a "romantic friendship" such as was common in those days?[4] Did they ever hold hands, or kiss? Did they move to Lagrange County together? In the early years of the new century, did they sit side-by-side on rocking chairs on the porch of Small Bill's farmhouse, and talk about old times, and smile? Joe didn't know. Whatever bond they had is lost.

What of those great-uncles and great-aunts, the brothers and sisters of his ancestors, who never married in spite of the social pressure and economic necessity?

Joe's great-great grand-uncle Nicholas Prater (1553-1589) was born at Latton Manor, Wiltshire, England, but moved to London during his teens. As an aristocratic man-about-town, he certainly attended the theatre, so he would have known gay playwright Christopher Marlowe, and probably a bisexual actor named William Shakespeare. He would have missed gay poet Richard Barnfield, still an Oxford undergraduate in 1589, but not the many other gay men who sought each other out in a society that rivaled Renaissance Florence for its openness to same-sex desire.[5]

Or did Nicholas Prater spend his entire 36 years on Earth bedding ladies?

There is no way to know.

Even if Joe did find out, he couldn't record the information. The major genealogy software packages don't allow for either sexual orientation or same-sex partnerships. Let's say Joe's uncle and his partner have been together for the past thirty years. They have had a Holy Union in the Metropolitan Community Church, and they have registered as domestic partners in their state. Or perhaps one of them is a Belgian citizen, so they are legally married in Belgium. How could Joe record them?

Family Tree Maker and *Ancestral Quest* allow only for male husbands to be married to female wives.

Brother's Keeper allows you to record up to eight marriages for each person, but all are of the male-female variety.

Family Historian uses the term "Spouse," but the spouse must always be of the other sex, so one of Joe's two uncles will have to be recorded as female.[6]

Joe was left with a family tree that fills a book, thousands of people who married or did not marry, who left evidence of several acts of straight intercourse, or only one, or none at all, yet genealogy software assumes that every one of them ached for the other sex, that same-sex desire or behavior did not exist in Shakespeare's London, or among the Cherokees of the Chowan River, or in Columbus, Indiana before the Civil War.

But Joe cannot even record the gay people that he knows exist today. Genealogy software is adamant: only the bonds of straight husbands and wives may be included. Gay people must be erased from history.

Should his brother's great-grandson someday become interested in family history, and start looking through old genealogy programs, he will find Joe's birth and death dates, his occupation, and a blank space under "wife." Perhaps he will wonder "Was my great-granduncle gay?" He will not be able to tell.

Settling Down

Service people and professionals, like the manager of Eye on Maine Bookstore in Derry, the hostess at Thai to Go in Boca del Gato, the checker at the Piggly Wiggly in Northland, and the clerk at CVS Drugs in Chester, never asked "Are you married?" at the first encounter; they said "Hello," took care of our business, and moved on to other customers.

But they certainly believed that Joe was straight. If he returned week after week or several times per week, they eventually began to feel a degree of intimacy that permitted them to butt into his life. If he came alone, or with a man at his side, then eventually they would feel free enough to advise, "You should get married!" or "You should settle down!"

In Kansas, the two concepts are identical. They both refer to growing up, leaving childhood things behind and taking on the big, important responsibilities of adulthood. Therefore, the question "Are you married?", which began this journey, is identical to "Have you grown up?"

When a student complained in a course evaluation about Joe's attendance policy, he said, "I shouldn't be forced to attend class like a *child*. I'm 26 years old and *married*." You are either married, or you are a child.

Marriage and maturity have been associated for hundreds of years. The fairytale ends with the wedding to indicate that childhood is over, adulthood beginning.

In a *Peanuts* comic strip from the 1950s, Violet asks Lucy, "What do you want to be when you grow up?" Lucy is unclear about the concept of "growing up," so Violet elaborates: "You know, big. . . *married*. . .a lady."

Fifty years later, Jerry and George of *Seinfeld* bewail their unmarried status: "What kind of lives are these? We're like children! We're not men!" They are rapidly approaching middle age. They have careers, homes, bank accounts, lots of friends, and a seemingly endless supply of sexual partners. Nevertheless, they are not grown up, because they have not "settled down," that is, married women.

In the science fiction series *Lost in Space* (1965-68), a family of space explorers is sidetracked en route to Alpha Centauri and spent three seasons trying to find the way home. Bill Mummy, who played eleven-year old son William Robinson, is now a singer/songwriter. On of the tracks on his album *Dying to be Heard*, "The Ballad of William Robinson," postulates that Robinsons are still chugging through the cosmos.

William, now forty-two years old, complains that he will never marry, never father children, never grow up and lead a "normal life."

There are no women in outer space except for his mother and sisters, so he is doomed to remain forever a child. "Show him mercy in this universe," he wails, "For I am lost in space."[7]

One would expect that a slight adjustment could be made for gay people: the entry into adulthood could become "settling down" with someone of the same sex. But no one in Maine, Florida, Wisconsin, or Ohio ever made that adjustment.

On the raunchy animated series *Family Guy*, one-year old Stewie is upset when his pretend-marriage doesn't work out. "Being grown up sucks!" he cries. "Why can't guys just live with guys, do the same things you would with a woman, but with your buddies?" His friend Brian tells him, "They can. It's called being gay."

Clearly they both believe that growing up is identical to being married to a woman. If a man sets up housekeeping with a man, he will always be a child.

Since being an adult means "settling down" into marriage, straights who admit that gay people exist at all are likely to place them into a sort of limbo of perpetual adolescence. Gay men constantly complain that their birthday and Christmas presents from relatives are appropriate for teenagers (a video game, a *South Park* dvd), or for new college graduates just starting out in life (a toaster, an electric grill). Since they have no wives, the gift-givers subconsciously think of them as "kids," far removed from the big, hard, important work of adulthood, and shop accordingly.

Even gay people tend to agree that they are still children playing house. They will call their partners "boyfriends" and "girlfriends" after living together for a decade. They will call sex "play" or "fooling around," to distinguish it from the real, important "making love" that the straights engage in.

When gay horror master Clive Barker revealed his "Five Most Important Books," *Peter Pan* was #4. Why? "The abiding myth of his childhood and of most gay men's lives: infinitely postponed adulthood. He will never have children; he will never take on adult responsibilities."

We are told over and over that adults who have not married and reproduced are worthless. As he approached a work zone on the highway, Joe saw a sign: "Slow down – my Daddy works here!" Apparently it is fine to careen into the unmarried, childless workers.

Two firefighters have died on duty. The newspaper mourns one as "leaving a wife." It is silent about the other. Surely he left someone behind as well -- parents, siblings, romantic partners, friends? No, the newspaper, insists: he was not married, and he had no children. No one knows, or cares, that he is gone.

In *Speed* (1994), a passenger on a runaway bus exclaims "I have a wife!" to emphasize how tragic his plight is; should he die, someone would actually care.

A hostage about to be executed on an episode of *24* cries "I have a wife!" to argue that he should be spared, that his life has value – they should execute one of the unmarried hostages instead, since they have nothing to live for anyway.

Security for Your Family

Sociologists love the straight nuclear family, that triad of husband-wife-children. Many first-year textbooks praise it as "basic unit of social life," yet at the same time the best, most efficient, most evolved family structure (both contentions are wrong: social life is arguably based on friendships rather than biological reproduction, and extended families are arguably more efficient at raising children). But at least sociologists realize that adults sometimes make other living arrangements.

Straights tend to believe that everyone, without exception, lives in a straight nuclear family: that every adult is either a husband or wife, a father or a mother, living in a huge ranch-style house in the suburbs; that every husband drives off to work in the morning, leaving his wife at home to raise the kids; that every boy grows up to marry a girl, and every girl grows up to marry a boy, and they start new nuclear families in huge ranch-style houses in suburbs of their own. There's an elegance to the arrangement: every boy finds a girl, every girl finds a boy, every husband and wife produce a miniature husband and wife, no one is left out.

But simple mathematical precision doesn't explain why "family," or the straight nuclear family, is used so often, in so many contexts where it doesn't belong. Joe checked the Barnes and Noble website for books with "Family" in the title, and found 41,742. But most were relevant to everyone, not just husbands and wives with kids:[8]

*The Bipolar Disorder Survival Guide: What You **and Your Family** Need to Know.*

*New Life Insurance Investment Advisor: Achieving Financial Security for **You and Your Family.***

*Choosing a Jewish Life: A Handbook for People Converting to Judaism **and for their Families** and Friends.*

Occasionally the text inside included gay people. In *Choosing a Jewish Life*, for instance, Anita Diamant uses the term "marriage" not only for husbands and wives, but for "committed partnerships that do not have legal sanction, including gay and lesbian couples."[9] Most of the time, however, there was no doubt: text and title both assumed that every adult on Earth is a straight husband and father or wife and mother, every child awaiting entry into marriage and maturity.

Family is not just a buzzword, with little precise meaning, added to a title or advertising slogan make straights feel warm and cozy. It has a specific purpose: it evokes an image of what life is like or should be like that assumes universal heterosexuality and eliminates any possibility that gay people might exist. And it appears everywhere, in politics, in entertainment, in business, in religion.

S. C. Johnson, producer of household cleaning products like Pledge, Glade, and Windex, calls itself "a *family* company," in every commercial, in every print ad. According to the official website, the "family company" catchphrase means that there is no public trading: all stock is owned by the biological progeny of Mr. Samuel Curtis Johnson, who founded what was then a parquet flooring company in 1886. But people who view the ads a dozen times a day will probably not take the time to research the S. C. Johnson Company's stock options: they will conclude that the products are meant for the exclusive use of husbands/fathers and wives/mothers.

"For over a century," the website explains, "The Johnson family has demanded the best for families everywhere." Oddly, the company also offers partnership benefits for gay couples. It sponsors Gay Awareness Week and Gay 101 diversity training seminars. Its Gay and Lesbian Business Council was named Employee Group of the year at the 2003 Out & Equal Organizational Workplace Summit.[10] One of the most gay-friendly companies in the world erases gay people in its advertising materials, unless we expand the term "family" in a way that most residents of Kansas will not.

A book by Dr. David T. Courtright blames unmarried men for most of the crime and injustice in the world: they have a tendency to be violent, impulsive, dishonest, and otherwise despicable, until they are rehabilitated by the love of a good woman. He does not mention gay people in his book, but no doubt, if apprised of their existence, he would suggest rounding them up and forcing them into shotgun-marriages with women to alleviate their criminal tendencies.[11]

In Kansas, children are awaiting straight destiny, adolescents are girl- or boy-crazy; gayness is something that happens in adulthood. But becoming an adult requires straight marriage and family, so gay people can never really grow up. There are no gay children, there are no gay adolescents, there are no gay adults. There are no gay people at all.

---

[1] Cover blurb, *All-Boy Scrapbook Pages,* compiled by Memory Makers. F&W Publications, 2004.

[2] *TV Guide,* Vol 56, No. 17

[3] Daldry, Jeremy, *Teenage Survival Guide.* New York: Little Brown, 1999: 53.

[4] Katz, Jonathan Ned. *Love Stories: Sex Between Men Before Homosexuality.* Chicago: University of Chicago Press, 2003.

[5] Alan Bray, *Homosexuality in Renaissance England.* New York: Columbia University Press, 1995.

[6]*Family Tree Maker,* http://familytreemaker.com; *Ancestor Quest,* http://www.ancquest.com; *Brother's Keeper,* http://www.bkwin.net; *Family Historian,* http://www.family-historian.co.uk/

[7] Bill Mumy official website, http://www.billmumy.com.

[8] Barnes and Noble Online Bookstore, http://www.barnesandnoble.com

[9] Diamont, Anita. *Choosing a Jewish Life*. New York: Schocken, 1998: 34.

[10] Press Release, SC Johnson website, http://www.scjohnson.com

[11] Courtwright, David T. *Violent Land: Single Men and Social Disorder from the Frontier to the Inner City*. Cambridge, MA: Harvard University Press, 1998.

Chapter Thirteen
The Boojum

After two years in Chester, Joe's temporary position was ending, and it was time to move on again. After ten interviews and many, many questions about his wife, he found a visiting position in Criminology, with courses like Policing, Corrections, and Criminal Law, and barely a moment for gay studies. It was at a small, conservative college in a small, conservative town in upstate New York, nestled among the Adirondacks, two hours from Oz.

By now Joe was used to the isolation and the loneliness of Kansas. But the erasure still came as a surprise.

Almost eight years to the day from when he first drove into Kansas, Joe ran into one of his colleagues in the mail room. Dr. Eppes was a tall, balding assistant professor who specialized in urban sociology.

Joe mentioned his upcoming brown-bag presentation on gay teenagers and the risk of delinquency, and Dr. Eppese replied, "If you're researching teenagers, you should talk to my daughter. She's in junior high, and all I hear is the Jonas Brothers, Zack and Cody, Zac Efron, all day long. [1] I know girls her age are all wild about boys, but she's obsessed! Have you ever heard of anything like that?"

Joe hadn't expected to hear that there are no gay children in response to a research project about gay children. But he managed to answer: "Of course. When I was in junior high, I couldn't stop talking about Bobby Sherman, Davy Jones, every *Tiger Beat* fave rave. I even belonged to the David Cassidy fan club. It was me and ten girls."

"You and ten girls, huh?" Dr. Eppes repeated with a lascivious grin. "You were a pretty smart operator back then!"

As often happens, Dr. Eppes had literally forced himself *not* to understand, to transform his evidence that gay people exist into its precise opposite. Why would a boy join a David Cassidy fan club? Obviously, to meet girls!

Undaunted, Joe pressed on. "But I had the biggest crush of all on Christopher Knight -- you know, Peter Brady, the middle boy on *The Brady Bunch?* I actually wanted to marry him when I grew up. I fantasized about us living together, cooking dinner, watching tv, waking up in the morning side by side, all sorts of romantic scenarios."

Now Dr. Eppes barked a short, nervous laugh, and his eyes darted about, searching for an escape. Joe wondered how he would try to render his crush on Peter Brady invalid.

He simply refused to hear. Joe *could not* be gay, period. "I'll bet your daughter is obsessed with Zac Efron, too," he responded.

"I don't. have a . . ."

"Sure she is. Just ask your wife!"

A few moments later, Joe was walking down the hall with his mail in hand,, still straight – and saddened. Doubtless no matter what Joe said, Dr. Eppes would refuse to face gayness head-on.

Why go through so much trouble, so much frantic ratiocination? Why not just relax and admit that some girls notice girls, some boys are attracted to male teen idols, and some men have male partners instead of wives? What was there to be afraid of?

For he was undoubtedly afraid.

The Monster in the Closet

What did Dr. Eppes think would happen if he admitted knowing that not everyone is straight, that a sizeable percentage of every human population experiences only same-sex desire, behavior, and romance?

A world where gay people are permitted to exist sounds completely harmless.

New acquaintances are simply asked, "Do you have a partner?"

Children are simply told, "When you start noticing boys or girls."

Movies feature masculine gay men and lesbians who are still lesbians at fade-out.

No one feels compelled to insist that a story about gay people is not a gay story. Easy.

Out-group competition has become the most common explanation for homophobia.[2]   According to this theory, racism, sexism, anti-Semitism, and homophobia are all strategies designed to justify or maintain inequalities in social, political, and economic capital between a group that has historically dominated and a group that has been disenfranchised.[3] The erasure in Kansas could have a similar effect on an institutional level, as policy decisions in health, education, and government are made for a world in which gay people do not exist.

However, the origin of erasur cannot not lie in competition over resources, since the out-group is not resented, but denied altogether. Gay people aren't evil or frivolous, they aren't anything at all. Homophobia and heterosexism say, "Your desires, practices, and romances differ from mine, therefore you are despicable or laughable," but erasure says,

"Your desires, practices, and romances *do not* differ from mine."

We can get a hint of their fear from the world of the imagination, where the villain is typically gay. Whenever a knight, freedom-fighter, secret agent, or Ninja is strung up in a dungeon, an elegantly-dressed, British-accented gay Girl is either administering the torture or more often standing in the shadows, licking his lips in voyeuristic delight, gayness literally attacking straightness.

Even Disney animated movies, from *Peter Pan* (1953) to *Ratatouille* (2007), invariably cast as their villains fops, gourmands, or lovers of the theater with long faces, long be-jeweled fingers, and the overmodulated, sophisticated accent of gay Girls.

In horror, the Bad Things that come in from the outside, the leering psycho-killers, the bug-eyed demons, the antique dealers who may or may not be vampires, are always gay Girls, usually transvestite, often pedophile as well, effeminate monsters plotting to kill, eat, or defile innocent gender-polarized straights.[4] The protagonists must then rise up, battle the effeminacy, banish the gayness, and restore gender-polarized straight normalcy to the world.

Maybe the cause of the straight erasure of gay people from every human and nonhuman venue is the fear of annihilation. Straights cannot conceive of gayness as an identity, but as an attack on identity.

If same-sex desire exists in the world, then cross-sex desire must not.

They must stop themselves before Saying the Deplorable Word, because even admitting that gayness has a name renders our identity chimerical, renders *us* chimerical. Lewis Carroll recounts a similar fear:

In the midst of the word he was trying to say
In the midst of his laughter and glee
He had softly and suddenly vanished away
For the Snark *was* a Boojum, you see.[5]

For this reason, we do not see substantial fear of annihilation in homophobia, in the contorted faces of the screamers, the shouts of "fag," the use of "gay" to mean anything wrong or bad. We do not see it in heterosexism, in the polite bigot's trivialization of gay people, insisting that they are concerned only with fashion and gossip, not concerned with, or qualified for, the big, important tasks of life. We see it only in erasure, the third strategy, the strategy of erasure.

Though erasure is extremely common in the everyday interactions of both homophobic and heterosexist individuals, it no less common among straights who are gay-friendly, or who at least give few other signs of antigay prejudice. It often appears in gay people themselves.

In the daylight hours of rationality, they may be gay-friendly, but in the subconscious, in the dark places of nightmares, gayness and straightness seem mutually exclusive. In the same way, Jane H. Hill notes that linguistic patterns of privilege and exclusion can force racism onto "tolerant" white and even nonwhite persons.[6]

Therefore, though I vote in favor of gay marriage and believe that there should be more gay-themed books in the library and affix a LGBT Safe Space sticker to his office door, I am certain that you, the person standing in front of me, could not be gay, or if you are, then one or more of the elements of your identity must be negated, or one or more of the spaces of your existence must be nullified. You must be barred from the public sphere or the private sphere, from childhood or adulthood, from the past or the future. If gayness becomes valid, essential, innate, then straightness becomes invalid, contingent, artificial. If gayness exists, straightness cannot.

In the end the fear is not the fear of an Other who storm into "our" world. The fear is the fear of sameness. Erasure worries that when straights, especially men, look into the face of gayness, they will not see monsters or clowns, but themselves. Calvin Thomas tells us, "The terror of being mistaken for a queer dominates the straight mind because this terror *constitutes* the straight mind." [7]

The glimmers of same-sex desire the straight perceives must be deferred onto a scapegoat, then demonized and destroyed through homophobia, or transformed into a clown through heterosexism, or rendered invisible through erasure. In the end, proclaiming "No one here is gay!" really means "I am not gay!"

Colonization of Kansas

We know the remedy for homophobia: come out, stay out, demonstrate that not all gay people are monstrous.

We know the remedy for heterosexism: march, picket, sign petitions, work toward equality in health care, government, education, and mass media representation.

But erasure does not require a closet; straight friends who heard Joe's "coming out" speech still were forced not to know, or to reject part of that knowledge, thinking, "You may be gay, but you are still attracted to women," or "You may be gay now, but as a child you were straight."

It does not require a disparity in capital; pro-gay and anti-gay churches are equally likely to proclaim "God's plan for straight marriage."

How does one go about resisting ideological presumptions that are so impervious to dispute?

We can find a clue by looking at Oz, where he lived without ever hearing a reference to "his wife," and comparing them with Kansas where, just a few blocks away, he heard of nothing else.

Gay people have always sought out rooms of their own. Typically they prowl small town library catalogs or the surrogate worlds of gay fiction, make a closeted jaunt to "that bar downtown," and then make the leap from gray dust-ridden Kansas to Oz. The straights who live there or nearby have met gay people before, recognize that sometimes men have no wives and women have no husbands. They may still be homophobic or heterosexist, but at least they recognize that same-sex desire and behavior exist. What causes erasure to falter?

It is not merely that Oz has a substantial number of gay residents, from 30% to 50% of the entire population; you can have thousands of gay residents who still appear in public in cross-sex dyads, and transformed lovers into roommates in office conversations. It is not an absence of homophobia or heterosexism; as we have seen, erasure requires neither.

If is not a matter of numbers or homophobia, what is unique about Oz that distinguish them from Kansas? Most noticeable is the utter absence of passing. In Oz, passing is anathema, the worst possible sin. Gay people do not "come out" to friends, neighbors, and employers; they were never in. They appear in public in same-sex dyads or cross-sex groups. They do not appear in public in cross-sex dyads, except incidentally. They occupy, they own public spaces. As a result, erasure is impossible, voiced only by newcomers or by intruders from Kansas.

But the gay people in the villages and cities and end-less sprawling suburbs of Kansas, or who simply move from one corner of Kansas to another without ever finding their true "home" in West Hollywood or the Castro, are almost without exception Discreet, at home, at work, among friends, or everywhere. Their friends may be all or almost all straight, and their public associations of necessity cross-sex.

If the gay residents of Kansas know any other gay people at all, they keep them strictly separated from their "straight lives," sneaking off for a few hours in "that bar downtown" or an organization named Friends of the Italian Opera.

If anything, they have D'Augelli and Garnett's model of "small, densely connected informal networks which operate without drawing the attention of others."[8] Thus they are easily able to accept erasure.

If they are asked, "Did your wife come with you?", they answer "No."

If they are assured that all girls start to "notice" boys, they respond, "Don't I know it!"

They write magazine articles proclaiming that a certain actress is "Every man's fantasy."

They write movie reviews beginning with "This is not a gay story, it is a human story." They readily contribute to their own negation.

Assimilation and Negation

Between 1850 and 1930, immigrants to the United States commonly formed territorial enclaves similar to gay neighborhoods, as friends, old neighbors, and distant relatives buy farms in the same county or rent flats in the same urban neighborhood. After a sufficiently large influx of immigrants, the demand for cultural and linguistically specific services, plus the strictures of prejudice, insures institutional completeness.[9] "Ghetto" residents rely on each other for their essential physical, social, economic, and spiritual needs. At the turn of the last century, the Illinois prairie boasted different weekly newspapers, hospitals, churches, elementary schools, and colleges for Germans, Swedes, Norwegians, and Danes. Except for taxes and run-ins with the law, they could conduct all of their daily affairs without every associating with English-speaking society (and of course, members of the main society "benefited" by never having to associate with one of *them*).

But as time passed and they acquired more social power, they moved out of the ghettos, became assimilated into the mainstream, and lost their specificity. Today being of Swedish, Norwegian, or German ancestry is a topic of conversation, a memory of candles on St. Lucia day, and nothing else.[10]

Many of the gay residents of Kansas have become in effect assimilated, without ever finding their gay homeland. In order to resist erasure, they must be convinced to affirm a gay identity again, colonize the public space of their home town, create a little Castro Street, create difference rather than the sameness that erasure fears. In the words of Toilette Eugene, "difference must make a difference" (1992:91),[11] It is not an obstacle to be overcome or minimized, but essential to the project of resistance.

If just a few gay people in every town refuse to pass as straight, become *different*, then the weakest of the axioms would fade, and the others would not be so intractable. But how does one convince someone who is de facto straight, who celebrates straightness in every instance and hides gay-ness from the world, to emerge into a public gay identity?

Every minority must choose between accepting assi-milation and embracing identity, but erasure makes the choice more difficult for gay people by denying that there is an identity to embrace at all. Existentialist theologian Paul Tillich described the human predicament as "the courage to be," "the ethical act in which man affirms his own being in spite of those elements of his existence which conflict with his essential self-affirmation." One must affirm one's own being, Tillich states, through encounters with others: "the place of this encounter is the community."[12]

Performing Identity

For Patricia Hill Collins, every person resides in a variety of relations of domination "structured by a system of interlocking racial, class, and gender oppression."[13] Depending upon the social location, any identity can be either oppressed or oppressor: that is, white gay men are subordinate in the relation of straight/gay, but dominant in the male/female and white/nonwhite; straight black women are subordinate in the relations of white/nonwhite and male/female, but dominant in the straight/gay.

One would presume lesbians of color would be entirely oppressed, and straight white men entirely oppressors, but other relations of domination, such as class, religion, dialect, handicapped status, masculinity/femininity, fetish interest, and age ensure that no one is entirely free from oppression, or from the guilt of oppressing. Moreover, each oppressed group attempts to maximize its power by presenting its dominant relations as unspoken yet axiomatic: thus, *gay* begins to mean *gay (white male)*, *black woman* begins to mean *black (straight) woman*, and so on.

Many conservative theorists, especially those who decry the end of "community," fear the proliferation of identities as a cacophony that can only lead to chaos and in the end prove a detriment to any attempts at liberation. They believe that solidarity must consist in recognizing a single subjection and retaining the structures of oppression for the others: gay people, including gay (white men) and gay (black women) should be concerned only with gay (white male) concerns.

Collins, however, locates it in "a conceptual space. . .for each individual to see that she or he is both a member of multiple dominant groups and a member of multiple subordinate groups."[14] Solidarity occurs not through recognition of sameness per se but through recognition of sameness within multiple structures of being and becoming: *gay* Native American handicapped female, *gay* white female leather enthusiast, *gay* Orthodox Jewish male lawyer, *gay* black male Snap! Queen, and so on. This entails "the straining to encompass in one's glance at the varied world the common threat, the unified theme through immense diversity."[15]

While there are hundreds of potential identities, affiliations, and interests which encourage solidarity, only a few are experienced by enough people, and in ways sufficiently similar to political activism-grassroots organizing model of the unaffiliated (white, middle class, male) gay mainstream to make quantitative comparison meaningful. Although they promise a profound colonization of a public space that is heterosexualized, racialized, and gendered, a colonization that is available in Kansas just as in Oz. All it takes is the choice of identity over nothingness.

Straight identity and gay identity are all organized and maintained through a discursive relationship between nodes of desire, constraint, habit, spontaneity, economic necessity, self-respect, the needs of peers and lovers, the normative glare of a million disapproving waitresses in coffee shops, what we heard in a university lecture three decades ago, and what someone shouted at us just today on the subway. In the midst of this cacophony of voices, we make a million trivial decisions that together affirm one or the other:

Where should I have dinner tonight?

What should I watch on TV?

How should I respond to the statement that "All boys are girl-crazy"?

Should I pick up a copy of *The Advocate* at Borders Bookstore?

Should I put a rainbow flag bumper sticker on his car?

Should I put my arm around my date as we wait in line at the Cinema 8?

The daily barrage of subtle exclusions and outright demonizations from both gay and straight, allies and enemies, Baptist ministers and professors of gay studies, may make erasure seem inevitable. However, one always has the freedom of resistance. No matter that it is fossilized, crystalized, embedded into the substrata of consciousness, pounded into the body along with childhood nursery rhymes, ritualized, repeated, absorbed with the air and light, no ideology is inevitable.

A thousand times a day, we can note or ignore the frailty and inconsistency of even the most powerful of the axioms, evaluate or dismiss its alternatives, decide through ignorance or malice or habit to behave as if it is true, or take a moment's thought to realize that it is not true at all. Resistance is an ongoing process, a thousand daily choices to tell the truth or to lie, to acquiesce or resist, to be part of a community or an individual. Some of us do not, cannot, and in the end *will not*, but most of us *must*. In the words of Alice Walker, "you yourself are your last hope."[16]

[1] Jonas Brothers, teen idols who appear regularly on the Disney Channel; Cole and Dylan Sprouse, stars of the Disney Channel series *The Suite Life of Zack and Cody*, and later *The Suite Life on Deck*; Zac Efron, star of the *High School Musical* movies.

[2] Hegarty, Peter, & Massey, Sean. "Anti-Homosexual Prejudice ... as Opposed to What? Queer Theory and the Social Psychology of Anti-Homosexual Attitudes." *Journal of Homosexuality* 52.1-2 (2006): 47-57.

[3] Bonilla-Silva, Edwardo. *Racism without Racists: Color-Blind Prejudice and the Persistence of Racial Inequality in the United States*. New York: Rowman and Littlefield, 2006; Feagan, Joe. *Racist America*. New York: Routledge, 2001; Laqueur, Walter. *The Changing Face of Antisemitism*. Oxford: Oxford University Press, 2008; Trepanger, Barbara. *Silent Racism*. New York: Paradigm Publishers, 2007.

[4] Benshoff, Harry. *Monsters in the Closet: Homosexuality and the Horror Film*. St.Martin's Press, 1997.

[5] Carroll, Lewis. *The Hunting of the Snark*. In Gray, Donald J. *Alice in Wonderland: A Norton Critical Edition*. New York: W. W. Norton, 1992: 234. Carroll did not have straight identity in mind, but "pure metaphor," everything at once and nothing at all. Cf. Holquist, Michael. "What is a Boojum: Nonsense and Modernism." Ibid: 388-398.

[6] Hill, Jane H. *The Everyday Language of White Racism*. New York: Wiley-Blackwell, 2008.

[7] Thomas, Calvin. "Straight with a Twist: Queer Theory and the Subject of Heterosexuality." Pp. 83-115 in Thomas Foster et al., eds., *The Gay Nineties: Disciplinary and Interdisciplinary Formations in Queer Studies*. New York: New York University Press, 1997; Warner, Michael. "Introduction." Pp. vii-xxxi in Michael Warner, ed., *Fear of a Queer Planet: Queer Politics and*

Social Theory. Minneapolis: University of Minnesota Press, 1993.

[8] D'Augelli, Anthony R., and Linda Garnets. "Lesbian, Gay, and Bisexual Communities." Pp. 293-320 in A. D'Augelli and C. Patterson, eds., *Lesbian, Gay, and Bisexual Identities over the Lifespan.* New York: Oxford University Press, 1995: 301.

[9] Breton, Raymond.. "Institutional Completeness of Ethnic Communities." *American Journal of Sociology* 70 (1964): 195-205.

[10] Daniels, Roger. *Coming to America: A History of Immigration and Ethnicity in American Life.* New York: Harper Perennial, 2002; Parillo, Vincent. "Diversity in America: A Sociohistorical Analysis." *Sociological Forum* 9.4 (1994): 523-545; Bruch, Elizabeth, & Robert D. Mare. "Neighborhood Change and Neighborhood Choice." *American Journal of Sociology* 112.3 (2006): 667-709.

[11] Eugene, Toinette. "On 'Difference' and the Dream of Pluralist Feminism." *Journal of Feminist Studies in Religion* 8.2 (1992): 91-98.

[12] Tillich, Paul. *The Courage to Be.* New Haven, CT: Yale University Press, 1952: 3, 91.

[13] Collins, Patricia Hill. *Black Feminist Thought: Knowledge, Consciousness, and the Politics of Empowerment.* New York: Routledge, 2008: 222.

[14] Ibid: 230

[15] Ibid: 236.

[16] Walker, Alice. *Possessing the Secret of Joy.* New York: Harcourt Brace Jovanovich, 1992.